Earthlight, Wordfire

Ivan Doig at the Jensen ranch near Dupuyer, Montana, described in **This House of Sky** *(1989).*

Earthlight, Wordfire

The Work of
Ivan Doig

by Elizabeth Simpson

A Publication in Northwest Folklife
Louie W. Attebery, General Editor

University of Idaho Press
Moscow, Idaho
1992

Design by Karla Fromm
Photographs courtesy of Ivan and Carol Doig.

The following publishers have generously given permission to use extended quotations from
copyrighted works:
    Extracts reprinted with permission of Atheneum Publishers, an imprint of Macmillan
Publishers Company: From *Dancing at the Rascal Fair* by Ivan Doig. Copyright © 1987 by
Ivan Doig. From *Ride With Me, Mariah Montana* by Ivan Doig. Copyright © 1990 by Ivan
Doig.
    Excerpts from *This House of Sky*, copyright © 1978 by Ivan Doig, reprinted by permis-
sion of Harcourt Brace Jovanovich, Inc. Excerpts from *Winter Brothers*, copyright © 1980 by
Ivan Doig, reprinted by permission of Harcourt Brace Jovanovich, Inc.
    Extracts reprinted with permission of Atheneum Publishers, an imprint of Macmillan
Publishing Company, from *The Sea Runners*, by Ivan Doig. Copyright © 1982 by Ivan Doig.
Extracts reprinted with permission of Atheneum Publishers, an imprint of Macmillan Publish-
ing Company, from *English Creek*, by Ivan Doig. Copyright 1984 by Ivan Doig.
    Permission to reprint one verse from "Lake Chelan," from *Stories That Could Be True*,
HarperCollins, 1977, has been generously granted by William Stafford.

Library of Congress Cataloging-in-Publication Data

Simpson, Elizabeth, 1951–
        Earthlight, wordfire : the work of Ivan Doig / Elizabeth Simpson.
        p. cm. — (Northwest folklife)
        "Works of Ivan Doig": p.
        Includes biographical references (p.   ) and index.
        ISBN 0-89301-156-8
        1. Doig, Ivan—Criticism and interpretation. 2. West (U.S.) in
    literature.   I. Title.   II. Series.
    PS3554.O415Z87 1992
        813'.54—dc20
                                                                    92-22634
                                                                        CIP

For Henning

Language is the light that comes out of us. Imagine the words as if they are our way of creating earthlight, as if what is being spoken by this man in a windswept dawn is going to carry everlastingly upward, the way starshine is pulsing constantly across the sky of time to us. Up through the black canyons of space, the sparks we utter; motes of wordfire that we glimpse leaving on their constellating flight, and call history.

—Ivan Doig, *Ride with Me, Mariah Montana*

Contents

Illustrations

Acknowledgments

Professor Mark Patterson of the University of Washington was my friend and advisor for many years and, in addition to careful guidance in the original work for this manuscript, supplied quiet confidence and constant support. Professor Harold P. Simonson taught me that literature is, above all, a moral study. I appreciate the commitment and passion he brings to his own writing, as well as his enthusiasm for this project. He and Professor A. Carl Bredahl, of the University of Florida, have provided valuable insights into the critical issues raised by contemporary western literature. I would also like to thank Professor Emeritus Eugene Smith of the University of Washington for allowing me to quote from his tape-recorded interviews with Ivan Doig.

I have had the rare privilege of working with an author who is both generous with his time and articulate about his work. When I got over my initial shyness about taking up the time of a busy man, I found Ivan Doig a marvelous source. He made his papers available to me, including private letters, original drafts of short manuscripts, the journal he kept during his work on *The Sea Runners*, and transcripts of speeches and addresses. Doig and his wife, Carol, provided the photographs included in this book. In addition, he and I discussed the book chapter by chapter, and our sessions were always stimulating and useful. For the friendship and warmth of Ivan and Carol, their hospitality, our celebrations together, I thank them again.

I am also extraordinarily fortunate to have a very patient husband who is also an outstanding teacher, scholar, writer, and critic. Professor Henning K. Sehmsdorf has guided my study of folklore and the ways it illuminates literature. He shares my pleasure in Doig's books, and our many spirited discussions were enormously helpful. His fine critical sense has shaped this work.

Introduction

This book has a four-parent birth certificate: It was born from two decades of my interest in contemporary western writing, from a strong sense that not enough serious critical attention was being paid to these new American voices, from my love for the work of Ivan Doig, and from my dismay when I read Wallace Stegner's essay, "History, Myth, and the Western Writer," published in 1967. There Stegner expressed an unwilling conviction that the West lacked a unified literary tradition, a body of writing that could be called "regional":

> As a westerner, I would love to believe that there is some spirit, attitude, faith, experience, tone, something, that binds all small-w western stories together as manifestations of a coherent regional culture. And yet I confess I have doubts. . . . Despite large individual differences, midwestern writers from Eggleston to Dreiser and Lewis have tended to be earthy, plain, and realistic. Southern fiction from Poe to Faulkner has had strong infusions of the gothic, the grotesque, the highly colored, the "tall," and it has had its consistent and repetitive themes: color, the lost cause, the persistence of the family fabric and tradition. But when one asks if there are comparable likenesses among western writers, one hedges (Stegner, *The Sound of Mountain Water* 1967, 61-62).

When Stegner wrote those words, western literature was just beginning to come into its own. Writers like Willa Cather, H. L. Davis, A. B. Guthrie, John Steinbeck, Mary Austin, and Wright Morris had worked in relative isolation from a regional tradition, and their work was evaluated according to critical standards that paid little attention to issues of context or to the significance of local knowledge. Fortunately, in the twenty-five years since Stegner's essay was published, western writing has begun to flourish in all of the genres and to make a significant contribution to national literature, regional writing has lost its status as the poor local-color cousin to mainstream writing (which means in part that mainstream writing has finally been recognized as regional), and New Criticism has died a natural death, freeing scholars to ask all kinds of contextual questions about literature. My purpose in this book is twofold: to provide an introduction to the work of a writer who, like Mark Twain, appeals to readers across the board and whose work is so recent that serious discussions about it are just getting under way; and to explore some critical approaches to western writing that are suggested by Doig's work. The audience I have written for is as varied, I hope, as Doig's audience: students, teachers, scholars, readers who love a good story and want to know more about it. For this reason I have avoided the technical aspects of critical theory and language and worked from what the texts have told me. Henry David Thoreau said, "Books should be read as deliberately and reservedly as they were written," and that has been my approach to Doig's work. Scholars will not find new critical theories in this book but still, I hope, some useful ways to think about western writing.

Doig's works are so rich that it would take volumes to examine all of them in detail. Therefore the chapters in this study are intended to be exemplary rather than exhaustive. In chapter 11, for example, there is a long discussion of the personal narrative structure of *This House of Sky*. The same analysis can be applied to *English Creek*, but I have used that novel to illustrate other aspects of Doig's use of folklore. The reader will recognize motifs throughout Doig's work that I have explored at length in only one of his books.

Part 1 examines each work separately. I focus on both the "separate selves" of the texts—the differences in structure, narrative strategy, theme, character, pace, tone, informing metaphors—and also on recurrent motifs that bind them into a canon.

Part 2, on folklore, is particularly important to a full appreciation of Doig's work. The body of his writing, especially the four books about Montana, has produced a detailed and accurate portrayal of life in the West, and this achievement is best understood through the methods of a folklorist. This section has two goals: first, to clarify for the reader what has happened in folklore studies in the last few decades and how those changes affect the study of folklore in literature; second, and more important, to explore how Doig overcomes the difficulties of incorporating folklore into a literary text and to examine the ways he uses folklore to solve certain problems. For example, Doig uses folklore motifs to create structural and thematic links among the three novels of the Montana trilogy (*English Creek, Dancing at the Rascal Fair,* and *Ride with Me, Mariah Montana*). These links illustrate the processes of acculturation as immigrants become Americans and demonstrate how cultural traditions create historical continuity.

Part 3 discusses Doig's use of western landscapes and places his work in the context of the writing of other western authors. These chapters provide a partial answer to Stegner's search for some "spirit, attitude, faith, experience, tone" in western literature that manifests a coherent regional culture. Doig's particular use of landscape to shape language, develop character, and inform the structures of his books is unique to his work, but also characterizes western writers' growing tendency to reflect contextual rather than literary antecedents in their writing. Scholars are just beginning to explore the literary possibilities of a relationship to landscape that is born of local knowledge. It is significant that although 84 percent of the population of the West is urban, the literary tradition now coming to maturity is almost exclusively rural, and that in the West's poetry, drama, fiction, and nonfiction, landscape is a powerful presence. The contribution of western writers to the national canon is in part their articulation of the interdependence of human and natural environments. It can be called a realization of continuity between internal and external worlds; Harold P. Simonson calls it "a sense of *place*," Carl Bredahl calls it "valuing surface."

Part 4, which discusses style, continues the earlier exploration of the importance of context in Doig's work, the significance of local knowledge in his use of language. But his achievement goes beyond his capturing the life of the West in the language of the West: Doig's genius lies in his ability to think, and write, like a poet. His work reflects an awareness that words are packets of sound and meaning within an ultimately self-reflexive system: it also reflects a unique skill for using language as a means not just to represent but to re-create experience. Ultimately, his style demonstrates the moral as well as the aesthetic power of language.

Doig's literary achievement is impressive: his first book, *This House of Sky*, was published in 1978; and his sixth book, *Ride with Me, Mariah Montana*, came out in the fall of 1990. Within that body of writing, Doig has explored new possibilities of genre and narrative structure and language, created unforgettable characters, and examined ways that history and landscape shape lives. He writes about many Wests and is sensitive to the differences among them but bridges those differences by developing themes common to them all: the challenges faced by people who leave one culture behind and establish themselves in a new country; the problems posed by landscapes that are seldom bountiful, sometimes hostile, and often fragile; the need westerners have for family and community; the definition and redefinition of the concept *frontier;* the roles of memory and story in creating a coherent cultural tradition. In Doig's work, in short, lies an answer to Stegner's lament. At the end of "History, Myth, and the Western Writer," Stegner notes that no one has yet created a western Yoknapatawpha County, traced in detail the historical continuities of the region. With *This House of Sky* and the Montana trilogy, it may be said that Doig has done just that.

But comparisons with Faulkner should be made cautiously, because Doig's voice, the western voice, is, unlike Faulkner's, ultimately realistic and positive. At the end of *Ride with Me, Mariah Montana,* which takes place in 1989, Montana's centennial year, the people of Gros Ventre raise a flag they have lovingly sewn from separate strips of material, each representing an important aspect of life in Montana: livestock raising, the headdress of a Blackfeet chief, homestead and ranch houses, town buildings, a range of mountains, and an enormous sun dawning in the center. As the flag is raised, a roaring Montana wind grips it, shakes and tugs at it, and finally tears its strips apart from one another. Here Doig creates a striking image of the past and present of Montana, of separateness and continuity, of human effort thwarted by the landscape. And the shouted laughter of the crowd in response to the flag's shredding captures perfectly Doig's perception of the spirit of the people of the West: strong, joyous, life affirming.

Part One
The Canon

"A person who is going to be a writer probably just cannot be stopped."

—Ivan Doig

Overleaf: *Ivan Doig at Dungeness Spit, Washington, doing research for* **Winter Brothers** (1980).

Chapter 1
Early Writing

Ivan Doig became nationally known in 1978 with the publication of *This House of Sky: Landscapes of a Western Mind,* and many critics and readers regard that book as the first work of a promising new writer. But *Sky* is as much a fulfillment as a beginning: most of Doig's life has focused on writing, each stage of his personal and professional development guided by his love for words on paper. Doig describes his youth as "bookish," a quality encouraged by his mother, who read to him by the hour so early in his life he has no conscious memory of it; by his father and grandmother, who told him innumerable stories and fostered his passion for language and his ear for western dialect; by neighbors who loaned him books and magazines that he devoured indiscriminately; and by teachers who recognized and fed his passion for learning.

Doig's inner life, bounded by books, was balanced by his outer life, spent working beside his father on various ranches. When Doig was sixteen, he realized that he had to choose between following in his father's footsteps and finding his own way. He chose to go to college, and, at the suggestion of a discerning football coach, decided to pursue a degree in journalism. He won a scholarship to Northwestern University, and divided the next four years of his life between summer jobs and academic work, taking courses in writing and reporting, not knowing where life would finally take him but being sure it would be somewhere he could work at writing. Although Doig's move to the Midwest separated him from his father and grandmother, his decision was faithful to the family pattern of individuals springing themselves free from the past. And he was aware of the importance of his success, for hopes were pinned on him, the first child on either side of the family to earn a college degree.

At Northwestern, Doig studied history and journalism and began to pursue the latter professionally. In his senior year, he wrote fillers for a magazine in Milwaukee and became the first undergraduate to place an article in the quarterly published by the school of journalism. After completing his master's degree in 1962 and serving a hitch on active duty in the air force reserve, he took a job in Decatur, Illinois, as an editorial writer for the Lindsay-Schaub newspapers (1963–1964). Despite his success there, he discovered that he did not have the instincts of a newspaperman and moved on to become assistant editor for *The Rotarian Magazine*, based in Evanston (1964–1966). In 1965 he married Carol Muller, a journalist, and they developed twin careers in Evanston, where they had first met. By 1966, Ivan and Carol Doig both felt they had accomplished as much as they could in their respective jobs and decided to make a major change. They moved to Seattle, where Doig entered the University of Washington as a graduate student in American history and Carol took a position teaching journalism at a local college. Doig earned a Ph.D. in 1969, but rather than taking the obvious next step into teaching became a free-lance writer. The handful of articles he had published before 1968 proliferated, and in the next five years he published four books. In 1972, in collaboration with Carol, he published *News: A Consumer's Guide*. This book was originally Carol's idea, growing out of her experiences in teaching a mass-media course at a local college in the 1960s. *News,* coauthored by Carol and Ivan Doig, is a discussion of the news as it is defined and disseminated by professionals and received by the general public. This book has been largely ignored by scholars, but Carl Bredahl considers it key to Doig's later work. He writes:

> Initially, given my interest in Doig's collected writings and his imagination generally, I was puzzled when I came across *News;* it certainly didn't seem to be anything like *This House of Sky* or *English Creek.* Today, however, I can't think of a more appropriate introduction to the work of an individual I consider one of America's important contemporary writers. The title of that first book—*News: A Consumer's Guide*—emphasizes three points: (1) event—*News* (2) the

consumption of event—*Consumer's* and (3) concern for understanding the interaction between event and consumption—*Guide* (Bredahl 1988, 1).

Bredahl's comment foregrounds Doig's debt to his training in journalism, which is particularly apparent in the Montana trilogy. The chapters of *English Creek* and *Dancing at the Rascal Fair* all begin with snippets from newspapers, and journalism is central to *Ride with Me, Mariah Montana.* Doig has the meticulous habits of a newspaper reporter and historian, always doing careful research and cross-checking his sources. More importantly, Doig's writing reveals a strong sense of the relationship between event and language that in shape and sound re-presents that event.

In 1975, Doig compiled and edited a collection of essays published under the title *The Streets We Have Come Down: Literature of the City* and in 1976 another, called *Utopian America: Dreams and Realities.* Both volumes were responses to intellectual and social issues raised during the tumultuous 1960s. In 1976, Doig was commissioned by the Forest Service to write a volume commemorating the fiftieth anniversary of forestry research in the Northwest. All the while, Doig free-lanced for magazines and newspapers. His files show that free-lance writing is demanding and difficult: the necessary research for even a brief article is extensive, and data must be cross-checked and verified. The writer is dependent upon the cooperation of other people, some of whom may have conflicting interests, and free-lancing must be conducted like a small business, in which expenses are closely accounted, remuneration bargained for, the product tailored to the market.[1]

The short pieces Doig sold (predominantly to *The Seattle Times* and *Pacific Search Magazine,* although he has published in more than forty different periodicals) reflect his academic interests and his dual regional loyalties, for he writes about Montana and the Pacific Northwest with equal ease. His training in journalism is manifested in technique: the articles are crisp, entertaining, and informative, often beginning with pun-laced titles such as "Rodeo: Sport of Flings," "Fenciful Artwork at the U.W.," and "Sound Reflections."

Doig conducted several tape-recorded interviews for *The Seattle Times* and *Pacific Search,* a means of gathering and presenting information that became an important device in writing *This House of Sky* and *Ride with Me, Mariah Montana.* He also experimented with form in many of his articles, juxtaposing journalistic reporting with historical notation and quotes from letters and diaries. These methods provide his articles with historical verisimilitude and a distinct structural rhythm, both of which he uses successfully in *This House of Sky, Winter Brothers,* and *Mariah Montana.* Doig's early experiments with oral narrative and complex structures matured in his later work into a sophisticated approach to history in his fiction.

As well as interviews, Doig produced articles on travel, ecology, humor, the craft of writing, local personalities, trends in education, interracial adoption. But by far the greatest number of his pieces are historical. Doig's doctoral dissertation was a biography of John Jay McGilvra, who served as U.S. District Attorney for the Territory of Washington during Lincoln's administration. Later, Doig mined his dissertation for articles, which he sold to several periodicals. He also wrote about Lewis and Clark; William Duncan (missionary to the Tsimshian Indians in Alaska); Edward Fox (a *New York Herald* reporter who witnessed the tragic ending of the Modoc Wars); Victor Smith (controversial customs official for Puget Sound); Ethelbert Oliphant (federal judge of Washington Territory during Lincoln's administration); and the writers Mark Twain, Owen Wister, and Robinson Jeffers. Although Doig usually focused on individuals, he also wrote about historical incidents: the devastating Bitterroot forest fire in 1910, an avalanche that buried a passenger train at Wellington that same year.[2]

In nearly all of his short pieces, even expository and travel articles, Doig writes from a historical perspective. He presents the past not only as "background" but as possibilities either fulfilled or ironically denied by the present. For example, in a short travel piece on Forest Grove, a community near Portland, Oregon, he shifts between the past and the present to show why the town is distinctive and what it stands to lose if it continues to grow. Doig does impeccable research for all of his writing: in his files, for example, are letters to acquaintances in Montana requesting their expertise on sheepskinning and forest fires, for scenes that became part of *English Creek.* Doig's passion for accuracy is reflected in this excerpt from a letter:

> I tried to use history...in *English Creek*...for veracity of detail. When you get to the forest fire section, for instance, the description of the pick-up fire fighters coming from "the bars and flop houses of Clore Street in Helena and Trent Avenue in Spokane and First Avenue South in Great Falls" is an almost-throwaway phrase (in appearance) which actually derives from 3 different sources—Dave Walter of the Montana Historical Society library tracked down for me a retired Helena Forest Ranger who "said the FS long had hired off the streets in the Park / Wood / Main area (of Helena). He referred to South Park as Clore Street—by which name the street became famous for bars, whorehouses and sleazy living. Then, in about 1911, the city fathers decided they would cleanse the reputation of Helena by changing the

name of Clore Street to South Park Avenue. An admirable attempt—but the same activities continued there, and most everyone still called it Clore Street." Which I decided to do in the book, too, to celebrate the defeat of good intentions. Trent Avenue in Spokane was provided for me by a friend who grew up there; and First Ave. St. in Gt Falls of course was notorious to me during my own boyhood. I tried to bring Missoula into the scene, hoping the Oxford would star, but one of my Missoula rangers said no, they hired the firefighters there down by the railroad tracks—rail-riding hoboes and such—instead of in any neighborhood. And, incredibly, I couldn't find anybody who knew which of Butte's sundry streets the Forest Service did its emergency hiring on. Anyway, the point is the "history" behind this single phrase of description, and while it's just one example, I did something similar time after time in the book.[3]

Doig's concern for authenticity emerges in the wealth of sensory and historical detail in his articles and books. For example, in *English Creek* the narrator comments that he and his father rely on canned tomatoes when they are packing in the mountains: "If you're thirsty you can drink them and if you're hungry you can eat them" (*EC* 1984, 88). In *Montana: A History of Two Centuries,* the authors describe the hard life and inadequate diet of the cowboy, and mention specifically that cowboys "relished canned tomatoes" (Malone and Roeder 1976, 127). Historical detail adds layer upon layer to the texture of Doig's work and provides the fabric of the daily lives of his characters.

Doig considers his chosen profession a craft, and he works at it with discipline and dedication. He believes that a writer who does not publish fairly often will lose his artistic edge, and as a result he averages a book every two to three years. In fact, he chose to write *English Creek* before *Dancing at the Rascal Fair* because even though the former book takes place a generation after the latter, it was the quicker of the two to write. When asked how he managed to meld the incidents and characters in the two novels since he wrote the first without a detailed outline of the second, Doig replied that he had left "windows of opportunity" in *English Creek* which could be explored and developed in *Rascal Fair.*[4]

Despite the personal nature of much of his writing, Doig is in no sense a "romantic" writer who awaits emotional inspiration before he puts words on paper. He says, "My imagination works off facts, by and large. . . . Once I do have a fact, I'm perfectly game to do something imaginative from it if I'm working on fiction. But apparently I need that seed of fact" (O'Connell 1987, 303, 304). He writes for five hours a day, and tries to produce at least

A horse race involving several Doigs through Sixteen, Montana, population about twenty. An unusual photograph, shot with a hand-held camera in the early years of this century.

Ivan Doig as a boy, counting sheep on a Montana ranch (early 1940s).

five pages each day. Publishing deadlines, however, do not prevent him from doing painstaking research, in libraries and on site, which results in his books' verisimilitude. In *At the Field's End*, Nick O'Connell asked Doig, "What's the value of that strict authenticity?" Doig replied:

> Well, intrinsic (laughs). It takes on a rightness in itself. I can't defend it financially. A lot of writers would not bother to defend it in terms of the time and energy it takes. But by God, you ought to do it right, it seems to me, even if it does take more time and energy. Nobody ever said this was going to be an easy business to be in. Some of this goes back to people I grew up around. There simply was a right way to build a haystack or fix a fence, in these people's minds—my dad among them (O'Connell 1987, 300).

"Doing it right" is an important part of Doig's work ethic. It means, above all, rewriting (the part of writing he likes best—achieving the "critical mass" so that he can play with the language) and researching carefully. In a talk before graduate student librarians at the University of Washington in 1988 Doig mentioned that he traveled all the way to Scotland to stand on the dock from which the protagonists in *Dancing at the Rascal Fair* embarked to America, to get a feel for the place and an ear for the dialect. He cross-checks information he is going to use; if data seems questionable or he cannot get a confirmation, he usually leaves it out of the text.

Because of his focus on the West, Doig can be described as a regional writer, and the lives of his characters are determined by, and reflective of, western experience. Doig's characters are invariably frontier people who live, as the Chinese curse says, "in interesting times." Because they are pioneers, they experience the excitement and hardship associated with being on the cutting edge of change: the clash of immigrant and native cultures, the opening and closing of the fur trade, the settlement of the West, the Civil War, the establishment of the national forests, World War I, the influenza epidemic of 1918, the Depression. His characters also suffer loneliness, loss of family security and cultural ties, alcoholism, bereavement, death. They are usually sponsored or controlled by large, impersonal forces, such as an eastern government that holds the purse strings and makes the regulations but is ultimately ignorant of, or indifferent to, the conditions of the frontier.

Doig's interest in people of the frontier, and the local knowledge he absorbed during his Montana boyhood, came to fruition in *This House of Sky*.

Chapter 2

This House of Sky: Landscapes of a Western Mind

Doig's first major work is a memoir of his years in Montana, of the lives of his father and grandmother.[1] In order to devote all of his time to *Sky*, Doig stopped free-lancing in 1975 and has written only a few article-length pieces since then. In an interview, Doig described his preparation of the book:

> It took me quite a while to accumulate the emotional ingredients of *The House of Sky* [sic], to get the material brought out of memory and taken back to Montana and expanded or verified by talking to other people and seeing the places where things actually took place. The work on the prose, of trying to make each sentence carry its weight, took two and a half years at the typewriter (O'Connell 1987, 304).

Doig began to collect material for *This House of Sky* while he was still free-lancing. He had wanted to write something about his father and had made a brief mention of him in an article he wrote in the 1960s about rodeos.

Then in the summer of 1968, while Doig and his wife were visiting his father and grandmother, Doig decided to interview Taylor Gordon, the black singer who lived in White Sulphur Springs, in order to write an article about him for the *Montana Magazine of History*. Before this interview, Doig took the opportunity to ask his father and grandmother questions and have them talk into the tape recorder. That impulse turned out to be truly fortunate, because it was one of the last times Charlie Doig was well enough for such a session. As inevitably happens during an interview, Doig's father and grandmother would say, "Well, you oughta ask so-and-so about that," and Doig began taping interviews with other people in the valley whenever he visited White Sulphur Springs. He ended up with at least two dozen tapes and several pages of notes, which turned out to be source material for *This House of Sky*.[2]

With the tapes, the notes, his own memories and his knowledge of the culture and landscape of Montana, Doig re-created his life from childhood to maturity, focusing on the two people who raised him—his father, Charlie Doig, and his grandmother, Bessie Ringer—and on ranch life in western Montana. But *This House of Sky* goes well beyond the conventions of biography and autobiography, for in it Doig explores some profound and elusive issues: the relationship of past to present; the nature and function of memory; the creation of personal identity; the political and ecological impact of the westering impulse; the cultural and personal qualities that permit one group to prosper on land where others starve out; the apparent arbitrariness of death.

All of Doig's books push the boundaries of genre, and some nearly defy classification. *This House of Sky* is no exception. Doig retells his story and explores these questions through intricate narrative and dramatic structures. There are three interlocking narrators: the author who crafts language, the man who looks back, the little boy (Ivan) who grows up again in these pages. The dramatic structure is thematically, as well as chronologically, inspired: *This House of Sky* begins with the death of Ivan's mother and Doig's search for her in stories and photographs, then flashes back to his father's family's experiences in the Tierney Basin, returns to Charlie and Ivan in the late 1940s, regresses again to sketch out his grandmother's story, and so on. The effect is like looking through someone's photo albums: the images are revitalized by musings, comments, family lore. Relationships between people and the connections between present and past are clarified by moving from one album to another, sometimes chronologically, sometimes thematically.[3]

The basic narrative of *This House of Sky* is the story of Charlie, Bessie, and Ivan's struggle to create a meaningful family life in the face of major economic and environmental odds, and often against personal inclination. Charlie Doig belongs to the second generation of Scots immigrants who left a hard, demanding country for one even more hard and demanding. The promise of productive land, which had beckoned Charlie's parents and uncles from Scotland, proved itself empty in one generation. Soon gone too

The Doig brothers. **Left to right:** *Claude, Angus, Charlie, Jim (1920s).*

was the illusion of government generosity, for homesteads of 160 acres were inadequate in that region:

> Simply, it came down to this: homesteads of 160 acres, or even several times that size, made no sense in that vast and dry and belligerent landscape of the high-mountain west. As well to try to grow an orchard in a window-box as to build a working ranch from such a patch. Quilt more land onto the first? Well and good—except that in an area of sharp natural boundaries, such as the Basin, a gain for one homestead could come only with someone else's loss. Simply go on summering the livestock in the shared open range of the mountains, as the Basin people did at first? Well and good again—except that with the stroke of a government pen which decreed the high summer pasture into a national forest, all that nearby free range ended. And promptly—*so fast it'd make your head swim,* my father would have said of such promptness—the allotments for forest grazing began to pass to the region's corporate ranches which already were big, and getting bigger (*Sky* 1978, 28).

This passage demonstrates one aspect of Doig's historical perspective, in which the lives of individuals are invariably bound with larger events and trends and are closely tied to the natural environment. The effect of politics, economics, and landscape on individuals is a major theme in the Montana trilogy as well as in *This House of Sky.*

Charlie's father, Peter, dies at the age of thirty-seven, and the efforts of his six sons to hold the ranch together are obliterated in one killing winter. Charlie becomes an itinerant ranch hand and proves to be such a good manager of livestock and men that he can pick and choose jobs for the rest of his life, though his work never provides much economic security. When he is twenty-seven years old he meets Berneta Ringer, the fifteen-year-old daughter of German-Irish immigrants from the Midwest, and after six years of courtship, they are married.

Their life together is abruptly ended by Berneta's death when Ivan is six. Charlie, devastated by his loss, has to raise his son by himself, and his choices in that regard shape Ivan's view of the world and possibly much of his personality. Charlie decides that Ivan's boyhood will be a copy of his own, an early assumption of adult responsibility and adult perspective. During the day father and son work on the ranch; at night they go to saloons, which are social gathering places for the men of White Sulphur Springs. The image of a seven-year-old spending his evenings in bars sounds crudely

Berneta Doig, in her first year of marriage (1934). The photograph is described in **This House of Sky,** *chapter 1.*

Charlie Doig and Berneta Ringer before their marriage (late 1920s).

Dickensian, but nothing could be farther from the truth of Doig's remembering. The men he meets are sometimes tragic, like the fat, joking Nellie, who is drinking himself to death, or pathetic, like the old timers, "gray and gimpy and familyless, making their rounds downtown, coming out for a few hours to escape living with themselves," but they are never grotesque (*Sky* 1978, 59). Doig does not write about them from the distant moral perspective of an outsider but from the memory of how he saw them as a little boy—with wonder, and warmth, and respect:

> For me, this span of episode at my father's side carried rewards such as few other times of my life. I cannot put a calendar on this time—more than a year, less than two—but during it, I learned an emotion for the ranchmen of the valley which has lasted far beyond their, and my, leaving of it. Judging it now, I believe what I felt most was gratitude— an awareness that I was being counted special by being allowed into this blazing grownup world, with its diamonds of mirror and incense of talk. I knew, without knowing how I knew, that there was much to live up to in this (*Sky* 1978, 66–67).

The bachelor lives of father and son end abruptly with Charlie's brief, stormy marriage to Ruth. This period is notable not only for the percussive relationship between his father and stepmother, but because it is during this time that Ivan's life assumes a pattern it will follow for the next ten years: boarding out with various families in town while he attends school, and when the weather permits, spending occasional weeks or weekends with his father and Ruth on whatever ranch they are working. Ivan, already introspective, turns even more bookish and becomes a solitary explorer of the small battered communities he lives in. As with the saloon episodes, the reader might expect some expression of moral outrage from a narrator whose boyhood was cut loose from basic moorings. Instead, Doig registers good-humored acceptance:

> The pattern to all this was jagged but constant: I would sleep on a couch in the living room of the moment, spend my day at school, roam town afterward as much as I wanted, come back to whichever house it happened to be—I once had a memory slip and returned to the one with the cellar toilet instead of the looming one across town—lose myself in a book or magazine until bedtime, dig the next morning's change of clothes from my suitcase behind the couch, and settle in for the night again. I found that everyone treated me fondly if a bit absent-

mindedly . . . and no one, least of all me, seemed to think there was much unusual about my alighting here and there casually as a roosting pullet (*Sky* 1978, 158).

Ivan's life is steadied by the introduction of another woman after the divorce of Charlie and Ruth. Charlie loves his son fiercely and has been determined that he will raise Ivan without interference. But a bleeding ulcer begins to sap his health, and he is forced to seek the help of his mother-in-law, Bessie Ringer, from whom he has been estranged since Berneta's death.

Bessie Ringer is as complex as her son-in-law, and as much a product of the frontier. Bessie is denied a formal education and while still a teenager marries a dour man twice her age who repeatedly drinks the family into poverty. But Bessie is strong. She travels from Wisconsin to Montana in 1914 with her husband and tiny daughter (Berneta) on the promise of steady work and immediately assumes a life of hard and thankless chores. By the time she enters Charlie and Ivan's life, she has separated from her husband, lost her daughter, and seen her sons grow up and move away. Hardworking, loving, scolding, temperamental, Bessie is nearing her sixties when she joins Charlie and Ivan. The uneasy alliance that knits a family out of this unlikely trio remains a mystery to Doig the remembering man (described in *This House of Sky* in italic typeface, used to comment on memories):

> *Here is a man and here a woman. In the coming light of one June morning, the same piece of life is axed away from each of them. Wounded hard, they go off to their private ways. Until at last the wifeless man offers across to the daughter-robbed woman. And I am the agreed barter between them.*
>
> *Not even truth brought down to bone this way can begin to tell what I long to of the situation shared by my father and my grandmother and myself during the years I call from memory here. For my father had to be more than is coded in the standard six-letter sound of father, he had also to be guardian-to-an-adrift-boy and as well, mate-who-was-not-a-husband to the daunting third figure of the household. In turn that figure, my loving thunder-tempered grandmother, who never had thought through roles of life but could don the most hazardous ones as automatically as her apron, had somehow to mother me without the usual claims to authority for it, and at the same time to treat with her son-in-law in terms which could not be like a wife's but seemed not much closer to any other description either. I believe that I inherited the clearest, most fortunate part in this, allowed simply to be*

myself-older-than-I-was, and to have the grant of a bolstered parent and the bonus of a redoubtable grandparent at my side as well. Yet even that lacks faithful wording: how can it be expressed that a boy's dreams of himself and his dream-versions of a threesome-against-life, yearnings so often drawn opposite each other in him, somehow were the same tuggings? (Sky 1978, 238–39).

Bessie unhesitatingly accompanies Charlie from ranch to ranch and job to job: working as a housekeeper, mother, cook, and ranch hand; trailing sheep; training dogs. Even after Ivan leaves Montana to attend college, Bessie stays on with Charlie, working with him and nursing him through his last illness. After his death, she asks to be buried beside him.

The life that Bessie, Charlie, and young Ivan assume in the pages of *This House of Sky* is created in a balance of dramatic and narrative scenes, punctuated by stories recalled and memories examined. The nature of memory—its disconcerting frailty, its tendency to become patterned and troped, its function in our lives—is one of Doig's major themes. In a letter to Mike Olsen, Doig explains his interest in memory:

One of the ideas I was toying with was that memory has a kind of half-life as radioactive materials do, but in a queer erratic way, not diminishing with mathematical regularity. Where that came from, I have no idea, and it never really worked out for the book, but it did get me farther into wanting to undertake what became *Sky*.[4]

In the book, Doig exploits all the tools of memory to re-create the contexts and incidents of his early life—photographs of his mother, his father's stories, his own sensory recall: *"A certain turn in my desk chair, and the leather cushion must creak the quick dry groan of a saddle under my legs—and my father's, and his father's"* (Sky 1978, 10). When his own memories grow dim and family stories are silent, Doig draws upon the recollections of friends and neighbors. His mother's schoolteacher recalls: *"The first morning of school, here I saw this girl coming up on a black horse, just coming as fast as ever she could. And it was your mother, and she was rushing up to tell me there were mice in the well, and not to use that water"* (Sky 1978, 7). A neighbor remembers: *"The first time I remember seeing Bessie Ringer was at the Caukins schoolhouse, at a dance out there, and I just admired her so, she always carried herself so straight and dignified"* (Sky 1978, 115).

In many ways, this is a book about memory, which Doig defines as *a set of sagas we live by, much the way of the Norse wildmen in their bear shirts. That such rememberings take place in a single cave of brain rather than half a hundred minds warrened wildly into one another makes them sagas no less. By now, my days would seem blank, unlit, if these familiar surges could not come (Sky 1978, 10).*

This House of Sky is predicated on the idea that personal identity is in part a function of memory. We know who we are and what we're like because we appear in certain roles in our own memories, in the memories of others, and in family stories, photographs, legends, and traditions, which are the products of collective memory.

Doig regards memory and oral narrative as primary texts: he seldom challenges their accuracy or consistency, not because he believes they are infallible but simply because *they are the texts we have.* Doig has pointed out that the recollective sections of *This House of Sky* are in italics rather than quotation marks, an editorial decision that emphasizes the ephemeral nature of the material.[5] Underlying his acceptance of memories and stories as they are told is the assumption that memory, like history, is a matter of selection and structuring. For example, he recounts his father's story of leaving foremanning positions on ranches that were badly run as a dramatic narrative, complete with dialogue, which his father told the same way each time for different incidents. Doig notes: "That the event did not always happen in just this fashion did not matter; it held that shape in Dad's mind, and left him free to revamp his routine of foremanning as promptly as he felt like it" (*Sky* 1978, 49).

Doig's literary uses of memory and personal narrative reflect his concept of history. History, for Doig, comprises the continuous interweaving of individual lives with major political, cultural, and economic events. Personal, regional, or national history assumes meaning according to how it is emplotted: the same event can be perceived as comic, tragic, romantic, or ironic.[6] The Homestead Act, for example, can be perceived as a noble attempt to populate the West with yeoman-farmers and their families, or as the first stage of feudalism. The stories that Nellie, Charlie's friend, tells about his own drinking bouts are intended to be comic, but to his companions they are tragic. Because events assume meaning not in themselves but according to how they are told, Doig uses many voices to examine a single event, such as his mother's death, from several perspectives. He also uses personal narrative to characterize his speakers: an individual's identity is often created in the text by the way he or she tells a story.

Another significant issue in the complex creation of identity is *region*. That is, who we are is in part determined by where we're from: the landscape and culture of a certain place define and limit our choices. On the first page of *Sky,* Doig establishes the fact that landscape is a powerful presence to the people of western Montana. The topography and climate are severe and weather swings from one extreme to another: it is dry country that floods at the wrong time; terrible winters thaw into springs in one afternoon of Chinook wind; hailstorms destroy a season's planting in a single deadly sweep. One summer storm, which takes the Doig family entirely by surprise, sets in a few days after their sheep have been sheared. Charlie has herded them into a corral for warmth and safety, but the pelting freezing rain panics them, and they begin to trample each other. Charlie, Ivan, Bessie and their dogs must loose 3,500 sheep, then herd them to safety. The sheep stampede, many of them drop back and freeze to death, many more hurtle off a cliff. Charlie, Ivan, and Bessie run after them, shouting, throwing rocks, clanking tins, siccing the dogs, in a desperate effort to save the animals. From noon to dusk, the three chase and cry out and finally collect most of the band. That day changes Ivan's life forever:

A hundred or more carcasses spotted the prairie behind us, dozens more strewed the base of the cliffs which the runaway clump had avalanched toward. If this was victory—and we had to tell ourselves it was, for we could have lost nearly all the sheep in a pushing massacre off the Two Medicine cliffs—I knew I wanted no part of any worse day.

I remember that I looked back from the mouth of the coulee toward the dusky north ridges, still smoked with gray wisps of the storm. As much as at any one instant in my life, I can say: *here I was turned* (*Sky* 1978, 221–22).

From then on, Ivan seeks the summer jobs and scholarships that will free him from the drudgery of ranch life and the unforgiving landscape. In so doing, he reverses the western migration pattern of both sides of his family, turning east to an education at Northwestern University and to jobs in flat, placid Illinois. When, a few years later, he can no longer live without mountains, he takes a larger western step and moves to Seattle.

The question, "Why West?" looms large in Doig's canon; in *Sky*, he ponders the westering impulse of his father's family:

Exactly what had plucked up the Doig family line from a village outside Dundee in Scotland and carried it into these gray Montana foothills this way, there is no account of. Dad simply wrote it off to Scots mulishness: *Scotchmen and coyotes was the only ones that could live in the Basin, and pretty damn soon the coyotes starved out.* I have but the rough list of guesses from the long westering course of this country's frontier: poverty's push or the pull of wanderlust, some word of land and chance as heard from those who had gone earlier to America, or as read in the advertisements of booking agents. Perhaps some calamity inside the family itself, the loss of whatever thin livelihoods there had been in laboring on a laird's estate. Or it may truly have been an outcropping of the family vein of stubbornness (*Sky* 1978, 24).

Certainly the Doig family did not prosper in America. Starved out of the family homestead, these people who had hungered for land became landless, the six brothers wandering off to make their way as best they could. The struggle of settlers in Montana is manifested in *Sky's* images: the grubby towns, their once-grand public buildings reduced to echoing shells; abandoned homesteads; desolate ranches where not so much as a tree has been planted to provide beauty.

A few people do succeed beyond subsistence level, like the colony of Hutterites, who run a collective farm so productively that their success is almost a reproach to single families who could not make it: "The Dupuyer people said the Hoots could thrive a hundred at a time on land where an ordinary family had starved out. They did not mean it as a compliment" (*Sky* 1978, 196). More reassuring are the Brekkes:

> Mr. and Mrs. Brekke both had been born in Norway, and both came young to the new life in America: they met and married, found a small ranch beyond Ringling where they endured through to prosperity. . . . The Brekkes owned the one house in all of Ringling that looked as if it truly had been built to live in rather than just to hold boards up off the ground (*Sky* 1978, 137).

What is it about the Doigs that dooms them to failure on the land? Or about the Brekkes that assures their success? The West was a proving ground for many immigrant groups. If the difference is cultural, can it be said that the Scots were less tenacious, less patient, less modest in the scale of their dreams than Norwegians? Less lucky in the land they claimed? Less skilled in husbandry and farming? Because Doig often talks about ethnic groups, the reader is tempted to speculate that cultural differences determine economic success or disappointment, but such generalizations are not borne out in his other books, nor in the historical record.[7] Luck, it seems, particularly luck with the weather, had more to do with success or failure than any other factor.

There is no mystery, however, about the prosperity of the large ranches, supported by government leases and subsidies. Doig's disgust with the inequities of the leasing system, which favors large ranches over small home-steads, crackles through his books, appearing in *This House of Sky* as occa-sional invective against Rankin, a rancher who pieced his holdings together out of failed homesteads, pastured too many animals on his land, worked his men too hard. The theme is developed more fully in the Montana trilogy.

Of all the issues that shape *This House of Sky*, none is more prominant than the mystery of death—whom it strikes and why. The story begins with the death of Ivan's mother, which, terribly and ironically, happened on Ivan's sixth birthday, a coincidence that echoed ever after in his father's re-dactions of the event.[8] In the second section of the book, Doig chronicles the deaths of several of his father's relatives, then pauses to contemplate Char-lie's own brushes with death. In 1918, on a winter hunting trip, Charlie and his cousin both contract pneumonia and influenza. The cousin dies, Charlie survives. Doig ponders: "Those two had started out even when they put their first footprints in the snow on that hunting trip. Why death for one, and not the other? No answer comes, except that even starts don't seem to count for much" (*Sky* 1978, 34–35). Later in his life, Charlie survives three accidents, all involving horses, all injuring him seriously. He survives, but two of his brothers die from similar accidents. Other deaths—of friends, rel-atives, working companions—dot the pages of the book, and the last full section recounts Charlie's final struggle with emphysema and Bessie's death. At the end Doig describes his own near-drowning on the Washington coast, which proves to be a last link to his father and grandmother.

It is startling to realize how much of *This House of Sky* is concerned with death, because the book is not morbid or grim or resigned. *Sky* is a book about coming of age, the creation of a family, the strengths and frail-ties of memory, ranch life in Montana. It is, in the best sense of the term, a regional book, which grew out of western experience and western language.

This House of Sky was nominated for the National Book Award and won the Christopher Award; it has been published in Great Britain and translated into German and has received consistently positive reviews.[9] The book has been praised for capturing the real West through the characters of Charlie Doig and Bessie Ringer; for its emphasis on the importance of the past in defining the present; and for its style, which captures the sound of western speech and the pace of western life.

This House of Sky is a superb literary achievement: many critics believe it to be Doig's best work. Although the book is carefully crafted and struc-tured—a balance of drama and narration, detail and generalization, story-telling and philosophy—the form never seems artificial. The story is both intimate and universal: all readers can empathize with the need of a child for a family and the need of an adult to break away from that family, the eternal tensions of love and responsibility and self-realization. His setting these themes in the West makes Doig part of a new generation of western writers. He feels that what these writers share is their sense of place:

> Socially and culturally, I'm aware of being part of a lineage, a family tree of Western writers, because I have read and know of Wallace Stegner and Mari Sandoz and Hamlin Garland. They are people whose growing up was somewhat along the lines of mine—on ranches, farms, homesteads. People who came out of rural places to be writers (O'Connell 1987, 301).

Doig emphasizes that writers can come out of rural places. But it is important to note that these writers have not fled to Paris or New York nor taken those places as their subjects. Bill Kittredge; A.B. Guthrie, Jr.; Gary Snyder; Marilynne Robinson; William Stafford; Norman Maclean; and James Welch (to name just a few) write about the Wests they know. Wallace Stegner expresses the wellsprings of their achievement in his essay "On the Writing of History," in which he recalls his early desire to "be the Herodotus of the Cypress Hills" of southern Saskatchewan, and his struggle to isolate material that would be regarded as "acceptable" history. Stegner notes that when he wrote *Wolf Willow,* he wanted to draw upon his own local knowledge: "I had lived in the hills myself, and my memories were sharp. It seemed legitimate, as a means of realizing the country for readers, to put my remembering senses in the book, and my own family's experiences" (Stegner 1965, 9). That phrase, "realizing the country," captures perfectly what contemporary western writers are doing, and particularly what Doig achieves in *This House of Sky.*

Chapter 3
Winter Brothers: A Season at the Edge of America

In his second regional book, Doig shifted his focus from Montana to the Northwest frontier. His proclivity for ignoring established conventions of genre is amply illustrated in *Winter Brothers,* which is a combination of memoir, biography, and history. The book examines the life of James Swan, a nineteenth- century pioneer, and through that medium describes life in the Northwest, past and present. As *This House of Sky* is a book inspired by and structured on the principles of memory, *Winter Brothers* is inspired by and structured on the principles of place. The first book may be likened to an exploration of family albums, the second to an archaeological dig: Doig excavates the layers of Northwest Coast history, then examines how the layers correspond, merge, and alter with time.

Winter Brothers is structurally intricate, thematically disquieting. Through Doig's evocation of Swan as a resident of the West, he makes the reader newly aware of what Crèvecoeur, Jefferson, and Frederick Jackson Turner knew: as Americans, we have turned our backs on Europe and defined ourselves as citizens of the West. But our citizenship has all too often resulted in thoughtless exploitation. Doig explores what our western identification has meant to us and to the land, using Swan as his guide.

Swan was both a typical and an atypical Northwest pioneer. He came, as did many, out of wanderlust, curiosity, and the desire to make his fortune. Unlike most settlers, however, he was deeply interested in native cultures, which were rapidly disappearing under the pressure of white settlement, and he left behind him a prodigious written record of his life and his involvement with the Indians.

Swan left his native Boston (and his wife and two children) in 1850, flirted with gold mining in California, claimed land on the Washington coast and spent a few months oystering there, and finally moved to Neah Bay and later Port Townsend, where he spent the rest of his life.

Today, Swan is remembered for his two books (both are still considered seminal texts by anthropologists, regionalists, and historians) and for his ethnographic work with the Haida and Makah Indians.[1] He collected their art and artifacts, most of which built the Indian collection at the Smithsonian. Some of them are still on display in the Provincial Museum in Victoria, British Columbia and in the Jefferson County Historical Society at Port Townsend, Washington. He also recorded linguistic information, tribal legends, lore, folk beliefs, and scraps of myth.

As well as being a pioneer, an explorer, and an ethnographer, Swan was a teacher, a government factotum, a sometime alcoholic, and an tireless diarist. *Winter Brothers* grew from Doig's interest in Swan's diaries, particularly from his discovery that they could not be shaped into the kind of work he had done on Oliphant, McGilvra, and Duncan—that is, they resisted synthesis into primary sources for short articles on Northwest frontier history. In his discussion of how *Winter Brothers* took shape in his mind, Doig recounts his discovery of the diaries in the collection at the University of Washington and his subsequent fascination with their author:

> I would write of him sometime, I had decided. Do a magazine piece or two, for I was in the business then of making those smooth packets of a few thousand words. Just use this queer indefatigable diarist Swan some rapid way as a figurine of the Pacific Northwest past.
>
> Swan refused figurinehood, and *rapid* was the one word that never visited his pencils and pens. When, eight, ten years ago, I took a segment of his frontier life and tried to lop it into magazine-article length, loose ends hung everywhere. As well write about Samuel Pepys only what he did during office hours at the British admiralty. A later try, I set out carefully to summarize Swan—oyster entrepreneur, schoolteacher, railroad speculator, amateur ethnologist, lawyer, judge, homesteader, linguist, ship's outfitter, explorer, customs collector, author, small-town bureaucrat, artist, clerk—and surrendered in dizziness, none of the spectrum having shown his true and lasting occupation: diarist (*WB* 1980, 4).

Swan's diaries are intriguing because they provide so much information about life in Washington Territory and its native cultures and also because, although they are by no means confessional, they reveal a great deal about the man who wrote them. What they reveal, however, does not necessarily conform to twentieth-century standards of literary achievement. If we take as a model the journals of Henry David Thoreau, for example, we find the diaries of James Swan much less poetic and philosophical, more impressive in quantity than quality. In his introduction to Swan's book, *The Northwest Coast*, Norman Clark discusses Swan's diaries, pointing out that they seem to have been written less from a desire to communicate to posterity than from an obsession with detail:

> The diaries he kept during these years are voluminous records of his day-to-day events and observations, even temperatures and tides, all of them neat, methodical, and literate. One wonders if he wrote all this with any conviction that his life in a muddy sawmill village glowed with a message or a vision that he would somehow, someday, cast into words and books. In these thousands of pages there is no hint that he did. Nor is there any implicit thrust or spirit, any insights, questions, or indignations. They are not the work of a dedicated artist or scholar or even of a self-consciously literary man (Clark 1972, xviii-xix).

Lucile McDonald, author of *Swan Among the Indians: Life of James G. Swan*, drew on the diaries for her biography and also used them to track down Swan's unsigned contributions to newspapers and his extensive personal and business correspondence. She points out that if Swan had not written so much, his claim to fame would be meager, though he was not a man to be modest about his own accomplishments:

> His writings reveal prodigious activity in more than a dozen different directions—student, adviser and partisan of the Indians, historian, promoter, folklorist, naturalist, lawyer, author of legislative measures, doctor, cook, teacher, musician, artist, journalist, boatbuilder's helper, and commission merchant. The writings also, in their entirety, disclose the man himself. Strangely enough, in his diaries Swan seemed bent on concealing his true personality (McDonald 1972, viii-ix).

McDonald speculates that Swan's reluctance to write very much about his personal life (particularly the periodic bouts of drinking, which are a matter of court record) was because of his anticipation that "his notes [would] be read by posterity and nothing should be written which would mar the image" (McDonald 1972, 196). But McDonald does not judge Swan harshly and believes that he was "basically a very human and lovable person" (McDonald 1972, ix).

Not everyone finds the old pioneer so disarming. Clark, for example, sums up Swan's accomplishments thus: "In all, he lived from hand to mouth, using his land claim as an annuity by selling small pieces, and performing odd jobs of simple literacy in a society where simple literacy was in demand" (Clark 1972, xx). Douglas Cole, in chapter 2 of *Captured Heritage,* which discusses Swan's ethnographic work, is even more severe: "Perpetually dissatisfied, always seeking any small honor that would help elevate his position to where his self-esteem placed it, Swan is an example of the shiftless, unsuccessful man of the territories" (Cole 1985, 15).

Doig's assessment of James Swan is neither sentimental nor critical. He set out to achieve empathy with Swan, to understand the meaning of his experiences. Intrigued by *text,* Doig re-created *context:* he read Swan's diaries, correspondence, and books; researched his life (relying on McDonald's biography and articles she had published in the *Seattle Times*); studied the Indian cultures Swan observed; and literally retraced the man's footsteps, traveling to Port Townsend and Neah Bay, to Ozette and to the Washington coast where Swan had held a claim. This field work precludes Doig's book's becoming a mere redaction of other scholarly and popular texts about Swan. After all, Doig does not uncover previously unavailable material, nor does he offer startling new interpretations of Swan's life. What he provides is an alternative to scholarly commentary on archived material: he articulates Swan's experiences in the West by comparing them with his own, a method that brings into focus the changes that one hundred years of history have made in this region.

The title *Winter Brothers* refers to the fact that Doig spends a winter season with Swan, with texts by and about him, visiting the places where he lived and traveled. The author sometimes makes Swan seem cozily avuncular by comparing Swan and himself: their decisions to invest their lives in the West, their need to put words on paper, even their physical similarities. And Doig sometimes makes Swan marvelous and strange, comparing his legacy of recorded experience to Patience Loader's or Lewis and Clark's, commenting on the coolness with which Swan faced tense encounters with the Indians and, at the age of sixty-five, embarked on a canoe trip up the treacherous western coast of the Queen Charlotte Islands. Because Doig writes in present tense, rather than retrospectively, Swan's life is not reified into historical artifact but rather unfolds before the reader like a drama.[2]

There are three basic structural patterns in *Winter Brothers:* temporal, generic, and contextual. Within those are more intricate structures. The overall movement of the book is chronological: Doig traces Swan's life from his arrival in the Northwest in 1840 to his death in Port Townsend in 1880. The first section of the book describes Swan's transformation from easterner to westerner, particularly his relationship with the Makahs at Neah Bay. The second section examines Swan's life in Port Townsend; the third, Swan's interest and involvement in collecting Indian art. These sections are also divided into the calendar of winter months and days that Doig spends on the relevant portions of Swan's diary. Hence, the sections are called "The Boston Bird: December-January," "The White Tribe: February," "The Cracked Canoe: March." Doig controls the wealth of material from Swan's diaries by focusing on themes about life in the West over the span of two centuries. Often these themes—such as native cultures, ecological exploitation, the act of writing—resonate in Doig's own life, and he is able to comment on Swan's experience from his personal perspective, as well as from the position of a scholar who knows the outcome of nineteenth-century dreams and efforts.

Within the temporal structure, which moves forward through Swan's life and, simultaneously, back and forth between the centuries, are structures derived from Northwest contexts. Indian art, particularly the art of totem poles, inspired one of the subtle patterns in *Winter Brothers*. Totem poles are simultaneously individualized and stylized, certain motifs and patterns reappearing on different poles and sometimes on the same pole. The reproduction of those patterns results partly from the use of templates, precut shapes that carvers use to replicate a pattern. When Doig's research on Northwest art revealed to him the existence of templates, he adopted something of the same practice in *Winter Brothers:* quotations from the diary are followed by Doig's thoughts, followed by more quotations, more thoughts, and so on. Words and phrases, like the shapes on a totem pole, are repeated, serving to echo back even as they move the book forward.[3]

Doig also uses a genre structure: because he is writing about diaries, *Winter Brothers* is written as a journal, a ninety-day record of "Swan and me and those constant diaries. Day by day, a logbook of what is uppermost in any of the three of us" (*WB* 1980, 4). Uppermost for Doig is his exploration of Swan's life, and his own, in terms of the West: why people were, and are, compelled by the westering urge; what it meant to live in the West a hundred years ago; what it means now. Doig's format provides a dual set of perceptions: we look over the author's shoulder as he looks over Swan's, and the two men and the Wests they inhabit fuse. Doig finds a perfect organic metaphor for this blending in the intertwining life forms of the Northwest rainforest:

Totem pole, one of the inspirations for the structure of **Winter Brothers** *(1980).*

The fascination of the rain forest is that all flows into and out of all else; here I can sense how the Haidas, whom Swan went among in their own clouds of forest, could produce art in which creatures swim in and out of each other, the designs tumble, notch together, uncouple, compress, surge. This forest's version is that an embankment with a garden of fir seedlings and ferns sprouting from it will turn out to be not soil, but a downed giant tree, its rot giving the nurture to new generation. Moss-like growth romps its way up tree trunks, and from amid the fuzzy mat spurts licorice fern, daintily leafing into the air sixty feet above the ground. Alders and broad-leaf elm are adorned with club moss, their limbs in wild gesticulation draped with the flowing stuff (*WB* 1980, 212–13).

The interpenetration of life forms was a common motif for Haida artists, who "weren't bound by the silly feeling that it's impossible for two figures to occupy the same space at the same time" (*WB* 1980, 195), and functions as a significant structural and thematic device of *Winter Brothers*. Doig occupies Swan's space, literally and literarily, which allows him to represent the past and to historicize the present. For example, on day forty-three of his winter with Swan, Doig spends the morning on Whidbey Island watching the sun rise over Admiralty Inlet, a setting that draws his eye "west onto the entire great bending valley of water. And south to the trim farmland where on a summer midnight in 1857, Indians snicked off a head" (*WB* 1980, 127). This brief section exemplifies the intricate structure of *Winter Brothers*, which moves from one historical period to another effortlessly, often within the space of a sentence. Doig describes the scene before him, discusses the incident when Tlingit Indians removed Mr. Ebey's head, and muses,

Peculiar, for a timber and water empire which appears so everlastingly placid and was explored by whites and yielded by the natives with perhaps less bloody contention than any other early American frontier, that the practice of beheading crops up so in the Sound and Strait country (*WB* 1980, 127).

Having thematized his dawn reverie, Doig reviews an incident of decapitation which Swan had recorded, that leads him to recall another, noted by Peter Puget, which had taken place one hundred years before Swan's time. Doig speculates about what Puget might have said about the Tlingit's treatment of Ebey's head, and then returns the reader to the present:

Come look from this eminence of bluff now in the soft hour before daybreak and you will declare on Bibles that the Tlingits' act of 122 years ago was the last sharp moment on this landscape. The island's farm fields are leather and corduroy, rich even panels between black-furred stands of forest (*WB* 1980, 128).

Doig speculates that all of the things that ever happen in a place remain there: "Across there, invisible yet imprinted, curves the canoe route which Swan traveled time on time during his Neah Bay years" (*WB* 1980, 128). Then Doig reverts to Swan's diaries, by turns paraphrasing and summarizing, quoting, musing on the entries, repeatedly coming back from the diaries to the scene before him. The section ends:

A second illumination of this sunrise. I realize that I bring myself back and back to this bluff because here scenes still fit onto each other despite their distances of time. Becoming rarer in the West, constancy of this sort. What I am looking out over in this fresh dawn is little enough changed from the past that Swan in a Makah canoe, coming or going on the Port Townsend-Neah Bay route, can be readily imagined across there, the sailing gulls slide through his line of sight as they do mine. Resonance of this rare sort, the reliable echo from the eye inward, I think we had better learn to prize like breath (*WB* 1980, 131–32).

"The reliable echo from the eye inward" depends upon our leaving the western landscape unaltered. Doig realizes, as Swan did not, that the landscape is fragile, but its exploitation is probably inevitable. He refers to Swan's ongoing flirtation with the Northern Pacific Railroad, which was inspired not only by Swan's dream of Port Townsend's becoming an important city, by also by his desire to make money. In this regard, Swan was, unfortunately, a fairly typical westerner. Doig writes:

It is the thing I would change first about the West, or rather, about an ample number of westerners. Their conviction that in this new land, just because it is new, wealth somehow ought to fall up out of the ground into their open pockets. Such bonanza notions began with the Spaniards peering for golden cities amid buffalo grass, and surged on through the fur trade, the mining rushes, the laying of the railroads, the arrival of the loggers, the taking up of farmland and grazing country, the harvest of salmon rivers, and even now are munching through real estate and coal pits and whatever can be singled out beyond those.

Besides a sudden population the West—the many Wests—have had to support this philosophy of get-rich-quicker-than-the-next-grabber-and-to-hell-with-the-consequences, and the burden of it on a half-continent of limited cultivation capacities has skewed matters out here considerably (*WB* 1980, 137).[4]

Doig, like Swan, preserves the West in the only way available to him—on his pages. He records the weather, the bird-life in his own backyard, the activities of local cats. He describes his camping and hiking trips, the suburban sprawl and "development" encroaching on his neighborhood. His observations have led some critics to label *Winter Brothers* a "self-conscious" book, and so it is.[5] It has the very self-consciousness, and historical consciousness, that Norman Clark found lacking in Swan's diaries. As well as different historical periods, Doig occupies different narrative spaces, conversing sometimes with the reader, sometimes with Swan. For example, when the diaries reveal that Swan has come down with Terminus Fever, a common enough disease in the railroad-hungry West, Doig writes, "Swan, I would turn you if I could from this railroad courtship. I know its outcome, and you would be better off spending your ink money and postage to bet on fistfights in your favorite waterfront saloon" (*WB* 1980, 136).

Doig then quotes from a letter Swan wrote to Thomas Canfield of the Northern Pacific (in which he proposed himself as a paid regional scout for the railroads) and comments to the reader, "Swan in this Port Townsend life is showing something I have not seen much of since his time among the Shoalwater oyster entrepreneurs. He has a little bright streak of hokum in him, which begins at his wallet" (*WB* 1980, 136–37).

The narrative and structural intricacies of *Winter Brothers* derive from Doig's use of Northwestern motifs: the life-and-death profusions of the rainforest, the world view reflected in a totem pole. These motifs, as much as the diaries, shape the book. And Doig's unique format precludes the impersonality of a historical novel or the distancing of a biography.

Winter Brothers did not enjoy the same enthusiastic reception as *This House of Sky*. Although many critics praised its elegance of style, others criticized Doig's attempt to fuse his experiences with Swan's.[6] Nevertheless, *Winter Brothers* is a compelling vision of the Northwest frontier, balanced between the author's personal experiences and his historical observations. Above all, Doig's ability to incorporate into his prose the organic and artistic forms indigenous to the Northwest is a major achievement and deserves serious critical attention.

In Doig's third book and first work of fiction, *The Sea Runners*, landscape again suggests structure and nearly becomes a character in itself.

Chapter 4
The Sea Runners

Like *Winter Brothers, The Sea Runners* resulted from a fortuitous find in a library.[1] Doig was reading through back issues of a regional newspaper for information about one of Swan's contemporaries when he came across an article about three Swedes who in 1853 had made a daring, twelve-hundred mile canoe run down the Northwest coast from New Archangel (now Sitka, Alaska), to Shoalwater Bay (now Willapa Bay) on the Washington coast. The article reported only their names, the fact that they were fleeing indentureships with the Russian fur company, and that a fourth man in their company had been killed by Indians along the way. Doig's imagination was sparked by this brief account, and his re-creation of the Swedes' journey became his first novel.

The Sea Runners, like all of Doig's books, is partly the product of research, much of it done on site. Doig and his wife, Carol, traveled to Alaska while he was preparing the manuscript. The descriptions of landscape in the book, which are some of the most powerful in his writing, derive from his own observations. In the Alaska Historical Library in Juneau he discovered maps that became the models for those Melander steals from the Russians and found information about the early fur trade. The first section, in which the conspirators plan their escape, is enlivened by details about the Russian outpost that Doig found in a diary kept by a visitor to Sitka in the 1850s—

Ivan Doig at an Olympic Peninsula Beach, Washington, the setting for Braaf's drowning in **The Sea Runners** *(1969).*

the fact that the officers drank champagne, that there were flowerbeds in the settlement, and that the sentries called out every hour.[2] The description of the little colony wedged between the mountains and the sea and the work routines and the patterns of the night watchmen, all gleaned from primary sources, are woven economically into the story.

The novel takes place during the nineteenth century, a time when Old World empires reached out to exploit territories they knew little about except that their resources could line the coffers of kings. The Russian colony, like the Hudson's Bay Company, existed for profit and remained isolated from the natives and the landscape that surrounded it. The officers maintained the rigid class system of the old country: the men who did the actual work were "seven year men," indentured as often by force as by choice. *The Sea Runners* is a novel dominated by the geographic, cultural, and personal distances that mark this period, and its heroes are four men who dare to challenge those distances.

The story itself is simple and compelling. Melander, a sailor from Gotland who left his first-mate's position aboard a Swedish trader and signed on with the Russians in the hope of serving aboard their steamship, has been assigned to catch and salt fish instead. Disillusioned, weary of the tedious work, and eager to be at sea again, he decides to escape in a native (Tlingit) canoe to Astoria, the American trading post on the Columbia River, where

Reconstructed blockhouse, the sea runners' gate of escape, Sitka, Alaska (1980).

he can find a ship bound for Sweden. Unable to manage such a journey alone, Melander chooses his confederates carefully: Karlsson, a woodsman and hunter, is skilled in handling canoes; Braaf, a thief, can steal the supplies they need from the stores of the Russians. It is Melander's talent to make these disparate personalities function as a unit. He notes, "The three of us are like a shock of rye when your Småland fields are harvested, Karlsson. Together we lean in support of one another. Take any one away and we fall" (SR 1982, 33). Their escape plan, masterminded by Melander, evolves smoothly over the months that follow. Braaf builds a cache of the supplies they will need, Karlsson chooses a canoe to steal.

The canoe, on which the men's lives will depend, marks an important shift away from the mentality of the Russian colony, which has cut itself off from wilderness and natives, closed itself behind stockade walls, protected itself with the guns of the steamship. The canoe, by contrast, is hewn from the forest, carved by a craftsman who worked within the laws of the natural world:

> Karlsson had eyed out a choice—a twenty-foot shell with a high bold bow, the sheer of its hull rising and sharpening into this cutwater as a scimitar curves in search of its point. High and pointy the stern, too, as though both the ends of this canoe were on sentry against the sea. Gunwales rounded and deftly lipped. Four strong thwarts. And encupping it all, that most beautiful stunt of wood, a great cedar taken down with reverence and wile—*I shall cut you down, tree. You will not twist and warp, tree. You will not have knotholes, tree. Black bear skins have been laid in the place where you will fall, tree* (SR 1982, 36–37).

Melander steals the maps they will need to find their way down the coast. Their plans progress smoothly until they are discovered by the blacksmith, Wennberg, a sour, sullen man who threatens to betray them to the Russians unless he is included in the escape. Despite the danger Wennberg's quarrelsome personality poses, the conspirators decide to take him along.

Part 2 of the novel begins with the first stage of the sea journey. The four men effect their escape on Christmas Eve while the Russians are feasting, and conclude rightly that because of the holiday, pursuit will be slow and half-hearted. That first night, they face the problems that will plague them throughout their journey: the wet, chilling weather, their inexperience as paddlers, the tension and fear that make tempers erupt, the terrible distance they face, fatigue and pain:

The paddler's exertion is like that of pulling yourself hand over hand along an endless rope. The hands, wrists, arms—yes, they tire, stiffen. The legs and knees learn misery, from the position they are forced to keep for so long. But where the paddling effort eats deep is the shoulder blade. First at one, then when the paddle is shifted to the other side of the canoe for relief, the ache moves across to the other: as if all weariness chose to ride the back just there, on those twin bone saddles (*SR* 1982, 78).

Their route takes them down the eastern side of the islands that lie in a broken chain off the Pacific coast. They face the worst weather possible in that region: gusting winds, fog, rain, snow. They suffer hunger too and augment their stores with fish and game when they can. But they must move with stealth, keep fires spare and gunshots few and far between. Worst of all, they must live with the clashing of four different personalities. Melander becomes skilled at making them work as a team; he scolds, teases, encourages, and the others come to rely on his leadership and tact. Each discovers previously unknown skills: Karlsson becomes the cook, Braaf the weather-reader, Wennberg the strongest paddler. Gradually and grudgingly, they begin to talk to each other. But Wennberg, particularly, is a dark, brooding man, given to dangerous fits of temper that occasionally threaten their safety. And they are not alone on the coast:

Until now, insofar as Melander and company could discern in their clamber down the precipice of coastline, not another human might ever have existed among these shore islands. Take the matter to truth, though, and their journey more resembled the course a late-of-night stroller might follow through slumbering neighborhoods. In tribal clusters, perhaps as many as sixty thousand residents inhabited this long littoral of what would become British Columbia: Tlingits, Haidas, Tsimshians, Bellabellas, Bella Coolas, Kwakiutls, Nootkas, peoples often at odds among themselves but who had in common that they put their backs to the rest of the continent and went about matters as if they alone knew the terms of life (*SR* 1982, 118–19).

The first death among the men comes from an Indian rifle, and costs them Melander—their leader, the experienced sailor and map-reader, who made them work as an efficient team and kept them from each other's throats. The remaining three then discover Melander's secret: the maps he stole from the Russians are incomplete and will not take them farther south than the half-way mark they have already reached. Now they must travel without Melander, and travel blind. In another catastrophe, Braaf is drowned. Karlsson and Wennberg, exhausted and near starvation, take the canoe a bit further south and then collapse. They are finally rescued by oystermen a few miles north of Astoria.

The Sea Runners differs markedly from This House of Sky and Winter Brothers in narrative technique. The first two books are shaped by the author's examination of his own experiences, and the perspective is one of personal discovery, unveiling. In The Sea Runners, however, the story is told by an omniscient narrator, whose impersonal, historical perspective emphasizes the relative puniness of the characters in contrast to the size of their endeavor:

> These four Swedes in a Tlingit canoe are attempting a thousand or twelve hundred miles—something of that range, by Melander's estimate—of this North Pacific world. Not all so much, you may say. A fraction of a shard of an ocean, after all. Ten or a dozen hundred miles: in fifty or sixty sturdy days one might walk such a distance and perhaps yet have a wafer's-worth of leather on one's boot soles. Except that much of this particular distance is exploded into archipelago: island, island, island, island, like a field of flattened asteroids. Except, too, for season being fully against these watergoing men, the weather of winter capable of blustering them to a halt any hour of each day and seldom apt to furnish the favoring downcoast wind needed to employ the canoe's portable mast and square sail. Except, more than that, current too being against them, the flow of the Alaska Current up this coast as they seek to stroke down it. Except, finally, for details of barrier the eye and mind just now are beginning to reach—forbidding bristle of forest on those countless islands, white smash of breakers on rocks hidden amid the moating channels—so greatly more complex is this jagged slope of the North Pacific than the plain arithmetic of its miles.
>
> In this picture, Melander as he raptly stashes his boxes of tea and swags of sailcloth amounts to a worker ant on the rock toe of an Alp (SR 1982, 89–90).

In this quotation, the narrator provides the reader with information the characters could not know: the exact topography through which they must pass. The narrator sets up a metaphor for the distance the characters will travel and then demonstrates, step by step, that the metaphor is inadequate. The novel is characterized by distance, both linear and spatial, and its perspective is on a large scale that emphasizes the relative powerlessness of the characters.

The novel opens with a map of the Northwest coast, and the narrator repeatedly focuses on that map from the height of a godlike cartographer. The voyagers' lack of a fourth chart to guide them south of Cape Scott therefore becomes not only a complication of the plot but a metaphor, as well. The landscape of the Northwest, magnificently described, is simply too large and daunting to be grasped and subdued by individuals. It may be traversed and survived, but even those achievements are miraculous, purchased at the cost of two lives.

The narrator occasionally shifts from macro- to microcosmic perspective, focusing for brief periods on the four Swedes, reporting their conversations (and occasionally interior monologues) but more often regarding them from a height that makes them look like insects crawling down the great, broken coastline. This narrative method succeeds wonderfully in conveying the adventure of the voyage, its singularity and its risks, but it also keeps the reader at an emotional distance from the characters.

In *The Sea Runners,* therefore, event is more compelling than character, and the book finally reads like a documentary. We never hear enough from or about the men to care very much what happens to them.[3] Their personalities are extrapolated from their professions. Melander, the sailor, is loquacious and imaginative; Karlsson, the woodsman, is silent and stoic; Braaf, the thief, is shirking and opportunistic; Wennberg, the blacksmith, is sullen and ill tempered. In a well-known discussion of the art of characterization, E. M. Forster describes "flat characters" as characters who are simply drawn, can be summed up in a single phrase, and cannot surprise the reader convincingly by changes in attitude or behavior. In *The Sea Runners,* event surprises the reader but the characters, once established, do not.

There is more creative energy in the descriptions of landscape. Beautiful, unforgiving, mysterious, the environment in this novel exists independently of human beings. In the following passage, for example, the characters exist only as observers of a landscape that has existed long before human memory:

> The fog was lifting from the forest and, abruptly, half a small mountain stepped into view: a startling humped cliff as if one of the cannonball peaks around Sitka had been sawed in half from its summit downward. This very top, start of the astonishing sunder, the pair of men could see only by putting their heads back as far as they could. They might have been peering through the dust of eons rather than the morning's last waft of sea mist. On the sheerness, clumps of long grass

somehow had rooted here and there atop basalt columns; together with moss growth, these tufts made the cliff face seem greatly age-spotted, Methuselan (*SR* 1982, 134).

In *The Sea Runners,* the landscape takes on a literary significance far beyond the traditional definition of "setting." In many passages, the laws of nature function as analogies for human experience:

The spaces between stars are where the work of the universe is done. Forces hang invisibly there, tethering the spheres across the black infinite canyons: an unseeable cosmic harness which somehow tugs night and sun, ebbtide and flood, season and coming season. So too the distances among men cast in with one another on an ocean must operate. In their days of steady paddling, these four found that they needed to cohere in ways they had never dreamt of at New Archangel. To perform all within the same close orbit yet not bang against one another (*SR* 1982, 101).

This passage is typical of *The Sea Runners* in the narrator's objectivity, the metaphoric use of natural law for human relationships, and the fact that this general introduction serves to prepare the reader for dramatic scenes to follow. The episodes of the novel are balanced between descriptions of the men's daily routines and longer narratives of specific incidents, such as Melander's death and the crossing of the Kaigani Strait.

The Sea Runners is an economical book. The journal that Doig kept while he was writing it shows that his revising process focused on three conventions: to distinguish the characters by assigning each of them particular habits of speech and gesture; to bring details into line with historical fact; and, most important for the overall effect of the novel, to achieve its swift clean pace. He collapsed scenes together, pared at paragraphs, cut sentences, made every word count in order to create the tension and movement that characterize the novel.[4] More leisurely is the pace of *English Creek;* published two years after *The Sea Runners.* In this book, Doig moves back to his native Montana, to a different landscape, a different century.

Chapter 5
English Creek

According to Doig's journal, the idea that became *English Creek* began to take shape in his mind when he was still at work on *The Sea Runners,* and he began doing informal research at that time, writing to friends in Montana who could give him information on sheep raising and forest rangering. The original notion of a novel about Montana grew into a trilogy, of which *English Creek* is the first book, *Dancing at the Rascal Fair* the second, *Ride with Me, Mariah Montana* the third.

English Creek takes place at the juncture of stock-raising country and the national forests of the Rocky Mountains. The juxtaposition of landscapes is an appropriate metaphor for this novel, whose setting, themes, and characters balance on edges of change. *English Creek* takes place in 1939, between the close of the Great Depression and the onset of America's involvement in the Second World War. In that pivotal summer, Jick McCaskill, the narrator, experiences the end of childhood and the onset of adulthood.

The novel is divided into three long sections. In each, the rhythms of daily life and work are set within personal and regional dramas: a break in the family, the celebration of the Fourth of July, a forest fire. There is a fourth, brief section in which the narrator, now a mature man, describes the intervening years.

In Part 1, which takes place in June, two conflicts are established. The first, which affects not only the McCaskill family but all the ranchers and farmers in the region, is the harsh, unpredictable Rocky Mountain weather. The Great Depression in the West was caused as much by long winters and dry summers as by the vagaries of eastern banks, and the preceding ten years have been hard ones. This June, the grass looks promising, and for Varick McCaskill, Jick's father, that news is doubly good: he is the ranger for the Two Medicine National Forest, and cattle and sheep men depend upon him for yearly grazing allotments; he is also responsible for controlling forest fires in his district. So far, Varick's record is spotless. But on his forest is a grim reminder of what can happen when a fire gets out of control—the Phantom Woman burn. The weather bodes well at the beginning of the novel, but its power to make or break people who raise crops and stock, and to create fire conditions, is clearly established.

The second conflict arises when Alec, Jick's older brother, announces that he is going to marry his girl, Leona, and establish his own ranch. Varick and Beth McCaskill know that Alec is sure to fail: even experienced ranchers and farmers have been going under. Moreover, Alec is a gifted mathematician and craftsman; his parents have been scrimping so that he could go to college and study engineering. Alec's decision creates a rift in a hitherto strong family. Jick says:

> I know now, and I somehow knew even then, that the fracture of a family is not a thing that happens clean and sharp, so that you at least can calculate that from here on it will begin to be over with. No, it is like one of those worst bone breaks, a shatter. You can mend the place, peg it and splint it and work to strengthen it, and while the surface maybe can be brought to look much as it did before, the deeper vicinity of shatter always remains a spot that has to be favored (*EC* 1984, 19).

The day after the quarrel with Alec, Varick and Jick pack in to the mountains for their yearly "counting trip"—checking the herds of sheep on the grazing allotments. On the way, they meet Stanley Meixell, who is camptending. Stanley is an old family acquaintence, but Jick knows little about him, and there seems to be some tension between Varick and Stanley. So Jick is surprised when Varick tells him to go along and help Stanley on his trip. This is no small request: Stanley has a wounded hand and a taste for alcohol, which prevent his doing much work. Jick's journey into the mountains is a major step in his journey toward adulthood. Hitherto dependent upon his father, he now has to single-handedly manage a recalcitrant pack-

Walling Reef, Montana, called Roman Reef in **English Creek** *(1983).*

horse, an eccentric sheepherder, and Stanley, and he finds himself equal to all of these.

The camptending trip not only is thematically significant but also establishes the tone, setting, and pace of the novel. Doig's understanding and enjoyment of his characters is refreshingly straightforward. Without resorting to epiphanies-in-the-wilderness, he celebrates the beauty of the mountains. Without sentimentality, he describes family life and the strong bonds created by shared work and play. Because he captures the texture of life through the language of his characters, the book is informative and often very funny. Typical of the novel's verisimilitude and humor is the scene where Stanley and Jick tend their first sheepherder. Canada Dan, as he is called, has allowed some of the ewes in his flock to get into poisonous fodder and then has let the carcasses lie in the rain for three days:

> "[We've got] about fifteen head of goddamn dead ones, that's what. They got onto some deathcamas, maybe three days back. Poisoned theirselfs before you can say sic 'em." Canada Dan reported all this as if he was an accidental passerby instead of being responsible for these animals. Remains of animals, they were now.
>
> "That's a bunch of casualties," Stanley agreed. "I didn't happen to notice the pelts anywhere there at the wag—"

"Happened right up over here," Canada Dan went on as if he hadn't heard, gesturing to the ridge close behind him. "Just glommed onto that deathcamas like it was goddamn candy. C'mon here, I'll show you.". . . .

I began to dread the way this was trending.

The place Canada Dan led us to was a pocket meadow of bunch grass interspersed with cream-colored blossoms and with gray mounds here and there on it. The blossoms were deathcamas, and the mounds were the dead ewes. Even as cool as the weather had been they were bloated almost to bursting.

"That's them," the herder identified for our benefit. "It's sure convenient of you fellows to show up. All this goddamn skinning, I can stand all the help I can get."

Stanley did take the chance to get a shot in on him. "You been too occupied the past three days to get to them, I guess?" But it bounced off Canada Dan like a berry off a buffalo.

The three of us looked at the corpses for a while. There's not all that much conversation to be made about bloated sheep carcasses. After a bit, though, Canada Dan offered in a grim satisfied way: "That'll teach the goddamn buggers to eat deathcamas" (*EC* 1984, 68–69).

As he had feared, Jick winds up doing the skinning and most of the hard work for the rest of the trip. In the process he develops self-reliance: faced with a broken pack on a runaway packhorse, he is torn between going for help and solving the problem himself—and he solves it himself.

"Son of a goddamn sonofabitch," I remember was all I managed to come out with to commemorate this discovery. That wasn't too bad under the circumstance, for the situation called for either hard language or hot tears, and maybe it could be pinpointed that right there I grew out of the bawling age into the cussing one (*EC* 1984, 85).

Stanley's acknowledgment of Jick's coming of age is reflected in the comments he makes ("Oh, to be young and diddling twice a day again"), in his introducing Jick to the dubious pleasures of whiskey, and his telling Jick something of his own history. Stanley has been a farmer, a hay hand, an association rider, a cowboy, a logger, a river pig. He was also the ranger who established the boundaries of the Two Medicine National Forest. The "forest arrangers," who preserved millions of wilderness acres against men determined to exploit that land for personal gain, were legendary. Jick is awed, then puzzled. In all of his father's stories about the Forest Service, he had never mentioned Stanley. At the end of the trip, despite unsolved mysteries and the trials he has endured, Jick is able to say to Stanley, "It's been an education."

Just as Doig communicates the beauty of the landscape without hyperbole and Jick's personal development without melodrama, so does he describe Jick's growing sexual awareness without explicit scenes. The mildly ribald jokes men make in his presence, as well as Jick's own observations about female anatomy and behavior, humorously capture the natural curiosity of the adolescent male. For example, his father's comment, "Let's keep our shirts on here" gives Jick "the vision just then of us all sitting around the table with our shirts off, Leona across from me in full double-barreled display" (*EC* 1984, 12).

Similarly subtle is the revelation of the ethics that inform the book, expressed in the phrase, "Well, we got it to do." These people are, for the most part, hard working and generous. Beth McCaskill not only cares competently for her own family but "comes out long on the baking" every week so that she can send bread and pies to neighbors. Jick assumes the less pleasant jobs on the camptending trip because, "In my father's universe matters fell that way." Characters who shirk responsibility or refuse to help a neighbor are treated with humor and contempt, like Good Help Hebner with his "oughtobiography" (ought to have done this, ought to have thought of that) and Canada Dan.

Part 1 is unified by the action, most of which centers on Jick. His narration of the events of June is punctuated by digressions about family lore and valley history, by anecdotes about minor characters, and by his speculations on the nature of adult experience. Like most adolescents, Jick is striving to understand the world beyond himself and to learn about the past. His curiosity about family lore—for example, the cause of the tension between Stanley Meixell and his father—is seldom satisfied. At one point he comes across a reminiscence in the local newspaper about his mother, his Uncle Pete, and his grandmother, who died before he was born. The article recounts a wagon trip they made to visit Beth's father, who was helping to build a roadbed. When Jick asks his mother for the details of the trip, she seems reluctant to supply them and tells Jick that she is worried about him:

All this interest of yours in the way things were. I just hope you don't go through life paying attention to the past at the expense of the future. That you don't pass up chances because they're new and unexpected ... there isn't any law that says a McCaskill can't be as forward-looking as anybody else. Just because your father and your brother, each in his own way, looks to the past to find life, you needn't.... Jick, be ready for your life ahead. It can't all be read behind you (*EC* 1984, 124).

Herein, two of the themes of *English Creek*: the role of the past in the present—what texts comprise history, who controls and shapes them, what effect they have on our lives; and second, how often we are ignorant about the people we should know best. Jick thinks: "They are beyond our knowing, those once young people who become our parents, which to me has always made them that much more fascinating" (*EC* 1984, 123). This second theme is more fully explored in *Dancing at the Rascal Fair* and *Ride with Me, Mariah Montana*.

On the subject of regional history, Jick's best source is Toussaint Rennie, a seemingly ageless man, part Indian, who lived through the final days of the Blackfeet before the destruction of the buffalo, who remembers the great cattle drives, the coming of the homesteaders, the fencing and domestication of the land. Toussaint serves as a kind of Tiresias, quietly judging the present by the standards of the past. At the rodeo, when Dode Withrow (who is Varick's age) rides a bucking bronc and puts on quite a show before he breaks his leg, Toussaint is there to evaluate and commemorate his ride:

> Toussaint was paying no attention to any of this conversation, nor to the process of Dode being put on a stretcher over his protestations that he could walk or even foot-race if he had to, nor to Coffee Nerves being tugged into exit through what little was left of the catch pen gate. Instead, he, Toussaint, was standing there gazing into the exact center of the arena, as if the extravaganza that Coffee Nerves and Dode had put on still was continuing out there. The walnut crinkles deepened in his face, his chuckle rippled out, and then the declaration: "That one. That one was a ride" (*EC* 1984, 195).

Part 2 of *English Creek* takes place on the Fourth of July and focuses on the community picnic, the rodeo, and the square dance. This section weaves together two major conflicts: the economic and environmental battles that characterize life in the West and the break Alec is making from his family. At the picnic, Beth McCaskill delivers a speech that shows that despite her concern about Jick, she too is absorbed in the past. In her speech, the significance of the title *English Creek* becomes clear. Ben English, for whom the creek was named, "honored the earth instead of merely coveting it" and husbanded the irrigation water that is the lifeblood of the arid West.

Contrasted with Ben English is the rapacious Wendell Williamson, who buys up failed homesteads or leases their range, exploits the land he owns and the people who work for him. (Those familiar with *This House of Sky* will recognize Rankin in the figure of Williamson.) In honoring Ben English, commemorating the families who have been driven out by hard times, condemning the men who have made their fortunes at the expense of those families, Beth McCaskill develops the public side of the private conflict. Alec works for Williamson.

At the rodeo that follows the picnic, Alec wins at calf roping, another demonstration of his determination to be a cowboy despite his parents' wishes. At the square dance, Alec and Leona are paired off against Varick and Beth as the stars on the floor. The struggle between the generations is beautifully and subtly developed in these "set pieces" as Doig calls them, and the descriptions of the scenes and the people who enliven them are masterful. The wealth of concrete sensory detail provides a sense that the story of the Fourth of July is not just being retold but relived and develops one of the most important thematic motifs of *English Creek*: the specialness of the ordinary. The measured pace of the novel, which emphasizes the rich details of daily life, disappoints some readers. In an interview, Nick O'Connell asked Doig:

> One of the reviewers of *English Creek* criticized the book as slow-moving while another reviewer contradicted this and said the pace was entirely appropriate for the period and the characters. Did you design the pace so that it would reflect the way life was during that time?

To which Doig replied:

> It never dawned on me that the actualities of life and how working people lived and went about their labors could be considered plodding; that you had to have green-eyed invaders from outer space before anything was happening. I thought, and still think, a lot of things do happen in *English Creek*.
>
> Along with its seasonal life had to go, I believed, description of the country—sense of the country, sense of the past, as people tell stories and listen to stories. This does not bother me at all as a reader and so it doesn't as a writer. But, Christ, you can edit Faulkner and Conrad and Shakespeare and everybody else down to a third their length and pretty much preserve what ostensibly happens. What you'd lose is the richness in life, and the richness in life is what I'm trying to get at (O'Connell 1987, 305).

The novel's measured pace and emphasis on detail encourage the reader to enter the world of English Creek with Jick's own sense of wonder and delight.

In Part 3, July gives way to August, and haying to forest fires. The haying scenes are depicted right down to the machinery and the way people from different parts of the region greet each other: "Hey," "How do," "How's she going?" and the different ways the phrase "son-of-a-bitch" can be expressed. In a lecture Doig gave at the 1988 Pacific Northwest American Studies Association conference, he commented that when *English Creek* had gone to the publisher, an overeager copy editor had standardized this phrase throughout the book, and Doig had to correct the galley proofs to ensure that the diversity true to the region's dialects was maintained. Much of the humor in the novel is provided by the eccentricities of the minor characters during the haying. These scenes are clearly drawn from Doig's own experiences and local knowledge.

Similarly, Doig's knowledge of forest fires, gleaned from his boyhood and from the research he did for articles on smoke jumping and the Forest Service, comes to play in the final scenes of *English Creek*, and here the novel's conflicts—the family quarrel, the mystery about Stanley Meixell, the treacherous weather—merge. A lightning strike at Flume Gulch begins burning out of control, and Varick goes up there to superintend the fire crew. Flume Gulch was a favorite fishing spot for the McCaskills, and the place recalls Alec and Jick's boyhood years and their bond with their father. Jick contacts Alec and pleads with him to join the fire crew, to use his knowledge of the area to help Varick. But even though Alec's life as a ranch hand has soured and he and Leona have drifted apart, he will not relinquish his independent status. He refuses Jick, and Jick feels the anguish of an irrevocably broken family.

Stanley Meixell volunteers to be camp cook, an enormously important job, given the number of men to be fed, and Jick goes with him to act as "cook's flunky" and to keep an eye on him—Stanley's alcoholism could be disastrous in this situation.

The fire reaches a state of crisis, and Varick has to decide where to move the fire line. A wrong decision could be a blot on his record, and worse, could mean a fire out of control and men at risk. Stanley steps forward and advises Varick to backfire an untouched slope, although this strategy goes against Forest Service regulations. The plan works. Had Varick not listened to Stanley, he and his men would have been incinerated in the gulch.

After the fire is out and the camp is breaking up, Jick demands to know the story of his father's relationship with Stanley. He discovers that Stanley was his father's mentor and friend when Varick had broken off with his own father and had given Varick his start in the Forest Service. Stanley was ranger and fire boss at the Phantom Woman burn. Incapacitated by alcohol, he let it get away from him. Varick had turned him in.

Jick and his father leave the fire camp and reach town in time to hear that war has broken out in Europe. The macrocosmic world looms over the microcosmic, with tragic implications for the people in the valley. In Part 4, a Jick who now looks back on his life instead of forward, reflects on what has happened to his family, and to him, since that innocent summer in 1939.

The story of Jick's family background, and the history of western Montana that shaped that background, are developed in the second novel of the trilogy, *Dancing at the Rascal Fair*.

Chapter 6
Dancing at the Rascal Fair

Dancing at the Rascal Fair **serves as a prequel** to *English Creek*. That is, its main characters, Rob Barclay and Angus McCaskill, belong to the generation that preceeds that of *English Creek*: Angus, who narrates the book, is Varick's father, a grandfather who died before Jick could know him.

The echoes between *English Creek* and *Rascal Fair* begin with maps of the area that embrace territory that is partly Montana, partly Doig's invention: English Creek, Noon Creek, Roman Reef, Jerico Reef, Rooster Mountain, Flume Gulch. The names of the ranches show the changes and the continuities in the history of the place. The chapters in *Rascal Fair*, like the sections in *English Creek*, are introduced by news clippings that provide a dispassionate perspective on the world of the characters and also serve as a thematic device. The clipping at the beginning of chapter 1 of *Rascal Fair*, for example, reports the drowning of a cart horse off the quay of Albert Harbour, where the westbound ship is loading emigrants. The drowned horse, a grotesque and comic image, returns as a tragic one at the end of the novel. As Jick does in *English Creek*, Angus, the first-person narrator of *Rascal Fair*, tells the story in retrospect, that most haunting of perspectives. But while Jick addresses the reader, much of Angus's narration is addressed to his friend Rob Barclay. Angus muses:

For I can't but think of you then, Rob. The Rob you were. In all that we said to each other, before and thereafter, this step from our old land to our new was flat fact with you. The Atlantic Ocean and the continent America all the way across to Montana stood as but the width of a cottage threshold, so far as you ever let on. No second guess, never a might-have-done-instead out of you, none. A silence too total, I realize at last. You had family and a trade to scan back at and I had none of either, yet I was the one tossing puppy looks up the Clyde to yesterday. Man, man, what I would give to know. Under the stream of words by which you talked the two of us into our long step to America, what were your deep reasons? I am late about asking, yes. Years and years and years late. But when was such asking ever not? And by the time I learned there was so much within you that I did not know and you were learning the same of me, we had greater questions for each other (*RF* 1987, 4).

In this passage are the seeds of several themes, that are, as is common in Doig's work, both national and particular, historical and personal. Angus McCaskill and Rob Barclay are part of the great nineteenth century migrations, in which half the populations of Ireland and Norway, and great numbers of Scots and Swedes and Germans and Danes, came to claim the lands of the West and wrestle new life out of them. The difficulties faced by these immigrants are addressed in *Crofutt's Trans-Atlantic Emigrants' Guide*:

Do not emigrate in a fever, but consider the question in each and every aspect. The mother country must be left behind, the family ties, all old associations, broken. Be sure that you look at the dark side of the picture: the broad Atlantic, the dusty ride to the great West of America, the scorching sun, the cold winter—coldest ever you experienced!—and the hard work of the homestead. But if you finally, with your eyes open, decide to emigrate, do it nobly. Do it with no divided heart (*RF* 1987, 3).

In *Rascal Fair*, the theme of the divided heart applies not only to emigrants facing the unknown, but to these two men. Through their experiences and relationships, this book develops the theme of personal epistemology introduced in *English Creek*: how well do we know anyone, particularly the people we think we know best? As Jick discovers a stranger in his brother, so Angus learns that he cannot fathom the two people he loves best in the world.

*Ivan Doig at Panbride Church in Scotland, doing research for **Dancing at the Rascal Fair** (1979). The Doig family originally came from this parish.*

The first chapter of *Rascal Fair* describes the trip to America, a sea voyage that Angus dreads because he is afraid of the water and cannot swim. This fact, like the drowned cart horse, also returns at the end of the novel.

After the crossing of the Atlantic and the journey to Montana, Rob and Angus begin their search for Lucas Barclay, Rob's uncle. Like many immigrants, they are following a relative who has gone before them. Lucas has owned a mine, and the young men set out to locate him, seeking him first in Helena, then traveling to Butte, questioning stagecoach drivers, examining public records, even visiting cemeteries. Their quest is both comic and disquieting, and emphasizes the sheer size of Montana, its emptiness, the long stretches of prairie haphazardly linked by freight wagons, the fact that people shifted around a lot. Mines changed hands frequently. Individuals who did not get rich fast enough often dropped one enterprise and moved on to the next—a pattern of instability perplexing to newcomers used to families living in one spot for generations.

Rob and Angus discover through a letter from Scotland that Lucas is living in a new settlement called Gros Ventre (pronounced "Grove-On," the Montanan pronunciation of the French appellation for the Indians there, which means "Big Belly") in the Northwest part of Montana.[1] On their journey there by stagecoach and freight wagon, they discover Montana's beauty and also its treacherousness: an April snow obliterates the faint wagon trail, an ominous foreshadowing of winters to come. In Gros Ventre they do find Lucas, but he owns a saloon, not a mine, and he has lost his hands. The maiming of Lucas is symbolic of the risks and hardships awaiting settlers: it is clear that Montana will demand its own price—physical, psychological, emotional—from those who try to wrest a life and livelihood from her soil. Lucas manages very well without hands, and what he can't manage is taken care of by the woman who lives with him. Nancy, whose real name is Buffalo Calf Speaks, is a Blackfeet Indian, niece-by-marriage to Toussaint Rennie, who colors the pages of both *English Creek* and *Rascal Fair*. Nancy is one of the few Native Americans who appears in the works of Doig, and she is silent, inscrutable, an anachronism in the white world, a reminder that when the whites moved in and slaughtered the buffalo, they killed the Indians just as surely as cavalry bullets would have.

Nancy's history was typical of the Indian experience in the late 1800s. Her family, among many others, died during the winter of 1883, aptly called The Starvation Winter. The buffalo had gone, the winter rations the Blackfeet were supposed to receive were stolen by an Indian agent, and smallpox had decimated the tribe. Toussaint and his wife had taken the orphaned Nancy into their own home. But the winter of 1886 was worse even than the winter three years before. Toussaint and his wife were not sure they could keep their own children alive and had to find another home for Nancy, so Toussaint brought her into town and gave her to the DeSalis family. Years later, Lucas bought their house and saloon when the family moved to Missouri. Nancy, grown by then, stayed on with Lucas. Rob and Angus are shocked by the story, but Lucas reminds them, "This isn't old Scotland, lads. Life goes differently here" (*RF* 1987, 60).

Nancy's story embodies one of the major themes of *Rascal Fair*: the contrast between the innocent hope that brought immigrants to Montana and the sometimes grim reality of their lives there. The land they had come to claim was not "free": it had been made available to whites by the disenfranchisement of the Indians. Many of the homesteaders themselves would be dispossessed—by death, by economic failure, by the encroachment of the big ranches, by the weather. Especially by the weather. The winter that starved the Blackfeet in 1883 was one of the "killing winters" in Montana— another like it, in 1919, would bring Rob and Angus close to disaster.

Rob and Angus stay on with Lucas and Nancy until Angus locates homestead claims for both of them near the mountains, where hay and stock can be raised. None too soon, for Rob has developed an interest in Nancy. Lucas loans them the money they need to begin building and partners them with their first band of sheep. The two men begin the necessary building and quickly come to understand that homestead land is anything but "free":

> Here then is land. Just that, land, naked earthskin. And now the due sum: from this minute on, the next five years of your life, please, invested entirely into this chosen square of earth of yours.
>
> Put upon it house, outbuildings, fences, garden, a well, livestock, haystacks, performing every bit of this at once and irrespective of weather and wallet and whether you have ever laid hand to any of these tasks before. Build before you can plan, build in your sleep and through your mealtimes, but build, pilgrim, build, claimant of the earth, build, build, build. You are permitted to begin in the kind delusion that your utensils of homestead-making at least are the straightforward ones—axe, hammer, adze, pick, shovel, pitchfork. But your true tools are other. The nearest names that can be put to them are hope, muscle and time (*RF* 1987, 90–91).

As Rob and Angus build their homes and fence their claims and tend their sheep, land is taken up around them by family after family, young women begin to appear, and Rob eventually marries one of them. Angus is asked to teach school and is grateful for the income, since prices for wool and lambs have been low.

The scenes in Angus's classroom are among the liveliest in the book: the children stand out as individuals, and there are incidents that are matchlessly funny. In these scenes Doig explores what it must have been like to be what Teddy Roosevelt called a "hyphenated American," knowing the history and geography of the old country but not of the place you live, feeling the clash of old-world orthodoxies in a new land, bringing Robert Burns into a classroom and having the children respond with cow-puncher songs.[2]

Angus, master of the South Fork school, falls in love with the new teacher of the Noon Creek school. Meeting Anna Ramsay proves to Angus that he was right to wait for a woman he could love, not to make a marriage of convenience. The love affair progresses through a season, and Angus proposes to her the night before she leaves with her parents to spend the summer cooking for a railroad crew. Anna asks him to wait for her answer until she returns in the fall, and he reluctantly agrees.

Rob in the meantime has sent for his younger sister, Adair, who arrives from Scotland expecting to marry Angus. Angus is furious at Rob's presumption. He avoids Adair and does his best to introduce her to other likely young men, even "throwing" a sheering contest so that Adair might find the winner attractive. For Angus is deeply in love with Anna, will never be able to love anyone else. His tragedy is that his love for her is not returned: she marries Isaac Reese, a local horse dealer. In a cruel stroke, Anna tells Angus, "If I ever see that Isaac and I are not right for each other, I'll know where to turn for better," a half-promise that keeps Angus hoping for years that they will someday be together (*RF* 1987, 192).

The loss breaks Angus, and he finds that he cannot go back to living alone. Three days after his meeting with Anna, he proposes to Adair. Because she came from Scotland to marry him and has nothing to return to, she accepts his proposal. Their marriage seems foredoomed. Angus is in love with Anna, now another man's wife. Adair, who is quiet and withdrawn, does not take to homestead life, nor to Montana. As she says to Angus after they have lived there for nearly twenty years, "There is so much of this country. People keep having to stretch themselves out of shape trying to cope with so much. Distance. Weather. The aloneness. All the work. This Montana sets its own terms and tells you, do them or else" (*RF* 1987, 332). But after two miscarriages, Adair and Angus finally have the child they desperately want, and Varick, their son, gives them the strength they need to stay on the land and stay together.

English Creek takes place in a single summer; *Rascal Fair* stretches over two generations. Rob and Angus witness Montana's statehood. They watch their own homesteading efforts flourish or flounder depending upon the weather and the wool prices. In 1910, a second land rush begins the immigration of the pathetic dryland 'steaders. Gros Ventre grows from a scratch on the map to the stable town of Jick's time. Stanley Meixell, young in this novel but already showing signs of the dissolute man of *English Creek*, establishes the Two Medicine National Forest on what was once open summer range for stockmen. World War I and the influenza epidemic claim lives in the valley. Doig deftly weaves the history of the nation and the region into the days of his characters without losing his focus on the drama of their lives.

Because this novel encompasses so many years, "set pieces"—in which an afternoon or an evening, a confrontation or a celebration is retold in vivid detail—are interspersed with years summarized in Angus's commentary: the hard winters, the dry summers, Varick's growth from child to man. What remains constant is Angus's love for Anna and with it grows Rob's anger toward the friend who he believes is betraying his sister. This is the part of family history that Jick is unable to pry from Beth in *English Creek*: that her mother and his grandfather loved each other, and one of their meetings took place on the wagon trip Jick asks about.

Angus's passion for Anna leads to the destruction of his friendship with Rob and a nearly permanent break with his son. Rob, determined to "bring Angus to his senses," tells the fifteen-year-old Varick about his father's love for another woman. Varick, who by that time is working for the Forest Service with his mentor, Stanley Meixell, rejects his father in an anger that lasts until he has gone through a hitch in the army and buried dozens of men who died from influenza. Angus survives a bout of the illness, but Anna dies.

Despite the final reconciliation of father and son, and Adair's patient acceptance of the terms of their life together, the animosity between Rob and Angus grows. Rob becomes ever more bitter and unreasonable, and the crises the two men face together do nothing to resolve their differences. Their enmity ends only with Rob's death, by drowning, on the back of a horse. Angus, who cannot swim, cannot save him.

Life provides its own terms of hurting and healing: Varick marries Beth, Anna's daughter, and by the end of the novel they are expecting their first child, who will be the Alec of *English Creek*. The patterns of rebellion and faith, of constancy and betrayal, of memory and history and story, established in *English Creek* and *Rascal Fair* are examined through contemporary lenses in *Ride with Me, Mariah Montana*.

Chapter 7
Ride with Me, Mariah Montana

The third book of Doig's trilogy, *Ride with Me, Mariah Montana,* takes place in 1989, the state's centennial year. In this novel, Jick McCaskill, now sixty-four, travels for four months around Montana with his daughter and her former husband, both journalists, who are putting together a centennial series for their newspaper. The places they visit are marked by events in Montana's history and often call up painful memories for Jick, who must come to terms with his own past and future in the course of the journey.

In perspective, *Mariah* is quite different from the first two novels of the trilogy. Despite all the hardships its characters endure, *Rascal Fair* looks forward, capturing the hopeful mood of the homesteading period when immigrants poured into a still open frontier and threw themselves into carving out homes and livelihoods, exploring possibilities, living on dreams. *English Creek,* set at the end of the Great Depression, looks around, examining daily life in rural Montana through the eyes of young Jick McCaskill. *Ride with Me, Mariah Montana* looks back, action yielding to reflection as an older Jick examines his own life and history and the life and history of the state.

Mariah fulfills some of the ominous premonitions of *Rascal Fair* and *English Creek:* the land of Montana has been exploited by mining and overgrazing, small ranches taken over by distant corporations, people out of work and moving away, small towns collapsing. The problems facing the state are mirrored in Jick's own life as he struggles with the sometimes grim consequences of the past. His mature perceptions are balanced by those of Mariah, his thirty-five year old daughter, a photographer for a Missoula newspaper, and those of her ex-husband, Riley Wright, a columnist, as they collaborate on the centennial series.

Photography and journalism, significant but subordinate in Doig's earlier work, are central to this one. Their alternative means of seeing and articulating suggest that any depiction of the world is an interpretation of the world, not merely captured but created by selection and representation.

Like *English Creek, Mariah* takes place in a relatively brief period, the action framed by the main characters' four-month journey through, around, into Montana. Three of the four chapter titles are engaging puns on the names of regions they visit: "The End Toward Idaho," "Motating the High Line," "East of Crazy." The familiar map that opens the book is not of the northwest corner of the state, as in the two previous novels, but of the whole state, and it is marked by sketches representing the places Riley and Mariah write about and photograph. (The relative scope of the maps indicate how the scope of the novels in the trilogy open out from Scotch Heaven during the homesteading period to the Two Medicine region in 1939 to the entire state in 1989.) The dramatic structure of the novel is picaresque, complicated by forays into history, story, and memory.

The novel opens on a Gros Ventre rodeo, Jick watching Mariah capture the day's events on film. But Jick, who once found rodeos exciting and significant, simply wants to get away from this one. His life, which had come together in running a ranch, raising his daughters and in his marriage, has fallen apart: keeping the ranch has become problematical, his daughters are grown, and his wife, Marcella, is dead. The loss has hollowed him out: "Her death was as if I'd been gutted, the way a rainbow trout is when you slit his underside all the way to the gills and run your thumbnail like a cruel little plow the length of the cut to shove the insides out" (*MM* 1990, 11).

If *English Creek* can be seen in terms of edges, *Mariah* can be seen in terms of angles: camera angles, the angle on a story, angle of vision, and especially the angled, three-in-one problem that Jick wrestles with throughout the novel: how to respond to Mariah's growing feeling for her ex-husband, how to live without Marcella, and what to do with a ranch he can no longer run.

Jick's problems are exacerbated by Mariah's pestering him to take time away from the ranch and drive her and Riley around Montana as they create the centennial series. Jick detests his former son-in-law for having made Mariah unhappy and for having turned down Jick's offer of the ranch.

Ivan Doig in rented motorhome, near Billings, Montana, doing research for **Ride with Me, Mariah Montana** *(1988).*

Small ranches in Montana, as Doig makes clear in *This House of Sky*, *English Creek*, and *Rascal Fair*, have ever been at the mercy of market prices and the weather. Ranchers borrow hope against the future, but there is never enough money or time or reliable, skilled help. When asked how his ranch is doing, Jick gives the answer his father-in-law always gave: "Doing good, if you don't count going broke." Even the large ranches around him, like the hated WW, have been bought up by "corporaiders," often as tax write-offs, and Jick is repeatedly pressured to sell. Nonetheless, Jick's offer to Riley was more than generous: the ranch is solvent, in good repair, and contains some of the original prairie grasslands that have, in most of the state, been grazed out of existence. With hired help, Mariah and Riley could run the ranch and still have time to pursue their own professional interests. Most of all, the ranch would provide continuity, for the land has been in the family for three generations. But Riley tells Jick that he and Mariah are splitting up.

Hard enough to absorb the shock of a child's divorce, even harder for a parent to accept the end of the family line. Although *Dancing at the Rascal Fair* promised dynasties (Isaac, Jick's maternal grandfather, bears the name of a Biblical patriarch), two generations later only Jick and his two childless daughters remain of the McCaskill and Reese families.

Jick has spent years building up the ranch, holding on to it, hoping to keep it in the family. But Riley urges him to sell out to the WW: "Jick, get out while you can. Ranchers like you aren't going to have a prayer. The pricks running this country are tossing you guys to the big boys like flakes of hay to the elephants" (*MM* 1990, 36).

Their conflict over the ranch typifies the personal differences between the two men. Riley is depicted through Jick's eyes, and therefore appears to be slick, wise-cracking, and insensitive. Riley has one blue eye and one gray eye, which Jick perceives as an image of two-facedness, or deceptiveness, and possibly of his tendency to perceive the world in polarities—good-guys-vs-bad-institutions. It is true that Riley often casts events in political terms, as battles in which large capitalist forces beat down people who have too little money or power to fight back. His columns, however, reveal him to be sensitive and compassionate, sides of his personality that Jick does not see but the reader comes to appreciate.

Despite Riley's disillusionment with contemporary Montana, his view of the world is more comfortable than Jick's. Riley may feel genuine anger at the injustices and stupidities he harangues against in his columns, but he can write about them from an emotional distance. Jick, on the other hand, responds to life in intensely personal, often sensuous terms, reflected in his memories of a first marriage that burned out when the passion did, his brief career as a smoke jumper, years of dawn-to-dark labor on his land.

Because of his feelings about Riley, it is with great reluctance that Jick agrees to be Riley and Mariah's driver and chaperon, donating the Winnebago he and Marcella had bought as their vacation home. He does so only because the outwardly tough and self-reliant Mariah has made a daughterly claim of need on him.

The conversation that settles this point is so brief as to be nearly codified. Of course, people who know each other well can talk in a personal shorthand, but as the book progresses, it is astonishing how little father and daughter tell each other of their deep needs and experiences. Their cultural habit of taciturnity makes them islanded and occasionally mysterious to each other, reinforcing the theme established in the first two novels of the trilogy, that people often don't know what goes on inside the people they should know best. Later in the novel, Jick muses:

That other side of things, I genuinely did have a long curiosity about. In the skin of a woman, how does life seem? I could remember speculating that about my mother, when I was still only a shavetale kid, fifteen or so: ranching and the Forest Service, male livelihoods both then—what did Beth McCaskill think of her existence in that largely man-run scheme of things? Certainly I'd had the occasions to mull McCaskill women since, too. Lexa, taking herself off to Alaska.

Mariah—God, you bet, Mariah. And even though I felt we knew each other to the maximum, sometimes even Marcella had stirred that skin-whisper question (*MM* 1990, 249).

In their silences, the characters in *Mariah* can be regarded, I suppose, as laconic westerners. But the very sparseness of their speech makes it precious, gives simple utterances emotional weight. Jick's feeling for his daughter is expressed in the phrase, "Ride with me, would you Mariah?" and hers for him in, "Jick. Jick, I need to have you along."

How little or how much is said in a given situation is a key to Jick's dual role in the novel: as a character, Jick is conventional in that he conforms to accepted norms of regional behavior, which include brevity of speech. Through his narration, however, Jick emerges as more than that: a keen observer, a poet, a philosopher, articulate and thoughtful. These two Jicks intersect and merge at the end of the novel, in the decisions he makes about his daughter, his future, his land.

One of the pleasures of reading *Mariah* is enjoying Doig's versatility as a writer, manifested here in his use of narrative voice. In *This House of Sky*, narrative is split between the colloquial expressions of Bessie, Charlie, the child Ivan and other people called from Doig's memory, and the literary language of the author. The difference in voice is appropriate to *Sky*, for it reinforces the theme of maturation, the distance between the adult Doig and the childhood he left behind, and also serves to demonstrate the evaluative function of personal narrative. (See also the discussion in chapter 11 about the evaluative function of personal narrative in *This House of Sky*.) But in *Mariah* these two voices, the experiencing voice and the reflecting one, come together in a single consciousness. The difference between what Jick says to the other characters and what he says in interior monologues emphasizes his inner conflicts. For example, fairly early in the journey, Jick tries and fails to tell Mariah why he wants to abandon the trip:

"Mariah," it broke out of me, "I don't think I can go on with this."
In the dimness of the Bago's cab her face whitely swung around to me, surprise there I more could feel than see.
A minute of nothing said. The pale glow of the dash lights seemed a kind of visible silence between us.
Then she asked, her eyes still steady on me: "What brought this on?"
Here was opportunity served up under parsley, wasn't it. Why, then, didn't I speak the answer that would have included her situation with Riley and my own with the memory flood unloosed by the sight

of Shirley in Missoula, the sound of Toussaint's voice ventriloquizing in me at the buffalo range, the war report of bald ghost warrior Ed Heaney, the return of Big Hole longings across fifty years, the ambush of Pat Hoy's lonesome death, the poised-beside-the-bar sensation again of Stanley Meixell and Velma Simms and the mystery of man and woman; the answer, simply but totally, "All this monkeying around with the past."

Instead I said, "I'm not sure I'm cut out for this rambling life, is all. With you newspaper people, it's long days and short nights."

"There's more to it than that, though, isn't there," Mariah stated.

"Okay, so there is," I admitted, wondering how to go on with the confession that I was being spooked silly by things out of the past. "It's—"

"—the ranch, isn't it," she helpfully spliced on for me. "You worry about the place like you were a mother cat and it was your only kitten."

"Well, yeah, sure," I acknowledged. "I can't help but have the place on my mind some" (*MM* 1990, 74–75).

Why can't Jick tell his daughter what is bothering him, when as a narrator he articulates it very clearly? Part of it is because of characterization, of course—later on in the novel Jick refers to Mariah as his "bossypants daughter." But Jick gives no indication that he fears a confrontation, that she will laugh at him or try to argue him into acquiescence. Instead we see a man in conflict with himself. Unlike the Ivan Doig of *This House of Sky*, Jick cannot distance himself from his own past, nor can he yet exorcise it by putting it into words for someone else. He must struggle to integrate separate parts of himself that relate to the past and the present, come to terms with consequences and possibilities.

The consequences of the past, embedded in the present, are precisely what Mariah and Riley are seeking on this trip, but the beginning of their quest is not auspicious. Already at odds in the aftermath of their bitter divorce, they cannot agree on how to approach topics for their series, or even what topics to approach. Just as Jick's personal quandaries mirror Montana's problems, here, too, character reinforces theme: one of the sad features of the state's history is a lack of agreement about how to use raw materials, what the results should be. Jick is put out by Mariah's snappishness and by the fact that, in Mariah's case, photography is not a gentle art.

Mariah's methods with her camera create much of the humor in the novel as she risks being bashed by buffalo, tromped by steers, or mauled by grizzlies in order to get good shots. She photographs a wedding from a six-story-high atrium skylight, capturing "the bride (as) a white blossom and the groom a plum sprig beside her and the minister's open book and the dot rows of the heads of the wedding-goers" and one upturned, open-mouthed bearded face—Jick's (*MM* 1990, 280).

In his descriptions of Mariah's photography, Doig opens the issue of epistemology and the limitations of the individual as a reference point. Photography is a special way of seeing and interpreting reality: Mariah captures a bridal party as a bridal bouquet, a buffalo through birdsong, a bartender through a beer glass. Watching her, Jick learns to see through lenses different from his own. At the rodeo, he finds himself "seeing the surroundings in the same bit by bit way she was through her picture-taking apparatus" (*MM* 1990, 2). Because Jick learns to see as Mariah does, when she kneels to photograph a flower he can describe the scene in poetic terms: "How a stand of foxtail was catching the sunlight—sprays of purplish green, like unearthly flame, reflecting out of the whisks of grass" (*MM* 1990, 29). Photography like poetry isolates images, contexts, and moments in time and permits us to perceive the familiar in new ways, to really see what we have only looked at.

Photography is a hedge against time, as well. Mariah tells Jick that she wants her pictures to preserve a world view, as the cave paintings of Lascaux and Altamira do:

> "Something people can look back at, whenever, and get a grasp of our time. Another hundred years from now, or a hundred thousand—the amount of time between shouldn't make any difference. If my pictures are done right, people whenever ought to be able to say, 'oh, that's what was on their minds then'" (*MM* 1990, 72).

The photographic moment Mariah waits for never reflects a conventional or stylized view. She snaps pictures of people when they have their guard down, when they are no longer self-conscious and are closer to revealing themselves. She takes many such pictures of Jick, to his vast annoyance—the novel begins and ends with her doing so. Near the end of their journey together, he loses his temper: "Mariah, goddamn that camera! You've about worn the face off me with it! You must have a jillion sonofabitching pictures of me by now, what the hell do you keep shooting them for?" Mariah answers, through tears, "Because I won't always have you" (*MM* 1990, 283).

Mariah, like Jick, is aware that the rest of his life is the last of his life, and the question of death looms large between them. Death is a central theme of *This House of Sky,* as well, but there it is untimely death, with no chance to plan the last years, no contemplation of immortality. In *Mariah,* those last years, and what will remain when they have run out, are major issues. Jick tells Mariah to carve on his tombstone, "Here lies all of him that could die." But what does not die? What remains of a person after death? Memory, certainly. But memory, in this novel, is a many-sided proposition. In *Sky,* Doig defined it as "a set of sagas we live by. . . . By now, my days would seem blank, unlit, if these familiar surges could not come" (*Sky* 1978, 10). Memory was the author's tool in reconstructing the lives of his father and grandmother and in making stories from his own; memory was, in short, a means of shaping identity. But to a man who has lost his wife and his joy in anticipating the future, memory is as painful as it is meaningful. When his wife's smile blooms on his daughter's face, it recalls him to his loss.

Painful as those memories are, they are a form of immortality: every child carries on a family. When Jick watches Mariah move around the farmhouse kitchen as if she is in her element, he is puzzled by how well she seems to fit there, despite her years away:

> Then it struck me. Mariah *was* the element here. The grin as she kept kidding with Darleen and Kenny and Riley was her mother's grin, Marcella's quick wit glinting in this kitchen once again. The erectness, the well-defined collarbones that stated that life was about to be firmly breasted through—those were *my* mother's, definitive Beth McCaskill who had been born on this ranch as a Reese. Born of Anna Ramsay Reese. . . . And on the Scotch Heaven side, the McCaskill side, Adair odd in her ways but persevering for as long as there was anything to persevere for. Mariah: as daughter, granddaughter, great-granddaughter, the time-spun sum of them all? Yet her own distinct version as well. The lanky grace that begins right there in her face and flows down the longish but accomplished geometries of her body, the turn of mind that takes her into the cave of her camera, those are her own, Mariah rara (*MM* 1990, 113).

Children are a form of immortality but stubbornly individual, as well; our endurance through our children is never more than partial. We may live on in the memories of others, but these, too, have limited lifetimes. On their journey, Jick meets Roger Tate, the rancher who found the body of Jick's sheepherder, Pat Hoy. Roger remembers the tragic incident but recalls the herder as "Pat Boyd." Jick is struck by the fact that, of all the people who had known this intense and colorful man, only he and Roger Tate remain, and their deaths will be Pat's "second oblivion."

Memory, as ephemeral as the spoken word, is sometimes surprisingly resilient, however. In Jick's memory are the words of Toussaint Rennie, the Remembrancer of the Two Medicine country. Jick's recollections of Toussaint's stories of the last buffalo hunt and of Gros Ventre's celebration of statehood are so vivid that he can pass Toussaint's exact words on to Riley, who promptly puts them into print. "Ink outlasts blood," Jick thinks.

To Riley Wright, ink *is* blood. Words are what we leave behind us; words recreate event, personality, history. Like Mariah, Riley seeks an angle (his newspaper column is called "Wright Angles") that will show the bone beneath the flesh, the history within story. He explains his efforts to Jick by telling him the joke about the person who believes that the earth is not suspended in space, but rests on the back of a turtle that stands on the back of another turtle, and so on—"turtles all the way down." Riley believes that too often history is perceived as a series of turtles, tidy stereotyped packages of historical trends: the brave pioneer turtle, the cattle kingdom turtle, the sheep empire turtle, the Great Depression turtle, the suffering farmer turtle, the dying little town turtle. Instead of stacking up turtles, Riley wants to get inside the turtle shell. He and Mariah do so in stories about Helena prostitutes turned real estate dealers, the bloody past of copper mining, the last battle of the Nez Percé, the removal and killing of a grizzly bear. They also write stories about contemporary Montana: a wedding in a Holiday Inn, the sale of western gear, the hills announcing in stone initials the names of towns below them.

Riley's angles on history in his column are as varied and creative as Mariah's photographs. Sometimes he summarizes the cumulative effect of an institution or economic trend: in his story on Butte, for example, he lists statistics about miners who were crushed or burned or slowly choked to death by silicosis. Sometimes he uses synechdoche, making one person's story recall the lives of many or re-present the flavor of a time. He writes of a wedding, unique to the couple, in the words of the Song of Solomon, illustrating the universality of love and bonding. He articulates the lives of individuals and weaves them into history.

The theme of history as *story* resonates throughout Doig's work. He reminds us of the rather unsettling fact that history is not a packaged truth but a human perception, and depends on the relativity and limitations of the human reference point. When the threesome arrive at the Chief Joseph Battleground, site of the last stand of the Nez Perce, who were trying to flee to Canada but were cut off by U.S. Cavalry before they could cross the border, Riley says, "Custer was a loser, and he's famous as hell. Chief Joseph fought longer and harder and didn't get his people killed wholesale, and all he's got is that plaque on a rock over there. Why'd it turn out that way?" (*MM* 1990, 178). Jick answers him by rubbing the back of his hand, the white skin there. Indians did not write the books. History is not a matter of fact but of perception and power—who interprets events, who writes them down.

Doig pursues the possible absurdities of this issue in a wonderful scene at the Gros Ventre Centennial committee meeting, where a television anchorman (called Tonsil Vapor Purvis by the scornful Mariah and Riley) tries to interview the infamous Good Help Hebner for a series on "Builders of Montana." All he can get out of Good Help about the work he did that made the state what it is today is that one summer Good Help was a "pigfucker," (a logging term referring to the man who throws the loose tools into a hollowed log in order to get them from one place to another). History written by a Good Help Hebner would be interesting, and, Doig implies with a lifted eyebrow, who's to say it hasn't been? Authority lies not in access to truth but in language, the words that outlive us. In the column he writes about the Gros Ventre celebration of the centennial, Riley demonstrates the power of language in his record of Jick's speech:

> His words climbed as he threw his head back to outspeak a gust that rattled his pages, to send his voice higher, stronger. Language is the light that comes out of us. Imagine the words as if they are our way of creating earthlight, as if what is being spoken by this man in a windswept dawn is going to carry everlastingly upward, the way starshine is pulsing constantly across the sky of time to us. Up through the black canyons of space, the sparks we utter; motes of wordfire that we glimpse leaving on their constellating flight, and call history (*MM* 1990, 312).

History, however, is what is recorded, not necessarily what happens. And events that happen—economic fluctuations, political upheavals, ecological disasters, wars, serene and prosperous times—all impact individuals. Jick finds that the journey through Montana is even worse than he had anticipated, because the sites they visit call up painful memories or reveal a part of the past that casts a new light on the present. Some of these memories are personal: he sees his first wife in a grocery store and relives the nightmare of their mismating; he finds the letters of his maternal grandfather and discovers that if his grandmother had lived through the influenza epidemic, he and his brother and his daughters would never have been born. Some of Jick's memories tap into broader events: he recalls the bitter times of the Great Depression, the skirmish in the Second World War when a bullet shattered his leg.

We live with the consequences of the past and must in retrospect reflect on the ignorance or carelessness with which choices were made. In

Winter Brothers, Doig speaks across the years to James Swan, telling him to cool his Terminus Fever, because "I know its outcome." But in *Winter Brothers,* although Doig may look back in sadness at a history that has had terrible repercussions for his own time and place, he can look back without guilt, a position of relative comfort denied to Jick in *Mariah Montana.* For example, Jick often feels his own unintentional culpability for a de-natured Montana. When he reads Riley's column on the buffalo, he thinks:

> I was pretty sure Toussaint would have gotten a chuckle out of seeing his words in the world, outliving him. That about the manmade herds, though. What, did goddamn Riley think I ought to have been in the buffalo business instead of the sheep business all these years? And Pete Reese before me? And my McCaskill grandfather, who withdrew us from Scotland and deposited us in Montana, before Pete? I mean, you come into life and livelihood with some terms set, don't you? The Two Medicine country already was swept clear of buffalo and thick with sheep and other livestock by the time I came along. So why did I feel the prod of Riley's story? (*MM* 1990, 39–40).

Even more disturbing to Jick is his recollection of baiting and killing a grizzly bear that was threatening his flocks and his family. Mariah and Riley want to record a bear-moving, the removal of a grizzly from inhabited land to wilderness. Despite all precautions on the part of the Fish and Game men, the bear is killed in the process. This incident brings back to Jick the horror of his own experience with the grizzly:

> All those years after, I could understand that Mariah was uneasy about that memory of the toe-caught but doomed grizzly. What the hell, I was not anywhere near easy about it myself, even though I yet believed with everything in me that that particular bear had to be gotten rid of. I mean, six-inch-wide pawprints when you go out to feed the chickens? But I knew that what was bugging Mariah was not just the fate that bear had roamed into on our ranch. No, her bothersome remembering was of us, the McCaskills as we were on that morning. Of the excitement that danced in all four of us after I had done the shooting— Marcella with her worldbeating grin, Lexa hopping up and down as she put out her small hand to touch the pale fur. Mariah stock-still but fever-eyed with the thrill of what she'd witnessed, myself breaking into a wild smile of having survived. Of our family pride, for in honesty it can be called no less, about the killing of the grizzly, with never a thought that its carcass was any kind of a lasting nick out of nature.

Late, now, though, to try to tack so sizable an afterthought into that Flume Gulch morning (*MM* 1990, 152–53).

Jick, an imaginative, sensitive man, is repeatedly overwhelmed by memories so vivid he seems to relive the events and feels at those times as if he is existing on two planes simultaneously. Jick fears these attacks of history, fears that during a centennial committee meeting he may begin speaking with the voice of Toussaint Rennie.

The hell of the past is not only that he must live with its consequences but also that it refuses to stay put. One of Riley's informants, Dale Starr, complains:

> Am I losing my g.d. mind or are things repeating theirselves? I've tried to do a little thinking about it. The way all the bad I've seen in my lifetime and figured we'd put behind us seems to be coming around again now. People losing their farms and ranches. Stores out of business. All the country's money being thrown around like crazy on Wall Street. How come we can't ever learn to do better than that? (*MM* 1990, 76).

This passage is the key to the thematic and narrative structures of *Mariah*. Jick is forced not only to examine the past in light of the present, as he does in his ambivalent feelings about the grizzly, but also to reluctantly witness the repetition of the economic disasters he saw during his boyhood—ranches going under, people having to leave the state. Structurally, the novel moves back and forth between scenes from the present and scenes from the past. And the intertwining of past and present becomes a miserably personal issue when Jick learns that Riley and Mariah are falling in love again.

Although at the beginning of the journey the two of them could barely tolerate each other (they had teamed up on the series only because each had suggested it independently and their editor had decided they should collaborate), as their work progresses they rediscover a mutual professional admiration that gradually becomes sexual. When Riley is offered a column on a newspaper in California, he asks Mariah to come with him, as his wife again. Mariah accepts. Jick is horrified. It means losing another daughter to distance, but, more important, it is like "watching a bad dream start itself all over again." Jick remembers their first, crippling misalliance and does what he can to prevent its recurrence. His most drastic step in that direction is to invite Riley's mother, Leona Wright, to join them for the remainder of their travels, hoping that the presence of two disapproving in-laws will put a damper on the romance.

Leona does not come unencumbered. Fifty years before, she was the Leona Tracy whose love affair with Jick's older brother Alec led to Alec's disaffection from his family and possibly to his death in World War II. At the beginning it is difficult for Jick to spend time with a person who caused his family so much grief. Surprisingly, however, Leona proves to be the influence that turns Jick's life around.

From the time she joins them, the focus of the novel changes. With the exception of the story of the wedding, which is developed as a full and charming (albeit misleading) foreshadowing of matings to come, the scenes involving the centennial series are collapsed together, as if the days are moving more swiftly now. Indeed they seem to be. Jick, who had been a deeply unhappy man with too much time on his hands, now says, "What a size life was these days. A person had to get up twice in the morning to begin to fill it" (*MM* 1990, 256). He relishes the work and travel partly because they forestall what seems to be waiting for him once the centennial is over, Mariah is gone, and he is faced with a choice between the loneliness of the ranch and the clutches of Althea Frew, a Gros Ventre widow who has decided she and Jick will make a perfect couple. There are wonderfully comic scenes where Jick struggles against Althea, evading her pats and adoring gazes, responding inwardly to her pursuing him (by fax, no less) with the old Forest Service response to orders from headquarters, "Fuck you. Strong letter to follow." But beneath the humor of Althea's cupcake coziness and Jick's bristly resistance is a sad possibility—that like his grandfather Angus McCaskill he might marry without love to avoid living alone.

The other McCaskill remarriage seems to be inevitable. Leona, to Jick's surprise and indignation, supports it. The smiling blond girl has become a strong, practical woman and, although she dislikes her former daughter-in-law, she believes that Mariah and Riley must determine their own lives: they are now old enough to know what they are doing and young enough to make a go of it. It is her first lesson to Jick that the past need not be a prison. Although he is at first dismayed that his plan has backfired, he finally decides that Leona is right and learns how to let go of his daughter, to accept loss as change.

Leona and Jick also come to terms with the old scars of her relationship with Alec. She tells him the whole story, and though her culpability is every bit as great as Jick had surmised, he finds himself able to set aside his anger and resentment at the way things turned out and focus instead on his own feelings for Leona, planted when she was his brother's sweetheart, blooming again in her presence. Jick's unhappy memories of "the blond lightning bolt that struck our family" alternate with, and finally yield to, those of the young woman he admired fifty years before, and these are expressed in unabashedly erotic terms: "As the younger onlooker during Alec's courtship, I'd regarded the Leona of then as the bearer of the eighth and ninth wonders of the world. Now she was stouter with the years, weatherlines at her eyes and mouth, but still a highly noticeable woman" (*MM* 1990, 220). He comments that the Leona of the present "would look dressed to the teeth with nothing on but her birthday suit," and points out that "the last person not to notice Leona must have been blind, deaf and on the other side of a lead door."

But Leona has qualities that extend beyond physical charm. Through her influence, Jick is able to merge his outward and inward selves and become a positive and powerful individual who is in control of his own life. Leona is instrumental in his transformation because he can talk to her, share his memories, and put them in perspective instead of being engulfed by them.

Jick becomes a new man, ironically because of the journey he was initially so reluctant to take. What he has learned from Riley and Mariah about new ways of seeing and interpreting reality and what he has learned from Leona about coming to terms with the past, enable him to make some unusual decisions. As soon as the journey is over and he reaches home, he calls the Nature Conservancy and strikes a deal with them. He will sell them his ranch if they will establish a buffalo preserve there and name it after Toussaint Rennie. Having settled the future of his land, he then calls Leona and proposes that the two of them try life together.

In so doing, Jick completes the cycle of pairing begun with his grandfather. Angus McCaskill loved Anna Reese and could not have her. The children from each family, Varick McCaskill and Beth Reese, had a long, successful marriage. But their son, Alec, loved and lost Leona. At the end of the cycle are Jick and Leona, whose relationship we feel will not only be successful but will, with the justice time sometimes affords, heal the family wound.

The last chapter of the novel, "Dawn Articulating," refers to the speech Jick gives at the Gros Ventre celebration of Montana's centennial. In Doig's usual fashion of packing phrases with multiple meanings, it also refers to a new dawn for Montana and a new life for Jick McCaskill. On the morning of the celebration he learns that Mariah and Riley have decided against remarrying, since their love for each other seems to be founded primarily on their admiration for each other's work. Riley will go to California; Mariah has parlayed her success on the centennial series into a job as "photographer at large" for the newspaper, breaking free from the restrictions of her former job and giving rein to her talent. She and Riley have given up the conventional way of doing things, the established paths of their professions, and Jick has followed them. In his centennial speech, he notes the outcome of their journey: "The automatic way of doing things isn't necessarily mine, any more. . . . I've maybe learned a little something about being usefully ornery, from the company I've been keeping these past few months" (*MM* 1990, 312). Jick has learned to see through Riley's words and Mariah's camera, and among the things he has learned is that people are not necessarily doomed to repeat the past, nor are they powerless in the face of impersonal forces. Riley may be correct in his estimation of power structures, but the individual is still capable of altering his or her corner of the world.

Of his decision about the ranch, Jick says, "I guess I see this as giving back to the earth some of the footing it has given to me and mine. . . . If we McCaskills no longer will be on that particular ground, at least the family of existence will possess it. That kind of lineage needs fostering too, I've come to think—our kinship with the land" (*MM* 1990, 314). He has also learned to recast memory as "stories our lives tell us." Finally he sees Montana whole, not just the parts that have been ravaged by mismanagement and exploitation, but as a magnificent country whose people are willing to struggle with difficulties because of the potential there, because they can "love a mountain with their eyes." The novel ends with a joyous affirmation of life, conveyed without sentimentality, exaggeration, or self-consciousness.

The tone of the novel's closure differs significantly from those of both *Dancing at the Rascal Fair* and *English Creek*. The homesteading novel begins with nervous anticipation of life in the New World but ends tragically with the disillusionment and death of one of the main characters. *English Creek* begins with the hope that the hard times of Montana's economic depression are over but ends with a sad retrospective on the Second World War, the death of a brother and the dissolution of a family. *Ride with Me, Mariah Montana*, in contrast, begins with the apparent end of a life and the downhill slide of a state and ends with a strong sense that both have rich and valuable times ahead of them.

There is a difference, too, in narrative consistency. In the first two novels, theme and tone are reinforced by voice, because both Angus and the adolescent Jick, as characters and narrators, have unified inward and outward lives: there is consistency between what they say to other characters and what they say to the reader. Narrative in *Ride with Me, Mariah Montana* is both more complex and more interesting: seriousness of theme is constantly undermined by the outward voices of the characters, who reflect a modern gift for understatement and ironic humor. Riley, for example, so eloquent and passionate in his columns, is characterized in conversation by his superficial pronouncements, conventionalized in the mock despair of

"Shit oh dear!" and the anonymity of "No problem!" as meaningless as the ubiquitous American phrase, "Have a nice day!" Doig fosters the double tone in incident as well as character: in the last scene, Jick's speech and the reader's realization of its implications are powerfully moving. But the danger of sentimentality is forestalled by the comic aspects of the moment, when in the dawn wind the centennial flag the committee has so lovingly sewn together shreds along its seams, and Althea Frew commemorates the event with her characteristic, "Oh, foo." The reader does not know whether to laugh or cry and most likely does both.

In Doig's hands, the contrast between what these people say to each other and what they think and feel inside, becomes a revelation of western, or rather American, norms. Outwardly conventional, these modern folk demonstrate a deep personal love for, and responsibility to, their world. American culture, so perfectly articulated in this novel, rests on a contradiction of responses: hope and despair, comedy and tragedy, humor and pathos. Outlanders seeking culture in America will not find it in museums and churches, in classical music or ancient buildings, but rather in the complex play between apparent callousness and the homogeneity of mass culture, and genuine concern for human and natural environments and the steady search for self-realization.

In their journey through Montana, the main characters come face to face with history through the filter of the present: the consequences of Montana's past, America's past. It's a world of landscape, both beautiful and scarred, and of culture expressed in the way people interact with the land and with one another. Subtly but clearly, *Mariah Montana* recreates the folk life of the West.

American culture is manifested in the common expressions and celebrations of its folk life: in rodeos, bluegrass festivals, coffeehouse poetry readings, in folk arts, in the ways people dress, the ways they do their work, the foods they eat, the stories and jokes they tell. The accurate rendering of this folk life is one of Doig's most important achievements.

Part Two
Folklore

McGrath has kept the count steady with his chopping hand. When Dad does the count, he stands half-sideways to the river of sheep, his right hand low off his hip and barely flicking as each sheep passes. I have seen buyers, the men in gabardine suits and creamy Stetsons, with other habits—pointing just two fingers, or pushing the flat palm of a hand toward the sheep—as they count. The one trick everyone has is somehow to pump the end of an arm at each whizzing sheep, make the motion joggle a signal to the brain.

—Ivan Doig, This House of Sky

Overleaf: *Dan Ringer, Doig's cousin, just bucked off at a rodeo in White Sulphur Springs, Montana (1960s).*

Chapter 8
Recent Developments in Folklore Theory

The scene of the sheep count in *This House of Sky* is one example of the folklore that enlivens all of Doig's work, most notably the books set in Montana. The faithful reproduction of how people lived and worked, the songs they sang and dances they danced, the jokes they told and the verbal expressions they used, gives his books texture and verisimilitude, provides the texts and contexts of his characters' lives.

Folk traditions have appeared in American literature ever since writers began trying to define American experience.[1] But until recently the study of folklore in literature has been dominated by concepts that date from the nineteenth century, according to which Doig's work would not be considered folkloric. It will be necessary to examine some of the changes in folklore theory in order to understand how Doig uses folklore and folklife in his books and the problems he has overcome in order to do so. Nineteenth century European scholars regarded the "folk" as the unlettered peasantry who had limited access to civilization and had therefore developed a "little tradition" free from the taint of formal education and cross-cultural influence. In America, which lacked a peasant class, folklorists defined their subjects of study in terms of cultural minorities. For example, in a manifesto published in 1888 in *The Journal of American Folklore*, William Newell, president of the American Folklore Society, designated the work of the society as:

(1) ...The collection of the fast-vanishing remains of Folk-Lore in America, namely:

(a) Relics of Old English Folk-Lore (ballads, tales, superstitions, dialect, etc.).

(b) Lore of the Negroes in the Southern States of the Union.

(c) Lore of the Indian Tribes of North America (myths, tales, etc.).

(d) Lore of French Canada, Mexico, etc. (quoted in Ben-Amos, 1984, p. 103).

The "folk," according to these principles, were "them" as opposed to "us," a definition that distinguished emic from etic, informant from collector, performer from interpreter. "Lore"—songs, dances, stories, medicines, art, architecture, and so on—was classified by genre and studied item by item, usually outside of the contexts of performance and community. These items were considered to be relics, "traditional" only if they had been passed down from generation to generation. They were regarded, therefore, as "survivals" of previous history and culture. In folklorists' desire to recover the past, they searched for, and sometimes reconstructed, the oldest or purest variant of an individual item: its *Ur*-form, in other words. The older the variant, the more authentic it was assumed to be. Because they believed that folk cultures were in constant danger of adulteration by the outside world, scholars collected and recorded items of folklore with the heroism and desperation of someone rescuing furniture from a burning house.[2]

Nineteenth-century American writers also often regarded folk tradition as something apart from and usually inferior to mainstream culture. Therefore the use of folk speech or folk belief in a text written in that time usually indicates not only class or ethnic differences between characters but also between characters and the reader. That is, the reader was intended to regard the "folk" as unlettered, exotic, quaint, or as members of a lower class.[3]

Nineteenth-century concepts of folklore dominated its literary uses (and the study of those uses) into the twentieth century. Within the last three decades, however, concepts of folklore have broadened and changed. Jan Brunvand's definition is *inclusive*, rather than exclusive. According to Brunvand, folklore comprises

the unrecorded traditions of a people; it includes both the form and content of these traditions and their style or technique of communication from person to person. The study of folklore attempts to analyze these traditions (both content and process) so as to reveal *the common*

life of the human mind apart from what is contained in the formal records of a culture that compose the heritage of a people (italics mine)
(1978, 1).

Similarly, Barre Toelken defines folklore genres as "those informal but traditional and recurrent ways in which the members of closely related groups
pass along the shared values and attitudes which animate their everyday
lives" (1987, 29).

The key to understanding the nineteenth-century approach to folklore
is the concept of *difference*—separation according to class and culture between the scholar and the folk, separation of the items into genre categories
and relegation of the items to a past that was ethnographically interesting but
not a vital part of the everyday life of mainstream culture. Now, however,
similarity rather than difference is the key to understanding folklore. "Folk"
is now defined as "us": that is, folklorists perceive that all of us are members
of many folk groups or communities, each of which maintains distinct traditions. "Tradition" (in the sense of transmission) is now perceived as a synchronic as well as a diachronic process: lore may be passed not only between
generations but between peers as well. "Lore" is still defined generically (as
folk song, folk belief, urban legend, for example), but the focus of study is
now on performance in context: what a tradition means to the people who
practice it, how it functions in their daily lives, and what it reveals about
them. The lines between emic and etic have shifted somewhat: the folklorist
is still often an outsider to the folk group, but the difference is not one of
Great Tradition examining little tradition, but rather of a trained observer
recording and analyzing the lore of a specific folk community or informant,
and often folklorists are participant-observers in the groups they study.

From the perspective of contemporary folklorists, then, folklore is
"the common life of the human mind," life as lived in a particular community. According to these guidelines, everything that is not artistically singular (such as the works of Shakespeare) and not formally transmitted (through
textbooks) is folkloric. The ways people work and relax, the clothes they
wear for different activities, the art they create, the stories and proverbs they
repeat, their foodways and celebrations—all the things that are shared by a
community and make up the texture of life—are folkloric. By studying folklore, the scholar comes to understand the values and patterns of behavior of
a given group and is able to trace the subtle shifts between tradition and
innovation, stability and change, in the life of that group.

For example, the traditional headgear of western stockmen has been
the Stetson, an item of folklore so evocative of the West that it is the key

image in advertisements of products that evoke the stereotype of the rugged western hero. But the headgear actually worn in the West today is likely to be a tractor cap (called "baseball cap" on the west coast). This alteration in folk costume indicates the acceptance of a new technology, which in turn implies a change in worldview. Cowboys may now ride a Harley rather than a horse, and most farm work is done from the seat of a tractor or combine, rather than from the saddle. This means that farms and ranches may employ far fewer people—the "bunkhouse community" is replaced by the machine shed—and that the human relationships to land and animals may have altered.[4]

The revolution in folklore studies that has taken place in the last thirty years is manifested in the fact that knowledge of folk traditions now provides a sense of both difference and similarity, of exclusiveness and inclusiveness. By describing the costume of the western rancher, for example, the writer makes the reader aware of the lifestyle and values unique to that group. By focusing on universal categories like costumes, storytelling traditions, dialects, beliefs, foodways, and so on, the writer makes the reader aware of his or her membership in a similar folk group: whether the reader is a doctor or logger or professor or office worker, he or she belongs to a group with its own costumes, beliefs, and traditions.

Writers who use folklore (whether or not they do so intentionally) can thereby express the worldview of a group that makes it—or an individual within it—distinctive, without denigrating the integrity of the group. The "folk" are no longer "them," in other words, but "us" as well. Now that folklore is freed from the onus of class and ethnic distinction, writers can and do use it more liberally, and for more complex and subtle literary purposes: to establish motivations, demonstrate sources of conflict, develop character, and explore the dynamics of "community."

Literary scholars who have some knowledge of folklore therefore have a powerful tool for the analysis of literary texts. But both writer and critic also face interesting problems because of the changes in folklore study. Writers using the nineteenth-century approach had to strive for authenticity, or, if they chose to violate a folkloric norm, they had to do so knowingly. Literary scholars had to establish that writers under consideration actually had access to the folk traditions they wrote about and then to demonstrate how those traditions functioned first in context (what historical incident a ballad referred to, for example) and then how they functioned as literary devices.[5] The problems that confront contemporary writers who use folklore in texts and scholars who study those texts, are more complex. These problems relate to the essential differences between folklore and formal literature and to the problems of authenticity and accessibility.

The differences between folklore and literature are profound. Folklore is the product of more than one mind: it is *shared* tradition, usually of anonymous origin. It reveals the common life of the group, common values and beliefs and habits. It tells us about groups we belong to and identify with, about aspects of our identity that we have in common with other members of those groups, and helps us distinguish one group from another. Folklore is lived tradition, a product of collective experience and worldview, that gives form to the daily lives of folk communities.

A literary text, on the other hand, is the product of a single imagination. Although it may draw upon the "little tradition," it belongs to the Great Tradition of literary antecedents. If we compare the work of Faulkner with the folk beliefs of Mississippi sharecroppers, the difference becomes clear. Faulkner may include some of these beliefs in his writing, but his manipulation of them is a literary decision and they will be subsumed to his literary purposes. Writers, in short, are usually not ethnographers (although they may be tradition-bearers, as Doig is). The writer may be not be concerned with authenticity, may alter traditions or even create plausible fakes. If this is done well (H. L. Davis is a master at it) and there is no inconsistency within the text itself, only the ethnographer will be dismayed.

The use of folklore in literature presents complex problems and fascinating possibilities, one of which is maintaining a balance between authenticity and accessibility. The writer creates a world about which the reader must, however briefly, suspend disbelief to enter and understand. In order to immerse readers in a sense of authentic time and space, a writer typically evokes the speech and customs and worldview of the people who live there. Authenticity (or a good fake), however, may result in inaccessibility. If the world of the text is *too* different from the reader's own, how can the reader hope to understand it? For this reason folklore in literature used to be regarded as appropriate and useful for scholarly purposes only in texts that were regional in origin and whose readers were also residents of that region.[6]

Chapter 9
Making It Work

Although the work of Ivan Doig is "regional" in the sense that it was inspired by and powerfully evokes a particular place and time and uses authentic folklore in order to do so, his writing is appreciated by readers who may have no notion of Montana outside of his books. Therefore his work may be examined with three considerations in mind: how Doig has overcome the problem of authentically recreating folklore; how he makes that folklore accessible to the uninitiated reader; and how he uses folklore for his own literary purposes.

In his books about Montana, Doig maintains the balance between authenticity and accessibility by having his narrators serve as tutors for the uninitiated reader. For example, Jick, the narrator of *English Creek*, speaks to the reader in brief asides to explain matters of local knowledge and specific items of lore as they appear in the text. In an early scene at the family supper table, for example, Alec, Jick's brother, is figuring out the total acreage of the Two Medicine National Forest. He asks his father, "How many sections does it have?" Jick immediately informs the reader, "You likely know that a section is a square mile, in the survey system used in this country" (*EC* 1984, 31). Such asides do not interrupt the flow of the narrative and do guide the reader in understanding the passage.

Often these asides are more subtle. When Jick first meets Ray Heaney, who will become his best friend, the boys get into a squabble and begin trading insults: "Beetle brain," "Sparrowhead," "Slobberguts," "Booger eater," and continue until Ray comes out with, "Turkey dink," whereupon Jick punches him: a clear sign to the reader that Ray had crossed the line set by adolescent boys. When they meet the next time, Ray greets Jick with, "Horse apple."

> I balled up both my fists, and my tongue got ready the words which would fan our creekside battle to life again: "Beaver tooth." Yet the direction of Ray's remark caught my notice. "Horse apple" was pretty far back down the scale from "turkey dink."
> For once in my life I latched on to a possibility. I held my stance and tendered back to Ray, "Mud minnow."
> It started a grin on him while he thought up: "Slough rat."
> "Gumbo gopher," I provided, barely managing to get it out before we were both laughing (EC 1984, 174).

Sometimes Jick's tutelage is direct, particularly in his explications of material culture, such as the haying scenes in *English Creek*. Because the novel takes place during the Great Depression, the methods and materials of local occupations are outside of most readers' experience. But Doig's narrator is telling the story of this summer of his life from retrospect—a perspective alluded to in asides throughout the novel and clarified at the end—so he is free to assume an uninitiated audience and to instruct them accordingly:

> It occurs to me: does everybody these days think that hay naturally comes in bales? That God ordained that livestock shall eat from loaves of hay tied up in twine by thirteen-thousand-dollar machinery? If so, maybe I had better describe the notion of haying as it used to be (EC 1984, 225–26).

Jick establishes intimacy with readers by addressing them in the second person as he describes the machinery and methods of haying in detail:

All in the world it amounted to was gathering hay into stacks about the size of an adobe house; a well-built haystack even looks as solid and straightforward as an adobe structure, though of course stands higher and has a rounded-off top. But try it yourself sometime, this gathering of ten or twelve tons of hay into one stack, and you will see where all the equipment comes in. Various kinds of stackers were used in various areas of the West, beaver slides, Mormon derricks, two-poles, jayhawks, but Pete's preference was an overshot. An overshot stacker worked as its name suggests, tossing a load of hay up over a high wide framework which served as a sort of scaffolding for the front of the haystack. If, say, you hold your arms straight out in front of you, with your hands clutching each end of a basket with hay piled in it: now bring your arms and the basket straight up over your head with a little speed and you are tossing the hay exactly as an overshot does (*EC* 1984, 226).

Another problem Doig faces is that folk tradition is dynamic, and this he also solves in the novels through narrative voice. Folklorists stress performance in context: that is, not only the item itself but why, when, and by whom it is performed, its role in the community. As Barre Toelken points out, the tale is in the telling:

> Folklore exists in the performance: not in what a dialect word looks like but how, and under what circumstances, it is said; not in the barn but in the barn raising; not in the quilt only, but in the quilting bee; not in the song text in the scholar's speech, but in the performance of the song within its traditional habitat (Toelken 1979, 21).

Toelken's point is further complicated by the fact that "performance" refers not only to setting but also to variables involving three overlapping factors: the performer, the text, and the audience. A folklorist working in the field examines the personal history of the performer, the place of the item in the performer's repertoire, the role of the performer in the community, and the relationship of one performance to others. There is no *Ur*-form of a given text (that is, no original or perfect paradigm from which all variants derive). For example, scholars who study urban legends (notably Jan Brunvand in America, Paul Smith in England and Bengt af Klintberg in Sweden) collect as many variants of an item as possible, examine how and where and by whom they have been transmitted, and from that information, analyze the social functions of the legends. The role of the audience is also a complicating factor. Some performances require audience participation, others require only observation. Some items of lore, such as family sagas, are most appropriate for an initiated audience; some, like the tall tale, work best with an uninitiated audience.

Considering these complexities, an item of folklore taken out of context is like a patch on a seamless garment. How can a writer faithfully render a dynamic process into a textual product, whose final goal is, after all, literary?[1] Doig solves that problem in three ways: he is faithful to the performance, rendering tales and narratives in the vernacular of the performers, and he provides as full a context for the performance as possible without burdening the reader with too much information. Finally, he always turns the item of lore to his own narrative purposes.

For example, Doig makes use of traditional stories in the Montana trilogy. One that appears in *English Creek* is a local variant of a western tale about a little boy whose brothers and sisters try to play a joke on him by putting horse manure in his Christmas stocking. But their trick is turned when their victim declares that the manure indicates that Santa has brought him a pony.[2] Doig includes this story in the context of a rodeo announcer's chatter and uses it to illustrate the general stupidity of the announcer: the story is lamely told, and received in kind by the audience.

Doig also includes an interesting version of the story of "Moose-Turd Pie" in *Dancing at the Rascal Fair*. The western variants of the story center on an occupation group, usually miners or loggers, who dislike having to do their own cooking. The bargain they strike is that one of them has to continue as cook until the others complain about the food. The cook sabotages his preparations every way he can but cannot get his partners to complain. Finally in desperation he bakes moose droppings into a pie. When his partners realize what they are eating, they cry, "This is—this is *moose-turd pie!*" and then, "Good, though!" The variant that Doig incorporates into his novel is less specifically regional: the protagonist is Methuselah's cook, doomed to keep on cooking for hundreds of years unless she can get Methuselah to complain. Finally she puts salt in his coffee, and hears, "By Jehovah!...the coffee is full of salt!" She's just ready to step out of that kitchen forever when she hears him say: "Just the way I like it!" This variant is appropriate to both performer and context: the teller is Angus McCaskill, from Scotland, whose lore is still more Scottish than western American. The context is that he and his partner are snowed in for the winter and getting more than a little tired of their own cooking and company. In this case, the presence of Methuselah in the variant suggests how long the winter seems to both of them.[3]

In *Mariah Montana* the traditional joke assumes thematic significance. Riley tells Jick the "turtle story" in order to explain his concept of the centennial series. According to the story, the earth rests on the back of a turtle, which stands on the back of a larger turtle, and so on—"turtles all the way down." Riley says he is tired of stacking up turtles in his column, discrete stereotyped concepts that simply go on and on, seemingly unconnected except chronologically—one knows that the "dying little town turtle" comes after the "brave pioneer turtle," for instance. Riley wants to get "inside the turtle shell": that is, to find causes, linkages, synchronic and diachronic patterns that will tell people in Montana something about who they are. The joke provides an image of how history is usually regarded and prepares the reader to think about the columns Riley writes as a different view of history.

Riley's frustration with conventional history and the fact that it presents people with tidy, respectable, idealized images of themselves and their ancestors is a feeling shared by some folklorists who discover that people tend to want to be polite about the past or at least that part of it with which they are connected. In "Northwest Regional Folklore," Barre Toelken points out that doing field work in folklore is sometimes difficult because people being interviewed tend to idealize their family histories. Toelken writes:

> The middle- to upper-class descendents of the Northwest pioneers have tried continually to depict their grandparents as farsighted, god-fearing folk who had no superstitions, sang no earthy songs, and who, if they had oral traditions, gave them up quickly as proof of their willingness to pull themselves up by their bootstraps (Toelken 1979, 23).

When people regard folk traditions as "backward" or undesirable, they are forced to substitute something else in order to create a history. The traditional "turtle joke," should be understood on that level: the explanation that turtles hold up the world is a substitution for understanding the laws of magnetism and gravity. Furthermore, the turtle is a clear image of duplicity, the shell covering up the animal inside.

The content and the imagery of this traditional story are thematically significant. The context of the performance of Riley's joke (in a bar, where he and Jick and Mariah are having a well-earned evening drink) prepares the reader for Riley's idea for their next story—bars and bartenders. Riley argues that nothing could be more typical of Montana than alcohol and writes in his column that "a considerable portion of Montana's history could be measured the way irrigation water is, by the liquid acre foot." Because of the turtle joke, the reader can also understand why Riley and Mariah pass up so many possible stories, one or the other saying, "Won't work."

One of the best examples of the balance Doig maintains between an accurate contextual rendering of a folk tradition and its literary function is in his re-creations of a folk performance that is central to the life of Montana—the rodeo. Derived from the work of an occupational folk group—cowboys—rodeos function as ceremony, contest, and celebration in which working people test their skills against each other and the animals they work with. Rodeos appear in Doig's writing from his days of free-lancing and in each of the books set in Montana. The rodeo scenes serve to develop character, accent conflicts, illustrate themes, and re-create the folk cultures of the region. Most of Doig's rodeo scenes climax with the "heart performance" of a rodeo, which is bronc riding. As Jick comments in *English Creek*, "I will say for saddle bronc riding that it seems to me the one rodeo event that comes close to legitimate. Staying on a mount that is trying to unstay you is a historic procedure of the livestock business" (*EC* 1984, 184).

In *This House of Sky*, Doig briefly describes an incident at a rodeo where Charlie was trampled by a horse and suffered injuries that laid him up for six weeks. Doig recreates parts of the scene in his father's own words: *Five or six of us were ridin', all had our girls there and were showin' off, ye know . . . Oh, he* [the horse that threw and trampled him] *was a bearcat, I'm here to tell you"* (*Sky* 1978, 41). The use of Charlie's voice has two effects: it recreates the scene in all its immediacy and informs the reader that the event had entered family lore—that is, the story of the rodeo was important enough to become part of the repertoire of stories that Charlie told his son again and again. Doig makes the scene accessible to the reader by summarizing and analyzing parts of it in his own voice: "The hill broncs which would be hazed in somewhere for this weekend rodeoing—the Doig homestead had a big stout notched-pole corral which was just right—were not scruffy little mustangs" (*Sky* 1978, 40). The story is part of the motif of death—and Charlie's courage in the face of it—that is developed throughout the book and climaxes in the final chapter. It is one of three stories set side by side that illustrate Charlie's "stalking by death." The other two incidents, also involving horses, take place while Charlie was working. The uninitiated reader may wonder, as the narrator does, why anyone would deliberately court disaster by making it part of recreational life. But the similarity of the rodeo incident to the incidents on the job illustrates that the occupational folk community to which Charlie belonged regarded risk taking as a necessary part of work and, therefore, of recreation. A man unwilling to mount a half-wild horse might also back down in the face of the hardships and dangers endemic to ranch life.[4]

In *Dancing at the Rascal Fair*, Doig uses a scene of bronc riding scene for thematic, tonal, and structural purposes. Varick has been estranged from his father, Angus, because of Rob Barclay's interference. Angus, desperately trying to reestablish himself with his son, attends one of the impromptu rodeos given by local ranchers, knowing that Varick will be there and hoping that the male camaraderie fostered by the event will break through the wall Varick has erected against him. The fact that Varick remains distant from Angus, even in the atmosphere of celebration and risk that characterizes the rodeo, emphasizes the depth of his alienation. The scene also serves as one of Doig's "set pieces." In these episodes, Doig describes a folk event in detail, such as the dance in *Rascal Fair* or the picnic in *English Creek*. These set pieces create much of the milieu in his books and allow him to explore his characters and their relationships in a controlled context. Structurally, they slow down the pace and momentarily relieve the tensions of building crises.

The rodeo scene in *Rascal Fair* emphasizes the pathos of the father-son relationship, but it is also humorous. Varick accepts the challenge of riding a steer, a trial that is both ludicrous and dangerous. He manages to go the time limit, but his struggles with the steer become more and more comic until finally his hazer, Dode Withrow, is thrown into a pool of liquid manure. The scene provides comic relief from the rising tensions in the novel by diverting the focus from Angus's pain to the actions in the corral. It also creates some of the texture of the history of Montana, which is one of Doig's subjects in the trilogy. Specifically, Doig uses this rodeo scene to particularize patterns of assimilation of immigrants to the American West. The inevitable growth of a child away from his parents is exacerbated if the parents are from the Old World. The fact that Angus still sees through Scottish eyes and is, to a degree, still a member of that culture, while Varick has embraced the values and traditions of the American West, is illustrated by the fact that Angus is only a spectator at the rodeo, and he is unable to appreciate the finer points of the sport at which his son is skilled. Rather than being able to comment on the quality of the horses to be ridden or the techniques used by the young men who ride, Angus can only think glumly, "It looked to me like a recipe for suicide." He feels that his son has become a stranger to him, not only because of the quarrel between them, but because of Varick's participation in a folk performance Angus does not understand: "What son of mine was this? Somehow this bronc rider, this tall half-stranger, this Sunday centaur, was the yield of Adair and me. I was vastly thankful she was not here to see our wild result" (*RF* 1978, 317).

The most fully realized rodeo scene takes place in *English Creek* during the Fourth of July celebration. The rodeo in general serves to emphasize the conflict between Alec and his parents, and the bronc-riding episode that follows Alec's success at calf-roping is one of the highlights of the novel. Doig does not miss a single contextual element in his depiction of this folk performance. The performer, Dode Withrow, (the same man who served as hazer for Varick's ride in *Rascal Fair*) was once a superb bronc rider; now he is older, out of practice, and in his cups. The performance itself is brilliant, for Dode has drawn a half-wild horse who could throw the best rider. Dode stays the limit (the performance is successful) and the response of the audience is overwhelming. Toussaint Rennie, the ancient arbiter of all such performances, gives it his highest accolade: "That one, that one was a ride."

In *English Creek* the rodeo scene illustrates both tension and continuity between the generations in this community. Alec demonstrates his determination to break away from his parents by entering the calf-roping. But unknowingly he is repeating the actions of his own father and grandfather, who also broke away from their families and established lives of their own. Dode's memorable ride links him to his own youth and to Montana's past.

The rodeo scene in *Mariah Montana* is given short shrift. Jick's lack of interest in the event signifies his sense of alienation from his own community since the death of his wife. The brevity of the scene and Jick's indifference to it also foreground Montana's changing economic and social patterns. In *This House of Sky, English Creek,* and *Rascal Fair,* rodeos were closely tied to economics: men pitted against animals was part of daily work. But in contemporary Montana, ranches have become agribusinesses, and ranchers rely more on machines than on animals. This means that the functions of rodeos have changed, and that the performers and the audience sometimes belong to different folk groups and appreciate the performance at different levels.

Chapter 10
Realizing the Country

Doig uses folklore not only to develop character and theme, to regulate pace and tension, but also to paint the life of a region—to "realize the country," as Wallace Stegner says. And here Doig faces a serious problem. Lore is generated by the daily life of people who share at least one common factor.[1] Therefore, each of us belongs to several folk groups: regional, ethnic, familial, religious, occupational, fraternal, artistic. The fact that each individual is a member of several folk groups simultaneously—for example, a Norwegian logger who belongs to the Lutheran Church and the Rotary Club, who has a large family and who does chainsaw carving on his day off—means that the recording of all of the group lore represented by even a single individual would be nearly impossible. Moreover, there is insider lore and outsider lore: that is, lore by the group, and lore about the group. In "Folklore in the American West," Barre Toelken describes the intricate web of folklore groups and interactions in the West:

> Not only is there sheepherder lore (both the lore of the sheepherders themselves and the ranchers who raised the sheep, and the lore *about* sheepherders passed along by those—for example cattle ranchers— who often saw the sheep ranchers as very odd people indeed, as outsiders to their own cultural views), but there is *Basque* sheepherder lore,

as well as Basque lore, and lore about Basques by non-Basque people. Along the Northwest coast there is not only the lore of the fishing people (the fishermen themselves, as well as their families at home); but also the lore of the Yugoslav fishermen as contrasted to that of the Scandinavian fishermen (Toelken 1987, 31).

Obviously Doig cannot include sufficient lore to do complete justice to a region, or even the part of the region he has isolated. He does succeed, however, in giving a broad and varied selection of the folk materials from which the life of the region is woven. For example, in *This House of Sky* he writes about Taylor Gordon, resident of White Sulphur Springs. Gordon is black, has a brother and sister who also live in the town and have their own family traditions. He is a talented storyteller, a disappointed author, a brilliant singer who after a season in New York was declared "the latest rival to Paul Robeson," and a spendthrift who sent himself right back into sheepherding in Montana when the Depression hit. Doig sketches this background quickly and deftly, and then focuses on a single item of lore, recalling that Gordon once told him

> Of how people in Harlem could tell where a man was from just by the scar on his face: *By the brand that was on him, y'see. They could tell where he'd been in a fight. If you were shootin' craps, you more or less would be bendin' down when you got cut and that way you'd get it across the forehead here. Whereas if you were playin' poker, you were more apt to be settin' up, then you'd be apt to get this one here across the cheek. Then if you were playin' what they called skin, why you'd apt to get this other. So y'see, if a fella was cut here, he was from Greechyland, if he was cut this other way he was from Selma, Alabama, and so on and so on* (*Sky* 1978, 90).

A black man from the community of White Sulphur Springs, Montana, member of at least seven distinct folk groups, transmits a bit of Harlem gambling lore. By telling that particular story, Doig relays the variety and complexity of life in a region that outsiders may have regarded as culturally homogeneous.

Doig keeps the complexities of such tales-in-context from overrunning each other by a consistent narrative point of view. Although the narrative structures of his books are elastic and occasionally multiple (see the discussion in chapter 3 of the narrative structure of *Winter Brothers*), the observing eye that guides the reader is singular and constant. But the use of a single narrative voice still allows him to record lore from more than one perspective.

In *This House of Sky*, for example, Doig recounts lore by and about the "Hoots" (Hutterites) who live on a communal farm close to a ranch the Doigs are leasing for a season. Charlie and Ivan are informed by the Hutterites that

> Heaven told them an endless amount that we had never heard of, such as that when one of their men married he had to grow whiskers along his jawline to make the face-circle which represented a wedding ring, or that their women were proper only when swathed in long skirts, aprons and kerchiefs, like walking mounds of fresh laundry (*Sky* 1978, 195).

Doig also reports lore about the Hutterites that articulates the initial disapproval of the local ranchers and townspeople: "Hoots" didn't pay taxes, refused military service, and intermarried to an alarming degree.

The balance that Doig maintains between insider and outsider lore gives the reader a broad picture of the attitudes and values typical of western Montana. People in Dupuyer are originally uneasy about the "Hoots" because they are culturally different. But the Hutterites win their way into the region because they meet the one unfailing standard by which everyone is judged: they are willing to work hard. Charlie is won over nearly at once; Bessie is more skeptical, "but eventually she too decided they were satisfactory neighbors. Certainly they were hard-working, and with her that nearly canceled out their quirks about soldiering and family line" (*Sky* 1978, 197).

The use of the single narrative perspective to relay insider and outsider lore also appears in *English Creek*, where for example Jick muses on the phenomenon of sheepherders' cairns:

> Just to be doing something a herder would start piling stones, but because he hated to admit he was out there hefting rocks for no real reason, he'd stack up a shape that he could tell himself would serve as a landmark or a boundary marker for his allotment. Fighting back somehow against loneliness. That was a perpetual part of being a sheepherder. In the wagons of a lot of them you would find a stack of old magazines, creased and crumpled from being carried in a hip pocket. An occasional prosperous herder would have a battery radio to keep him company in the evenings. Once in a while you came across a carver or a braider. Quite a few, though, the ones who gave the herding profession a reputation for skewed behavior, figured they couldn't be bothered with pastimes. They just lived in their heads, and that can get to be cramped quarters (*EC* 1984, 42).

In this passage, a single item of lore (the cairns) is analyzed from the point of view of the sheepherder (the insider) and the narrator (the outsider) and serves to illustrate the problem of the occupation—isolation and loneliness.

Sheepherding is the regional occupation Doig explores most thoroughly, and a solid ethnography of that vocation could be reconstructed from his books about Montana. In *This House of Sky* he recounts in detail the lore that sheep ranchers share: methods for lambing, castrating, docking, "jacketing," shearing, doctoring, counting sheep, training a dog that will "run on wool." He also recounts lore about sheepherders, frequently immigrants who took up the lonely work because they could do it without learning English:

> Countless of them went through life trapped in their homeland language; it was a historic joke that the eastern end of the county originally had been populated entirely by Norwegian herders who knew but two words of English: *Martin Grande,* the name of their employer. Fairly or not, the numbers of Romanians who arrived as herders had a particular reputation for shunning any language but their own. Their chosen set of bywords was simply *no savvy.* There exists the exasperated report of an early forest ranger who came upon a Romanian herder placidly spreading his sheep across an allotment of cattle range: *All I could get out of him was 'No savvy' until I applied a shot-loaded quirt . . . it was surprising how quickly the incident got to all the Romanians in that district (Sky* 1978, 169–170).

This particular redaction represents an outsider's perception of immigrant sheepherders but is mitigated by Doig's phrases: "historic joke," "fairly or not," "reputation," "exasperated report." The lore as actually passed from person to person would, like the lore about the Hutterites, probably be expressed in unqualified terms of ridicule or disapproval. But Doig's redaction expresses as much about the informants' attitudes and world view as it does about the sheepherders' lifestyle.

Doig also describes other occupation groups in his Montana books: cattle ranchers, homesteaders, haying crews, teachers, forest rangers, fire fighters, bartenders, miners, journalists, and "cow-chousers." He writes about each of these groups in its own vernacular, thereby reducing the distance between the folk group and the reader. Doig also writes about family lore, ethnic lore, and regional lore, all of which serve his literary purposes, and here his use of the vernacular is subtle and masterful, functioning to create some of the most memorable characters in American literature.

Readers who believe that the most engaging heroes are "of the folk"

Charlie Doig, branding calves near Ringling, Montana (early 1930s).

will find themselves justified by Doig's characters, particularly Bessie Ringer and Charlie Doig. It is certainly possible that Joseph Campbell could trace in their lives the patterns of initiation common to heroes in all cultures, and to an extent Doig does just that: his authorial voice sketches their life histories according to patterns familiar to the mythographer: unusual circumstances of birth and rearing, initiation by experiences of loss and death, return to society and useful function within the community.[2]

But the delineation of that pattern alone would produce archetypes, whereas Doig creates fully realized characters by allowing them to speak for themselves. The potential problems inherent in that decision, and its final significance, can be demonstrated by examining Bessie's and Charlie's speech patterns and analyzing the functions of those patterns. Because Doig is writing about people from his own past rather than creating fictional characters, his problem here is one of selection: obviously in his years with his father and grandmother they did and said a great many more things than could be included in one book, and Doig had to select those aspects of their lives and speech that would characterize them most fully and consistently.

Doig begins to sketch his characters by describing the early lives that shaped them into the people he knew. Bessie came to Montana from Wisconsin and found herself in a primitive, wild land governed by brooding

mountains and severe weather, accompanied by a husband who was more li-
ability than asset. She responded to adversity by hard work:

> In this total rind of determination, Bessie was not like many of the val-
> ley women, or most of the men either. Down through the valley's his-
> tory, such settlers had expected something of their work, and sooner
> or later uprooted themselves if it didn't come. Bessie only chored on
> (*Sky* 1978, 116–17).

Denied a formal education, Bessie formulated her life and raised her children
according to the precepts of practical folk wisdom. When Ivan went to live
with her in the tiny house in Ringling, he discovered that his grandmother
was a rich source of useful lore and folk remedies. The stories she told him
were not part of the literary tradition he was later to absorb through endless
reading and formal training but stories about family and neighbors. They
told him about his origins and taught him that there was mystery and meaning in the world around him.

Bessie's forceful, positive approach to life was tainted by the threat of
losing Ivan, which would happen if the shaky family structure came apart:

> Beneath it all was a hard unsaid truth we all knew. The three of us by
> then had been together long enough, and closely enough, that if my fa-
> ther and my grandmother parted ways, I now could have the choosing
> of which one I would live with—and I would choose at once to go
> with Dad again (*Sky* 1978, 156).

Confronted by that possibility, Bessie rests uneasily on the edge of authority, both claiming it and denying it, asserting herself against a son-in-law
with whom she is often at odds, but never allowing a serious breach to split
the family. Bessie's sense of her own situation is described when Doig points
out that she *"had somehow to mother me without the usual claims to authority for it, and at the same time to treat with her son-in-law in terms which
could not be like a wife's but seemed not much closer to any other description
either"* (*Sky* 1978, 238–39). The ambivalence she feels about her place in the
family and her role with Ivan is reflected in her speech, specifically in her use
of proverbs and aphorisms.

Bessie's speech patterns (and those of other characters in the book)
have been singled out for some criticism. In a paper given before the 1988
Western Literature Association meeting, Sanford Marovitz of Kent State
University pointed out that the author's voice in *This House of Sky* differs
notably from the voices of the people he recalls:

Although [Doig] alternates between a heavily metaphoric, formalistic style and a more casual one, the difference between his voice and those of the recalled people he profusely quotes is obvious. Their manner of expression as he cites them is characterized by cliché, pictorical but stale language, in contrast to an imaginative literary voice (Marovitz 1988, 7).

Marovitz's point is that although cliché "may well have been the colloquial speech of Doig's family and their neighbors when he was a child," it serves to distinguish the writer from his characters—to imply a separation of Doig from his own background. This is perfectly true; in fact, Doig's complex relationship to his own childhood is one of the themes of the memoir. But it is disturbing to modern readers that characters who are so vivid and appealing speak in clichés, given a contemporary attitude toward cliché that denigrates it as the expression of stale or false sentiments. But if we examine the verbal patterns of his characters according to the functions of folk speech we can regard their turns of phrase somewhat differently. Bessie's "clichés" are actually often proverbs. In *Sky,* Doig notes:

> Her sayings too took their own route of declaring. That it was time to get a move on: *Well, this isn't buying the baby a shirt nor paying for the one he's got on. . . .* Neighbors were rapidly tagged with whatever they deserved: *She goes around lookin' like she's been drawed through a knothole backwards. . . . That pair is as close as three in a bed with one kicked out. . . . That tribe must never heard that patch beside patch is neighborly, but patch upon patch is beggarly (Sky 1978, 130–31).*[3]

The role that proverbs play in Bessie's speech, and by extension what they reveal about her character, are elucidated in Roger Abrahams's study of traditional conversational genres. Abrahams points out that the motivating force behind proverbs is the issue of authority and that the speaker of proverbs simultaneously asserts and disclaims authority. Abrahams's analysis rests on three premises: a social problem exists and the speaker uses a proverb to suggest a solution to that problem; the speaker asserts authority by using a speech format that is time honored (and therefore authoritative); and the speaker also avoids claiming authority because the "solution" is couched in impersonal rhetoric. (Abrahams 1968, 50). Proverbs also serve as a way to take control of a situation, to create order out of chaos or difficulty by describing an unfamiliar situation in familiar terms.

When Bessie states, "Patch beside patch is neighborly, but patch upon patch is beggarly," she is not merely passing judgment on the sartorial habits of her acquaintances, she is citing a formula that tells her, and Ivan, how to live.[4] The other speeches that Doig repeats reveal Bessie's gift for dealing with difficult circumstances in practical terms. When she and Ivan are left alone in charge of the sheep on the summer range, they discover that their fat ewes are dying. The owner of the sheep has cut costs by neglecting to spray them for ticks, and the sheep, rolling on their backs to scratch and unable to scramble to their feet again, are bloating up in the summer heat and expiring from the buildup of internal gas. The situation is potentially disastrous, and Ivan chokes out, *What the hell are we going to do?* Bessie does not stop to bewail their predicament: "She snapped: *I don't like to hear you say 'hell.'* Then: *We're gonna have to stay right with the sheep and turn 'em off their Godblasted backs*" (*Sky* 1978, 206).

Bessie's talent for action and for piecing a coherent life out of fragments is also manifested in the folk art she begins to practice in her later years: quilting. Quilting has long been acknowledged to be a primary artistic expression of women in rural North America, the elegant gift of making something useful and beautiful out of scraps that would otherwise be thrown away. It is significant that Bessie takes up this art during the time that her son-in-law is struggling against emphysema and she and Ivan, as well as Charlie, must deal with the emotional and physical trauma of life-threatening illness.

> What Grandma turned out now, in the living room as Dad watched from his haven of chair, danced with brilliant colors—snipped-and-sewn diamonds of ragwork marching and playing and jostling like a meld of rainbows, or some resplendent field of tiny flags from all the universe. To come out of our ungaudy family, this was an absolute eruption of bright art, and I blinked in wonder at this gray-haired woman I thought I knew so entirely. For her part, Grandma simply produced each quilt, demanded *Now then, isn't that pretty?* and gave it to Carol and me or someone in her sons' families. When we all had quilts galore, she began selling them, and there are valley households now with half a dozen blazing in their rooms (*Sky* 1978, 285).

Bessie's voice in *This House of Sky* complements the image of her that the narrator provides in his more formal and literary style: she emerges as a straightforward, down-to-earth woman, loving and temperamental, heroic in her ability to take life as it comes. Doig credits her for shaping his own ear for language, and the reader can perceive in the forms and cadences of her speech a kind of folk poetry.

In one sense, *This House of Sky* is about the apprenticeship of a writer.

One of the consistent traits throughout all of Doig's work is his evident love for language and his ability to create meaning through sound and pattern as well as connotation and denotation. Also evident is his love for storytelling: stories are embedded in all of his narratives, and weave with the threads of the plot in complex ways. He credits Charlie, his father, with much of his sense for story: *"It was you, in your burring troubadour's way of passing to me all you knew of the valley and the Basin, who enchanted into me such a love of language and story that it has become my lifework" (Sky 1978, 273)*. As he does in his re-creation of Bessie, Doig sifts from a lifetime of material those speech patterns that best characterize Charlie and illuminate his responses to problems and challenges. These are folk patterns: vernacular speech, jokes, aphorisms, and most notably, stories. Most of Charlie's stories are personal narratives, which can be analyzed in terms of their functions in the text and within the context of their original tellings.

In *This House of Sky*, Charlie's speeches have great entertainment value. Like Bessie, he often uses aphorisms and proverbs but alters the traditional formulas in order to make his own jokes. Charlie's modifications of traditional forms reveal an approach to life that is wry, sometimes rueful, often humorous. His proverbs and aphorisms begin traditionally but end with an ironic twist, a punchline of his own: *"As the fellow says, a fool and his money are soon parted, but ye can't even get introduced around here . . . I never saw anybody so big I couldn't take him on in a fight, anyway. . . . He might of cleaned my clock when I took him on, too, but that didn't matter. Oh, as the fellow says, I'm awfully little but I'm awfully tough" (Sky 1978, 19, 31)*. By balancing insider and outsider lore, accurately rendering work traditions, and recreating the sound and significance of folk speech, Doig realizes the country and the people he grew up with and brings into focus the life of a region. His use of folklore in this regard is masterful and serves him in another way as well: using folklore as a literary convention, Doig creates complex characters and shows how they interact with one another and come to terms with their world.

Chapter 11
Personal Narrative

Storytelling is an important part of Doig's work, and his books are graced by master storytellers. Foremost among them is Charlie Doig. Most of Charlie's stories are personal narratives. Reproduced in his own words, they meet the aesthetic criteria of "coherence and delight" that folklorists suggest are central to a successful storytelling performance [1] Charlie tells both "other-oriented" and "self-oriented" stories. Sandra Stahl notes that "other-oriented" storytellers

> tell stories that resemble representatives of the various legend categories. They underplay their personal role in the story to emphasize the extraordinary nature of things that happen in the tale. These stories might easily be categorized as memorates rather than as the more secular personal narratives, or perhaps as anecdotes in which the narrator serves mainly as witness and recorder of incidents in which other people are the primary participants. Like Luthi's "legend character," such a storyteller hopes to impress the audience with the testimony that life does indeed confront us with some of the strange and awesome happenings hidden behind the beliefs and rumors of earlier generations. The "self-oriented" tellers delight in weaving fairly elaborate tales that build upon their own self-images and emphasize their own

actions as either humorous or exemplary. These tellers tend to offer the audience stories that resemble the tall tale, joke, parable, or realistic *novella* (Stahl 1983, 270).

Charlie's "other-oriented" stories are never "memorates" (personal accounts of experiences with the supernatural), but they are often extraordinary, such as his description of schoolmates who came from so far back in the hills that they were "more like the coyotes which watchfully loped the ridgelines than like the other Basin youngsters."

> One family's boys, he remembered, started school so skittish that when someone met them on an open stretch of road where they couldn't dart into the brush, they flopped flat with their lunchboxes propped in front of their heads to hide behind. *Thought we couldn't see 'em behind those damned little lunchboxes, can ye feature that?* (Sky 1978, 32–33).

Charlie's "self-oriented" stories fall into several categories: reminiscences about his family or the pastoral idyll that he and Berneta lived out in their mountain summers; occupational stories that succinctly (and often humorously) characterize skinflint ranchers or half-crazy sheepherders or recall mishaps on the job; tales of adventure, such as the story of his fight with a bear. His stories are strongly marked by his voice and by opening and closing formulas: "Oh, as the fellow says . . . I'll tell ye a time . . . I'm here to tell ye. . . ." Charlie's stories are also formulaic in that he never altered them. Doig comments: "It was my father's habit to say and resay a version as it had first taken shape in him" (*Sky* 1978, 14).

In *This House of Sky,* Charlie's stories re-create the man himself and much of the life he knew in the valley. In Charlie's own life, stories served as part of his solution to the major problem he had to face after the death of his wife: how to raise his young son by himself. His decision about Ivan came from his own past:

> It may have been that he thought back to what his own boyhood had been like after his father died, how quickly he had grown up from the push of having to help the family struggle through. It may have been only habit, out of his years of drawing the fullest from those reluctant crews. Or maybe simple desperation. From whatever quarter it came, Dad took his decision about me. My boyhood would be the miniature of how he himself lived (*Sky* 1978, 54).

Charlie made Ivan his partner, keeping him by his side and teaching him all he could about life, particularly life in the valley. Ivan's early education took the form of traditional apprenticeship—learning by seeing and listening and doing, mastering skills by working with the master. Ivan also learned ethics and attitudes and values from the stories his father told him. Unlike those parents who create separate worlds for adults and children, Charlie told his son the truth about jobs and employers and risk taking, and about his own strengths and fears and loneliness. And through his stories, he opened himself to his son. One of the generic qualities of the personal narrative, according to Sandra Stahl, is the vulnerability of the storyteller:

> Nothing creates intimacy quite so well as some confession or exposure of the self; the storyteller offers a welcome gift to a cold world, a moment by the fire of self. The conventions of the story make self-revelation acceptable and entertaining, but the courage of the storyteller in articulating usually covert values makes the storytelling an engaging experience, for the teller and the audience. In effect the narrator tests personal values—practical, moral, social, aesthetic—with every story repetition. The willingness to bring forward values for the scrutiny of the audience makes the narrator vulnerable (Stahl 1983, 274).

His early attained knowledge about life and about his father did not burden the child, because it came in the form of parable, metaphor, aphorism, tale. Doig attests to the efficacy of his father's heritage of storytelling by ending *This House of Sky* with a personal narrative of his own, describing his near-drowning on the Washington coast. This incident echoes experiences from both Charlie's and Bessie's lives and also recalls their making those experiences meaningful by shaping them into stories.

The significance of Bessie's and Charlie's contributions to Doig's work as a writer can be illustrated in the metaphor of quilting, a literary process of "piecing" much like Bessie's steps in producing a quilt. From scraps of memory and voices recalled, bits of information gleaned from archives and books and his own observations, more "scraps" are made—the notecards that fill his file cabinets and cover his study tables. He matches and pieces them according to the patterns they suggest and makes them into something whole and new. Doig's materials are not derived from the exploration of the writing *process* (as postmodernists' materials may be said to be) nor from abstract ideas. Conventions of his writing, such as structure and style, derive from the patterns he perceives in the world around him. The structure of *Winter Brothers*, for example, recalls the interpenetration of life forms in the

Olympic rainforest, the art of Native American carvers. The structure of *This House of Sky* corresponds closely to the structures and conventions of personal narrative, a folk genre "storied into" him by his father.

David Stanley asserts that personal narrative is a form that bridges the gap between folk performance and certain literary genres, particularly those he calls "personal novels," including *Moll Flanders, Portrait of the Artist as a Young Man, Great Expectations,* and *Huckleberry Finn.* Although *This House of Sky* is a memoir rather than a novel, it can be analyzed according to the same criteria Stanley uses, which establish its formal and functional ties to oral tradition:

> Such narratives are, in essence, the stories we tell each other about our everyday experiences, stories which center themselves in decision-making, conflict, ethical ambiguity, and danger, so that the personal narrative is more often than not a tale about the teller as much as it is about his experiences (Stanley 1979, 108).

Doig's memoir is clearly "a tale about the teller": not only the facts of his life but his apprenticeship as a writer, his processes of decision making, his perspectives and personal values. These emerge not just in what Doig says but in how he says it, in the interweave of voices, the play of language. The complex narrative, dramatic, and temporal structures in *This House of Sky* all bespeak the balance that Doig, like all good storytellers, maintains between the world of the story and the world of the author.

Personal narratives are usually chronological, but the forward movement of the story is interrupted by flashbacks, reminiscence, and comments that evaluate action in light of what the narrator has learned since the action took place. Therefore their content is not only the redaction of experience but experience reconsidered. Stanley points out that no matter what the plot of a particular narrative may be, the subject is the self:

> Personal narrative and personal novel alike are concerned with defining the self as it emerges from the past and as it demands correlation with the self-perceived person of the present. Evaluation is the functional element which permits the narrator to observe that self as perceived historical fact, but fact of a frustrating, quicksilver elusiveness. The experiential focus of both personal narratives and personal novels, then, is on the emergent self (Stanley 1979, 112).

Doig's work is notable for this back-and-forth movement: the narrative is continually interrupted by the author's evaluative comments, in which experience is analyzed from the point of view of the mature narrator: "I know now . . . but I did not understand it then; I believe what I felt most was gratitude; the pattern is gone now . . . but in its time; what I gained. . . ." *Sky* is filled with Doig's mature ruminations and evaluations of past experience.

These evaluations take place in the reader's mind as well. Personal narratives are usually told in the context of conversation, members of the group taking turns to tell their own thematically similar stories and to pass judgment on the actions of others as they unfold in narrative. Stanley asserts that the same process takes place in reading:

> This scanning of one's own file of experiences and potential narratives, I think, matches the reading process as we experience literature in general and personal novels in particular. . . . Personal fiction invites just that kind of activity, a continuous process of comparison and consideration on the part of the reader, who imaginatively stands ready to contribute to this interaction with the text with his own store of personal narratives (Stanley 1979, 115, 116).[2]

This House of Sky is particularly suited to this kind of reader interaction because its themes are familiar to everyone: maturing, coping, learning, apprenticeship, family, independence, and responsibility. Most readers will have experienced many of the same conflicts, crises, and times of decision making that Doig explores in his memoir. As we read, we remember our own stories about ethical struggles, the difficulties of growing up, of finding a life partner, of dealing with the illness or death of a parent.

Finally, the audience of the personal narrative and the reader of this memoir are aware of the balance between fact and fiction in the narrative. Even though both oral and written forms announce themselves to be true, the listener and the reader know that fictional techniques invariably shape narrative: selection, condensation, evaluation, hyperbole, and understatement are used to make a good story, which is "true" on a different plane than that of the merely factual.

Ride with Me, Mariah Montana, like *This House of Sky*, is structured as a personal narrative—the entire novel is Jick's story—in which shorter narratives are embedded. As in *Sky*, these narratives reflect personal values, methods of decision making, perceptions, ethical ambiguities, qualities that are re-created by the teller with each retelling of the tale. In *Mariah*, however, personal narrative functions not only as a method of characterization but also as a powerful thematic device, a reinforcement of Doig's vision of history.

The issue of what history is, who controls it, and what effect it has on our lives is central to the novel. Doig makes it clear that often there is a conflict between formal history—as it is recorded and disseminated—and the remembered pasts of individuals. This conflict is articulated in the novel's subtle dialectic between formal history and personal narrative. It can be seen in Jick's disgust for Virginia City, which has been made into a sort of "outdoor western dollhouse," and in the fact that Riley and Mariah spend all day tramping Virginia City and do not find anything worth photographing or writing about. It's all "turtles"—neat packages of prefab past.

They do find meaningful stories, however, in the personal narratives of "the geezers"—seven men they meet along the freeway. These men are retired and spend their time driving used cars from overstocked to understocked car lots. When the "Baloney Expressers," as they call themselves, pull off the highway to investigate the Bago's flat tire, Mariah and Riley see a golden opportunity: "Five hundred years' worth of geezers in one bunch" (*MM* 1990, 70). So Riley, riding with each of them in turn, records their stories: the rancher's son whose drunken father drove Model T Fords through miles of fences; the farmer's son whose memories of a plague of grasshoppers left forever in his mind the sickening sound of their eating through a season's crop; the packer who brought frozen bodies, victims of a plane crash, out of the Bob Marshall Wilderness; the father who lost a daughter in Vietnam; the retired farmer who feels the country in his blood but has been transplanted to the city; the immigrant who took one look at Montana and made it his home.

Personal narratives, in this case, stand in contrast to collective history; that is, the memories and stories of individuals are often quite unlike generalized histories that find their way into books or take the form of legends. Whether or not they are historically based, and despite their fictional formulations, legends are often accepted as factual.[3]

Legends, which do not appear very often in Doig's work, come in several kinds. Urban legends are bizarre, often horrific tales about modern life. Riley captures their essence perfectly when he protests Jick's and Leona's telling tales of his and Mariah's childhoods, saying, "You know, folklorists just put numbers on stories that crop up time and again. Number 368, The-Chihuahua-Who-Took-One-Nap-Too-Many-In-The-Microwave-Oven. Parents ought to do that. Just call out the numbers. Save yourselves the trouble of doing the telling" (*MM* 1990, 241). Local legends are stories that center on a particular place and may tell how it got its name or recount some unusual sacred or secular event that took place there. These legends convey how people feel about the place they live, what standards from the past they accept as authoritative. In *Winter Brothers* Doig notes that the Makah and Haida Indians told James Swan many such legends.

The legend type that appears in *Mariah* is, in Riley's parlance, a type of heroic legend, one that exaggerates the accomplishments of the past. Riley believes that these legends have created an unrealistic standard of achievement for the people of Montana. In his story called "Twilight of the Rancher?" Riley focuses on the image of the tan line made by the Stetson, saying that it used to make the rancher "stand out at the Saturday night dances, as if a man needed to be bright-marked at the top to be able to schottische and square dance so nimbly...now worry fits on at that line...." Worry about the weather, about market prices, about hired help, about the toll ranching is taking on his body. Riley points out that Montana's legends about its past have betrayed the rancher:

> If the legends of his landed occupation are to be believed, a century and more ago Montana ranching began heroically, almost poetically, splendid in the grass. Yet even then, here and there a rancher twinged with the suspicion that legends are what people resort to when truth can't be faced. In 1882, cattleman Charles Anceny contemplated himself and his neighbors in Montana's new livestock industry with just such skepticism: "Our good luck consists more in the natural advantages of our country than in the scale of our genius" (*MM* 1990, 200).

What truth there might have been to the legend has been eroded by the exploitation of the land and the gradual consolidation of global economic structures that put the small rancher at a big disadvantage. The tan line left by the Stetson, once a mark of pride, is now a mark of worry:

> The rancher goes back and forth in his mind—give it up, tough it out. The past stretches from him like a shadow, recognizable but perplexing in the shapes it takes. He knows too well he is alone here in trying to look from those times to this. He rubs at that eclipse-line across his forehead and wonders how he and his way of life have ended up this way, forgotten but not gone (*MM* 1990, 200).

That such legends about Montana's heroic past abound today is noted in the comic scene where Riley, Mariah, and Jick, with mingled horror and delight, watch a television special on the centennial cattle drive, touted as a "true taste of the Old West," which features twenty-seven hundred head of cattle driven by twenty-four hundred riders. "You know, maybe this actually is a historic event," says Riley. "The biggest herd of clichés that ever trampled the mind."

Personal narratives act as correctives to heroic legends, describing lives as they were lived rather than as the collective mind imagines they were lived. Many of the personal narratives in *Mariah* are sad, even tragic, but Doig also includes stories that leaven the novel with warmth and humor. Jick's recollection of the "shivaree" that friends and family gave him and Marcella on their wedding night, complete with wheelbarrowing the new couple around their house, dancing, toasting, and the symbolic presentation of newborn twin lambs, illustrates the joy of this union and reminds us of the role of family and community in a marriage. At the end of the novel, Jick says, "Memories are the stories our lives tell us." Personal narratives are the articulations of those memories, our way of creating ourselves and finding our place in the world.

Chapter 12
Solving Problems

Doig's use of folklore can be examined not only from the perspective of how he solves the problems of incorporating folk traditions into a literary text, but also according to how he uses folklore to solve literary problems. One such problem is the establishment of necessary links between the first two books in the Montana trilogy. *Dancing at the Rascal Fair* precedes *English Creek* by a full generation, and one of Doig's purposes is to sketch out the changes in life in Montana that took place between the time of homesteading in the 1800s and the time of the Depression in the 1930s. This particular problem is complicated by the fact that Doig wrote *English Creek* first and had to work backwards in order to develop links in the second novel from suggestions he had planted in the first. Many of these links are items of occupational, family, regional, and ethnic folklore introduced in *English Creek* and then developed in *Rascal Fair*.

For example, Jick, ever curious about family history, notes the paucity of it and clings to the scraps he has learned:

I possessed no firsthand information on my father's parents. Both of them were under the North Fork soil by the time I was born. And despite my father's ear to the past, there did not seem to be anything known or at least fit to report about what the McCaskills came from in

Scotland. Except for a single scrap of lore: the story that a McCaskill had been one of the stonemasons of Arbroath who worked for the Stevensons—as I savvy it, the Stevensons must have been a family of engineers before Robert Louis cropped into the lineage and picked up a pen—when they were putting the lighthouses all around the coast of Scotland. The thought that an ancestor of ours helped fight the sea with stone meant more to my father than he liked to let on (*EC* 1984, 27).

That "single scrap of lore" that is a source of family pride for Varick McCaskill is developed into a full-blown family saga in *Dancing at the Rascal Fair*, where it becomes a personal talisman for the protagonist and narrator, Angus McCaskill. At the beginning of the novel he recounts the story in full—about his great-grandfather working with Stevenson on Bell Rock, a treacherous place covered by the tide every evening. The story centers on the crisis that ensued one night when their boat did not come. The men isolated on the barren rock were close to being drowned but were saved by the unexpected appearance of another boat. The story serves to remind Angus, who is afraid of the water, of the tested courage of his ancestor.

Doig uses the story to signal crises in the narrator's life: Angus recalls it when he crosses the ocean and fears drowning every moment of the crossing; he tells the story to the parents of Anna, the woman he is courting, in order to impress them; when Anna marries someone else, he encapsulates his despair with the phrase, "This was my Bell Rock. My time of stone, with obliteration all around." He envokes the saga again as he watches his son go off to war. And finally, when his friend and enemy, Rob Barclay, is drowning, Angus has to overcome his terror of the water in order to try to rescue him, and the family story becomes linked with his own time of testing, his fear of drowning when he crossed the Atlantic from Scotland to America: "*You ask was I afraid*, the McCaskill family voice ever since the treacherous work on the Bell Rock lighthouse. *Every hour and most of the minutes, drowning was on my mind*" (*RF* 1987, 396). The family saga of the Bell Rock Lighthouse serves the novel particularly well in this instance. The scene is "underwritten"—that is, the narrator does not describe what a fear of water feels like. Readers who have no such phobia would be unable to grasp the significance of Angus's attempt to save Rob without his evocation of the incident at Bell Rock, the terror of which any reader can understand.[1]

The use of this saga also demonstrates the relationship between the two books, which depends in part on the order in which they are read. The reader who reads *English Creek* first is likely to pass over the single reference to the Bell Rock Lighthouse because it does not connect with anything else in the novel. The reader who reads *Dancing at the Rascal Fair* first will pick up on the Bell Rock reference in *English Creek*, in which case it will enhance the character of Varick. Fighting the forces of nature, "the sea with stone" or fire with fire, becomes a matter of family history, courage a family trait.

Doig also creates links between the novels in "set pieces" of folk performance: rodeos and dances. The Dode Withrow who is thrown into a pool of manure at a rodeo in *Rascal Fair* takes a grander fall in *English Creek* and breaks his leg. Toussaint Rennie, present at both events, recalls the days of Dode's youth when rodeo was rough and crude and more dangerous perhaps than in the 1930s, by which time some of the cowboys on rodeo circuits were professionals, and he is qualified to praise Dode's ride. The development of rodeo from an impromptu Sunday sport to a major community celebration bespeaks the growth of the town and, to some extent, its stability: a generation later, many of the same people are there.

In *English Creek,* a special dance takes place on the Fourth of July, during which Jick is reminded that dancing is in his family's blood: "What little I knew of my father's father, the first McCaskill to caper on America's soil instead of Scotland's, included the information that he could dance down the house" (*EC* 1984, 205). The link exists not only in the family tradition of loving to dance but in their tradition of falling in love at dances: just as Angus had cemented his feelings for Anna at a schoolhouse dance, so Jick's own parents had fallen in love at a dance, and when he dances with his mother this Fourth of July, Jick is reminded of the family heritage: "She came for me, eyes on mine. I was the proxy of all that had begun at another dance, at the Noon Creek schoolhouse twenty years before" (*EC* 1984, 213). Like the story of the Bell Rock Lighthouse, the rodeos, dances, and references to Beth's and Varick's parents will have a different effect in *English Creek*, depending again on which book is read first. If the reader is not familiar with Angus's personal tragedy in *Rascal Fair* and the healing significance of Varick's marriage to Beth, he or she will be as mystified as Jick about family history. If the reader has read *Rascal Fair*, however, all of the allusions in *English Creek*, such as Beth's wagon trip with her mother and brother, become very significant indeed and make possible a more complicated relationship between the reader and the narrator. In this case, the reader "knows the answers" to the questions Jick asks about his own background, which creates a silent dialogue between reader and narrator.

Doig also uses complementary set pieces to show the differences between two generations—one immigrant, the other native. Folklore is a fortuitous choice for this purpose, evoking as it does both continuity and change. The dances in *Rascal Fair* are imports from Scotland. The residents of "Scotch Heaven" dance to the music they brought with them: "Tam Lin" and "Sir Patrick MacWhirr."[2] The dances in *English Creek* are pure Americana: square dances guided by a caller to western songs like "The Dude and Belle," whose lyrics are filled with regional references and lingo.

English Creek takes place in a single summer; *Rascal Fair,* however, spans two generations. Among other devices, Doig uses folklore motifs in order to bind together the sections of the longer novel: the Scottish toasts periodically offered by Lucas, which usually mark times of crisis or change in the lives of Rob and Angus: "broth to the ill, stilts to the lame"; "wives and sweethearts"; "rest our dust." They are traditional, and it is typical of Lucas to pour the whiskey and offer a toast when Angus and Rob come to him to share good news or bad. He becomes a foil for their responses, usually the older more mature voice in their partnership. "Toasting," in this case, remains the constant; the toast itself reflects the particular issue at hand, signaling turning points in the men's lives. "Broth to the ill, stilts to the lame" is a reference to Lucas's maiming and a reminder that he has been able to carry on his life successfully despite it. He offers "wives and sweethearts" during a conversation in which he urges Angus to marry and wisely points out that although Rob's choice of a wife will be relatively mechanical because Rob is already infatuated with himself, Angus needs to choose carefully. Lucas's advice is ironic in light of his own situation with Nancy and because of Angus's later, life-long love for his sweetheart, Anna, who will never be his wife. "Rest our dust" is a pun on settling the literal dust that coats westerners inside and out during the summer and on the dust of the dead. In this instance, Stanley Meixell has arrived to set up a national forest on what had been open grazing land; Lucas may be thinking of the possible demise of sheep ranching.

Most important are the variants of "Dancing at the Rascal Fair," the song that appears throughout the novel to grace romances and weddings.[3] It is one of the motifs that binds the book together, and each time it appears it has a different resonance: Rob and Angus sing it as they embark for America, and here it is a light-hearted song, full of young men's hope for a prosperous future. When the song appears in connection with Anna, it takes on a richness because of Angus's love for her. But the song is also sung at Angus's marriage to Adair, and there it becomes ironic in the eyes of the reader because the couple is mismatched and the groom is in love with somebody else's bride. Each time the song appears, it takes on a new layer of meaning, moving from hopeful innocence to tragic experience. When the song is sung for the last time, at the wedding of Varick and Beth, it has come full circle— a joyous song again because these people are right for each other, and the families are at last united in the marriage of Anna's daughter to Angus's son.

As he does with the song, Doig uses tradition as a thematic and structural device; he juxtaposes Scottish lore with American lore in order to mark the stages of assimilation of his characters to this new land. Angus as schoolmaster teaches his pupils traditional songs like "Flow Gently, Sweet Afton," and they counter with purely American folk songs, such as the Texas-born ballad, "Zebra Dun." The Scottish folk beliefs invoked early in the novel, such as the good-luck omen on Hogmanay, are later replaced by American tall tales, like the story of the fillyloo bird (*RF* 1987, 103, 374).[4]

Chapter 13
Folklore and History

Doig also uses folklore to suggest a solution to one of the problems faced by all contemporary western writers: the issue of western history. In his classic essay, "History, Myth and the Western Writer," Wallace Stegner argues that western writing has been hampered by two historical factors: the "mythic petrifaction" of one brief segment of western experience (the "Wild West" of cowboys, Indians, cattle drives, and walkdowns) into an enduring legend that dominates much American thinking about the West, and the discontinuity of settlement patterns:

> Settlement in the West was not only late, it was irregular. The mining West, and to a degree the timber, the grazing, and the homestead Wests, were raided, not settled; and sometimes raided for one resource after another, by different breeds of raiders. Despite their colorful history, there has hardly been a *continuous* community life in an Aspen or a Telluride; and when oil fields are superimposed on cattle country in Texas, or subdivisions superimposed on orchards in California, something disruptive has happened in the life of both people and towns (Stegner 1967, 62, 76).

Western literature, according to Stegner, has responded to the first pattern by producing formula westerns; to the second by representing the past as a prelapsarian ideal and the present as industrialized, vulgar, and disgusting. Stegner calls for western writers to break with these patterns by finding viable links between the past and the present that will provide westerners with a sense of a "possessed past," an understanding that the present is meaningful in historical terms.

Interestingly, Stegner does not regard folklore as capable of supplying those links:

> Folklore, more often than not an improvisation on an occupational theme—logging, riverboating, railroading, cowboying—is *only* an improvisation, and though it may be curiously lasting, it lasts as the Western lasts: it is cut loose like a balloon from the actual and continuing lives of men and women (Stegner 1967, 76).

In the twenty-five years since Stegner wrote this essay, writers in the West have been exploring ways to link a viable past to a meaningful present, and the expanded concept of what folklore is and how it can be used in literature has been a useful tool for them.

Doig, a historian himself, makes it clear that a sense of the past is crucial to a sense of personal and community identity. In *English Creek*, Jick's continual prodding of his parents to tell him the history of their families is motivated by a need to know more about himself and the person he will become. In *Dancing at the Rascal Fair*, the need for a sense of the past is articulated in a book of stories that Angus has his students read aloud:

> "One more sun," sighed the king at evening, "and now another darkness. This has to stop. The days fly past us as if they were racing pigeons. We may as well be pebbles, for all the notice life takes of us or we of it. No one holds in mind the blind harper when he is gone. No one commemorates the girl who grains the geese. None of the deeds of our people leave the least tiny mark upon time. . . . Why is it that the moon keeps better track of itself than we manage to? And the seasons put us to shame, they always know which they are, who's been, whose turn now, who comes next, all that sort of thing. Why can't we have memories as nimble as those? Tell me that, whoever can (*RF* 1987, 131–32).

The king solves his problem by appointing a "remembrancer," and Doig solves his problem in the same way. The character of Toussaint Rennie, who appears in both *Rascal Fair* and *English Creek*, is the "remembrancer." Part Indian, part white, very old but still vital during the time of Jick's youth, Toussaint belongs to two cultures and two centuries. By his own account, he has witnessed most of the history of Montana: the decimation of the Indian tribes and the buffalo herds, the great cattle drives, the construction of the Valier irrigation project, the establishment of homesteads, the growth of Gros Ventre. The stories Toussaint tells remain alive in Varick, Alec, and Jick, who feel the resonance of history when they look over the hay fields that once fed buffalo and then cattle herds. Historical significance for these people is not nostalgia for the past but an understanding of how they themselves fit into the life of the valley that preceded them and will go on after they are gone. When Toussaint Rennie teases Jick about camptending with Stanley, Jick has a sudden, not altogether comfortable, sense of what it means to become part of the history of the valley as recorded by the remembrancer:

> Better or worse, part of me now was in Toussaint's knowledge, his running history of the Two. In there with Phony Nose Gorman and the last buffalo hunt and the first sheep and the winter of '86 and Lieutenant Black Jack Pershing and the herded Crees and—and what did that mean? Being a part of history, at the age of fourteen years and ten months: why had that responsibility picked me out? (*EC* 1984, 153).

In all of Doig's Montana books, "history" is not restricted to formal texts complete with theories and interpretations but includes *oral* history—"his story," "her story"—the memories and achievements of individuals that collectively recapture the past and bind it to the present.

In the Montana trilogy, Doig records both the continuities and changes in the folklife of the region. The continuities, like the changes, are registered in the land itself and in the fact that life in rural Montana has always been structured on the rhythms of seasons and days:

> *One shard of time repeats itself like the snow-helmets of mountains across each season of my memory. An edged piece of the day, that is, in the strictest sense—the high sun-point called noon.*
>
> *It seems curious now that this one daily interval counted for so much. Daybreak did not, nor dusk; days arrived and went with an unnoticed ease then. But noon climbed up like a crier to a tower, and my father reckoned his life, and those of his ranch crews, and mine at his side, by its powers. . . . For so potent a piece of time, noon was not exact at all. It never meant to us high twelve o'clock, any more than to the*

early English countryfolk who accounted their noon at three P.M., the ninth hour after sunrise. Noon meant instead the controlled curve of the day from morning into afternoon, where the beginning of labor crossed into the lessening of labor. (Sky 1978, 175, 176).

The calendars of folklife are set by natural seasons in *This House of Sky* and *Rascal Fair:* lambing, summering in the mountains, shearing, wintering; or by the demands of rangering in *English Creek*, in which the year of work begins in early spring, follows the summer migrations of animals, climaxes in the haymaking and fire danger of summer. Thus folklife is irrevocably tied to weather, land and landscape, and the ways people meet their patterns and demands.

Part Three
Landcape

They call it regional, this relevance—

the deepest place we have: in this pool forms

the model of our land, a lonely one,

responsive to the wind. Everything we own

has brought us here: from here we speak.

—William Stafford, "Lake Chelan"

Overleaf: *Tom Salansky's ranch, on a fork of Dupuyer Creek in northern Montana, setting for* **English Creek** *(1983).*

Chapter 14
Re-Visioning the West

Western writers, perhaps more than writers from any other region, are associated with "place." We think of the brooding lake in Marilynne Robinson's *Housekeeping;* the Rocky Mountains in A. B. Guthrie's *Big Sky;* the Oregon rainforest in Ken Kesey's *Sometimes a Great Notion;* the Montana mountains and valleys in Ivan Doig's *This House of Sky;* the Saskatchewan prairies in Wallace Stegner's *Big Rock Candy Mountain;* the Wyoming grasslands in Gretel Ehrlich's *Solace of Open Spaces.* All of these are western landscapes, and they, more than culture or history or industry, characterize the West, define it in the American imagination.

The concept *West* has altered during three centuries of migration and settlement and before the late nineteenth century was often linked with the concept of *frontier:* to seventeenth-century colonists on the eastern seaboard the entire continent, unknown and alluring and threatening, was "West." Now that the frontier is closed and patterns of settlement are established, the West can be defined geographically as the land lying west of the one hundredth meridian, where rainfall slackens and mountains begin.[1] But the simplicity of that division of West from East is misleading, for there are many Wests. The arid West, consisting of mountains, high plains, and deserts, breaks off at the Rockies and yields to the West of the Pacific Coast states, which have a semiarid climate on the east side of the Cascade Mountains, a marine climate on the west side. Texas and Alaska are both part of the West but seem to have as little in common as Massachusetts and Nebraska.

Because of the region's geographic diversity, scholars disagree about how it should be defined and on what grounds it can be divided into subregions, and whether, indeed, there is sufficient unity in the landscapes of the West to warrant their being considered a single region. In *Winter Brothers* Doig notes that there is a common factor shared by the subregions of the West, although it is difficult to name:

> There are and always have been many Wests, personal as well as geographical. (Even what I have been calling the Pacific Northwest is multiple. A basic division begins at the Columbia River; south of it, in Oregon, they have been the sounder citizens, we in Washington the sharper strivers...) Swan on the Strait has been living in two distinct ones, Neah Bay and Port Townsend (and sampled two others earlier, San Francisco and Shoalwater Bay) and neither of them is the same as my own Wests, Montana of a quarter-century ago and Puget Sound of today. Yet Swan's Wests come recognizable to me, are places which still have clear overtones of my own places, stand alike with mine in being distinctly unlike other of the national geography. Perhaps that is what the many Wests are, common in their stubborn separatenesses: each West a kind of cabin, insistent that it is no other sort of dwelling whatsoever (*WB* 1980, 109–10).

Doig's observation does justice to the "otherness" that most western residents feel about the place they live but leaves the scholar unsatisfied. If the region is geographically multiple (and, to a degree, culturally and historically diverse) is there a unifying factor that defines the West? Can that factor be said to shape the distinct contemporary writing of the region? Although regions within the United States can be defined geographically, historically, sociologically, or politically, there is usually one major factor, such as Puritanism in New England or slavery in the South, that unifies those regions. The most important factor in the West is landscape, including its spaciousness and diversity, and that factor is probably the most important single influence on western writing. George Venn argues that "environment and the human response to it will emerge as one source of continuity in the region's literature that cannot easily be dismissed" (Venn 1979, 99). Venn limits his discussion to Northwest writers, but his argument can be extended to writers from other western states. "Western writers" are not just those who write about the West, nor those who employ the popular stereotypes of the cowboy romance, but writers who are aware of the interpenetration of landscape and human life in this part of the country.

Landscape is, of course, an important factor in American life in general, and certainly the East has its share of weather and landforms. But western livelihoods, such as mining, farming, ranching, fishing, and logging, are all tied to the land—and western environments are characterized by an extremity that affects daily and seasonal life:

> In addition to low rainfall, the Western states share climatic extremes, a comparatively high elevation of land, and wide expanses of either plains or mountains. Weather is easily visible and has a direct effect upon the people. Most of the land is open and unprotected, so that the Westerner must always confront his total environment. . . . In the West towns are far apart, violent storms swing suddenly across the plains, snow comes early in the mountains, and the wind blows hard enough to be a factor in the behavior of the people. Life can be a physical and spiritual ordeal, or it can be seen in terms of purity as symbolized by the clear and dry air which is undefiled by industrial civilization (Milton 1967, 267).

The impact of the landscape on the people who live in the West can be regarded in terms of two overlapping arenas: environmental and psychological, and in each of these, "influence" is a two-way street: humans change their physical environment and are changed by it, humans interpret their world, mediate it by the ways they see and describe it, and in turn are psychologically shaped by that world.

In the West, human beings and their enterprises can appear to be dwarfed by the sheer size and spaciousness of their environment, which is so large in scope it seems utterly indifferent to human affairs. In the following passage from Ken Kesey's *Sometimes a Great Notion*, for example, Jonas Stamper expresses his frustration at the insignificance of human effort in the Oregon rainforest:

> For *one* thing, Jonas couldn't see all that elbow room that the pamphlets had talked about. Oh, it was there, he knew. But not the way he'd imagined it would be. And for *another* thing, there was nothing, *not a thing!* about the country that made a man feel Big And Important. If anything it made him feel dwarfed, and about as important as one of the fish-Indians living down on the clamflats. Important? Why,

there was something about the whole blessed country that made a soul feel whipped before he got started. Back home in Kansas a man had a *hand* in things, the way the Lord *aimed* for His servants to have: if you didn't water, the crops died. If you didn't feed the stock, the stock died. As it was ordained to be. But there, in that land, it looked like our labors were for naught. The flora and fauna grew or died, flourished or failed, in *complete* disregard for man and his aims (Kesey 1965, 20–21).

On the other hand, the power of western land to regenerate itself is a misleading notion, at best. Fragile ecologies, especially in the arid West, have sometimes collapsed under the impact of human interference. In *The Sound of Mountain Water,* Wallace Stegner notes:

All of the West's resources, even water, even scenery, are more vulnerable than the resources of other regions . . . the basic resources of soil and water, which can be mismanaged elsewhere without drastic consequences, cannot be mismanaged in the West without consequences that are immediate and often catastrophic, and that reach a long way. Overgrazing or clear-cutting in a watershed on the Yampa can send consequences clear to Yuma; abusing the range on the Big Horn can do things to the Missouri that alarm St. Louis. And the entire history of the West, when we hold at arm's length the excitement, adventure, romance and legendry, is a history of resources often mismanaged and of constraining conditions often misunderstood or disregarded. Here, as elsewhere, settlement went by trial and error; only here the trials were sometimes terrible for those who suffered them, and the errors did permanent injury to the land (Stegner 1980, 19).

In *Ride with Me, Mariah Montana,* Doig comments on the despoiling of the state, the strip mining and overgrazing that have left permanent scars on the land. The "get-rich-quicker-than-the-next-grabber-and-to-hell-with-the-consequences" attitude Doig describes in *Winter Brothers* is reflected in Montana, as well, exemplified in the photograph Mariah takes of the Berkeley Pit in Butte:

Enormous above Riley's words, Mariah's Butte photo was of the Berkeley Pit, the almost unbelievable open-pit mine which took the copper role from the played-out mineshafts everywhere under the streets of the city: a bulldozed crater a mile wide and deeper than the

Empire State Building is tall. Ex-mine, it too now was, having been abandoned in favor of cheaper digging in South America (*MM* 1990, 58).

The pun Doig uses to describe the depth of the mine, "Empire State Building," is ironic: the empire here, owned and run by Anaconda Copper, has not built the state but literally gouged it out and left the wound still gaping. "Miners never put the earth back," Jick thinks. The fact that the land is considered, in the crudest sense, a "resource," is illustrated in the fact that according to Riley the Pentagon has requested eight million more acres in the western states for tank maneuvers and artillery and bombing ranges. An undersecretary of defense has called these lands "a national treasure" (*MM* 1990, 244). The disease of exploitation is not limited to faceless corporations and branches of the government. Riley writes about a big farm operator who, during a time of crop surpluses, plowed up thousands of acres of virgin grassland and then let it lie fallow for the winds to rip away, "farming the farm program" (*MM* 1990, 33).

The difference between the exploiters of the land and people like Jick and Riley is one of perception: seeing the land in terms of dollar bills as opposed to seeing the land itself. About the plans of the Pentagon, Jick thinks, "This country of the Big Dry did not appeal to me personally. Yet why couldn't it be left alone? Left be empty?" (*MM* 1990, 244).

The psychological impact of the western landscape is also a matter of mutual influence between human beings and their environment. In Parts 1 and 2 it was noted that people shape their realities by the way they emplot them in storytelling: foregrounding or ignoring details, choosing a viewpoint and tone, allow the storyteller to create meaning from experience. The same process takes place in the perception of the environment: the raw material takes its shape and assumes significance as it is interpreted by the seeing eye. In their study of eighteenth-century British perception of the Northwest Coast, "Pleasing Diversity and Sublime Desolation," Douglas Cole and Maria Tippett argue convincingly that the way a landscape is seen and described will vary, age to age, depending upon cultural training and expectations:

Man looks at the landscape through conditioned eyes. Perceptions of beauty in land forms are molded by the taste of the age, and the emotions which a landscape inspires are learned reactions. "We see what we have been taught to look for, we feel what we have been prepared to feel" (Cole and Tippett 1974, 1).

Conversely, the outside world shapes inner human life. Although a scene in the landscape may be perceived by different individuals as elating or depressing, beautiful or frightening, the landscape *affects* people. In *The Solace of Open Spaces*, for example, Gretel Ehrlich makes it clear that in the West, the outer environment shapes the inner person:

> Dryness is the common denominator in Wyoming. We're drenched more often in dust than in water; it is the scalpel and the suit of armor that make westerners what they are. Dry air presses a stockman's insides outward. The secret, inner self is worn not on the sleeve but in the skin. It's an unlubricated condition: there's not enough moisture in the air to keep the whole emotional machinery oiled and working (Ehrlich 1984, 78–79).

The complex interplay between westerners and the landscape they live in is an artistic gold mine. But the very richness of the material makes it difficult to handle artistically. Studies by scholars like George Venn and Douglas Cole demonstrate that eighteenth- and nineteenth-century explorers and pioneers tended to record their impressions of the West romantically, even hyperbolically, and that in western writing of the last century, environment often eclipsed character. John Milton writes: "[The West] is a land of extremities and relatively few people, tempting the writer to focus his attention upon the landscape and to view the people either as pawns of nature, or, if they survive, as heroes" (Milton 1967, 267).

This problem was addressed by Ivan Doig at a meeting of the Pacific Northwest American Studies Association in Seattle in spring 1988 when he spoke to teachers and scholars of western literature on the topic of "place" in his writing. Doig said, "Today's writing about the West of America is sometimes thought of as a focus on the *land* rather than on the *people*." This perception is due in part to book titles that feature landscape images, such as *The Solace of Open Spaces, The Big Sky,* and *A River Runs Through It*. It is also due to the geography of the West, its powerful landforms and extremes of weather and immense distances, all of which have a tremendous impact on the imagination. In his speech, Doig noted that the landscape does figure large in the work of many western writers, including his own. "But," he added, "I don't particularly think it's at the neglect of the people, the human stories, the characters who carry on their lives against the big bold landscapes of those books." Doig listed over a dozen characters from contemporary western novels, including Norman Maclean's flyfishing brother in *A River Runs Through It*, the Stamper family in *Sometimes a Great Notion*, the men of the Montana reservations in the works of Jim Welch, the women of Fingerbone in *Housekeeping*, "all of them *characters* of modern western literature who seem to have found a continuing life in the minds of readers." Doig's assertion that place in western writing does not overshadow character can be taken one step further. In western writing, landscape and character are inseparable: "landscape" assumes meaning through the perceptions and responses of characters, and character is shaped by landscape. Landscape is seldom expanded to symbol or reduced to setting but rather treated as *context*: a causal force in human life.

In order to gain some perspective on how Doig describes and uses landscape in his books, how he achieves a balance between the inner and outer worlds of his characters, it will be helpful to examine his work within the context of the body of western writing being produced by his contemporaries. Although Doig may not have been influenced directly by these writers, his work is shaped by the same forces as theirs. As William Kittredge and Steven Krauzer point out, writing in the West is coming of age, and, as diverse as they are, western writers share a common literary milieu:

> The current status of western writing is similar to that of southern American writing in the early 1930s when a major regional voice, in the persons of such authors as William Faulkner, Robert Penn Warren, Eudora Welty, Andrew Lytle, and Katherine Anne Porter, was beginning to be heard. Just as the old south was gone, the old west is gone. Freed of the need to write either out of the mythology or against it, the writers of the new west, responding to the variety and quickness of life in their territory, are experiencing a period of enormous vitality (Kittredge and Krauzer 1980, 13).

Keeping in mind the great variety of landscape and lifestyle within the region it can still be argued that writers like Ken Kesey, Marilynne Robinson, William Kittredge, James Welch, Norman Maclean, and Ivan Doig have one powerful thing in common: they are all native to the West and therefore work from local knowledge. They write about the land and people of the West out of their own deep and intimate relationship to place. That common factor creates recognizable literary patterns and motifs: the sensuality of their writing, their attention to detail, their sense of profane and sacred space, and their emphasis on community.

To rural westerners, the forces of nature are a reality, not an abstraction. As Doig points out:

> You can't be around that landscape without it being on your mind. The weather governed our lives on the ranch, often determined

whether the entire year was a success or not. Our lives turned on the weather, in combination with the landscape. This carries over into my writing (O'Connell 1983, 305).

In examining how the landscape influences his writing, it is important to realize that because Doig respects the facts of weather and landscape, he records them in careful detail and avoids literary conventions that would abstract those facts or convert them into symbols. During one of my discussions with him, I quoted a passage from Ken Kesey's *Sometimes a Great Notion* that seemed to articulate Doig's approach to landscape. In this passage Hank Stamper, the novel's protagonist, (and in this case, one suspects, the author's spokesperson) talks about the need to confront the river as a physical reality, to avoid imposing categories onto something already meaningful in itself:

> I know, for instance, that, if you want to play this way, you can make the river stand for all *sorts* of other things. But doing that it seems to me is taking your eye off the ball; making it more than what it is lessens it. Just to see it clear is plenty. Just to feel it cold against you or watch it flood or smell it when the damn thing backs up from Wakonda with all the town's garbage and sewage and dead crud floating around in it stinking up a breeze, that is plenty. And the best way to see it is not looking behind it—or beneath it or beyond it—but dead at it (Kesey 1965, 105).

Doig commented that this passage demonstrates local knowledge, the wellspring of his own writing:

> I think it comes back to the fact that that's where I was *born*, that's what I *saw*, that's what I go *back* to see, that's what I try to describe, and so, yeah . . . the essential part of the quote from Kesey strikes very nicely with me—I wish I'd thought of that—so if you can find a way to tell the world that you're looking at this from what seems to *be* there rather than what the critical frames around it would say is supposed to be there, that is certainly something I would appreciate and hope you can do.[2]

"What seems to *be* there," in Doig's words, is the re-creation of the West as experienced by a person who has internalized the landscape he or she grew up in.

The apparent straightforwardness and simplicity of this approach result in complex literary crafting, particularly in the use of narrative voice. In *The Sea Runners*, for example, Doig creates an omniscient narrator who assumes varying perspectives, sometimes "overhearing" the characters' conversations and interior monologues, sometimes observing them from historical or physical distance. The impersonality of the latter point of view sets up an antagonistic relationship between the characters and the landscape they are traveling through: they are not granted the power of defining for the reader what they see. They are in awe of the natural world, but they cannot really touch it or know it—it is not meaningful to them as it is to the Native Americans who call it home—so for the protagonists it is an impersonal order that two of them do not survive. In the following passage, for example, the reader is given information that the Swedes have no access to:

> Vaster stretches can be found on the earth, but not all so many, and none as fiercely changeable. Most of the weathers imaginable are engendered somewhere along the North Pacific's horizon coast, from polar chill to the stun of desert heat. Within this water world the special law of gravity is lateral and violent. Currents of brine and air rule. Most famous and elusive of these is the extreme wind called the williwaw—an ambusher, an abrupt torrent of gust flung seaward from the snow-held Alaskan mountains. But times, too, the North Pacific flings back the wind, gale so steady onto the coast it seems the continent has had to hunch low to keep from swaying (*SR* 1982, 88).

In this passage the voice of the verbs is not active, but passive: "can be found," "are engendered," which contributes to the impersonality of the description. The items compared are opposites: "polar chill"..."desert heat"; the descriptions convey extremes: "vaster," "chill," "stun," "extreme," "abrupt." And the only presence is the landscape, in battle with itself. The effect of such passages is to create a glacial distance between landscape and character that emphasizes the miraculousness that the journey had been made at all.

In his other books, Doig uses first-person narrators, so that the reader's perception of landscape is always mediated by the point of view of someone living within that landscape. This method effectively re-creates the environment but precludes its overshadowing character and emphasizes the interrelationship between landscape and the people who live in it.

In the following passage from *Dancing at the Rascal Fair*, for example, there is subtle interplay between the land and the narrator, and the reader becomes aware of the land's physical as well as aesthetic impact:

Not an hour after we were underway the next morning, the trail dropped us into a maze of benchlands with steep sides. Here even the tallest mountains hid under the horizon, there was no evidence the world knew such a thing as a tree, and Herbert pointed out to us alkali bogs which he said would sink the wagon faster than we could think about it. A wind so steady it seemed solid made us hang onto our hats. Even the path of wagon tracks lost patience here; the bench hills were too abrupt to be climbed straight up, and rather than circle around endlessly among the congregation of geography, the twin cuts of track attacked up the slopes in gradual sidling patterns (*RF* 1987, 45).

In this passage the landscape is active, vital, nearly personified: "The trail *dropped* us... the tallest mountain *hid*... the world *knew*... alkali bogs *would* sink the wagon... a wind so steady it seemed solid *made us hang onto our hats*... the path... *lost patience*... the twin cuts of track *attacked* up the slopes."

But the narrator is not a victim of this landscape, as were the fugitives in *The Sea Runners*; he describes the landscape as he perceives it and is thus able to come to terms with it, to shape it, literally to *realize* it. This narrative technique reflects the worldview of people living *with* the land, not merely moving across it. The intimacy between people and environment in the West is manifested in the sensuality of western writing: the force of the wind, the pain of a sunburn that cracks and peels the skin, the sound of mountain water are re-created not as symbols or abstractions but as physical sensations.

Western writers exploit all of the senses but especially emphasize seeing, often from the vantage point of mountains and ridges. Gary Snyder climbs Mount Rainier and marvels with irony that in Washington, D.C., lives a senator who claims to "represent" the forests and rivers below; Bill Kittredge scales a cliff and looks down onto his property with bitterness, reflecting on the destruction of natural order in the name of husbandry. What is distinctive about this kind of seeing is that it is outer-directed; these writers do not gaze into Walden Pond to reflect on themselves. The point should be made here that much canonical American writing focuses on the self, and Nature becomes myth or symbol or adversary or metaphor for the inward journey. Contemporary western writing explores the self, but it is a self shaped by and in constant interaction with a living world.

Living with the land requires the ability to perceive and interpret its rhythms. Ranchers and farmers must be able to predict the weather, to "read" the mountains to know when to move their herds and flocks to upland pastures, when to plant and when to harvest, to know whether a rustle in the brush is a deer or a bear. Clear-sightedness implies insightfulness, not only about nature but also about people. Western towns usually have a small core population and a large itinerant population of ranch hands, hay hands, sheepherders, and the like who move from job to job. Westerners value the ability to "size someone up" quickly, to trust or mistrust them on sight. In *This House of Sky,* for example, Charlie must be able to gauge the characters of men, their strong and weak and breaking points, when he hires them. Bessie turns her grandson over to a total stranger, who in turn accepts a total stranger to board in her home, on the strength of a few moments' "sizing up."

The relationship between seeing with one's own eyes (as opposed to visualizing or imagining) is significant to both the process and the product of Doig's writing. His research for each book always includes seeing the places he writes about: in his preliminary work on *Dancing at the Rascal Fair,* he traveled to Scotland to stand on the dock at the mouth of the River Clyde, where his characters set off for America, in order to find "the resonance in actuality." For *The Sea Runners,* he traveled to Alaska and committed to paper his impressions of the landscape: "From eye to [note] card to novel," he commented in a speech, and then quoted from a long set of notes he had taken that, revised again and again, became a brief scene in the book. "Six hundred words achieved at an enormous cost of travel and time." For *Winter Brothers,* Doig traveled to nearly all the places James Swan had lived, worked, and visited in order to comprehend those sites and their significance to Swan and to western history.

For *Ride with Me, Mariah Montana,* Doig made several visits to his home state, crisscrossing it to explore the places that appear in the book. He and his wife, Carol, who photographs many of the sites Doig writes about, rented a motorhome one summer and spent sweltering days traveling in it, finding out about life in this modern version of a sheepherder's wagon as well as about life in contemporary Montana. Some of Doig's personal experiences during those trips made their way into fiction: on a cold evening at the Chief Joseph Battlefield "fifteen miles from anywhere," Doig locked himself out of his rental car, a maneuver he let Riley take responsibility for in the novel.

In Doig's world, a clear perception of outer forms becomes synonymous for the perception of inner forms. In a passage from *English Creek,* Jick puzzles over his brother's aberrant behavior as he rides to check the herding cabin of Walter Kyle. Walter has taught him the use of a spyglass for seeing long distances in the mountains, and Jick plays with the idea that because of his "vision," Walter can see inside people as well; Jick carries on a monologue with the absent sheepherder, asking him to explain the things that are worrying Jick and confounding his family. Jick also wishes that a

Ivan Doig in the Beartooth Mountains, Montana (1987).

painter could do a portrait of the people at the Fourth of July picnic: "That would convey every one of those people at once and yet also their separateness. Their *selves*, I guess the word should be" (*EC* 1984, 151). In other words, for the relationship between individuals and community to be comprehended, it must be captured visually. In *Mariah*, Jick learns that the world looks different through the lens of his daughter's camera. In *This House of Sky*, Doig begins his reconstruction of family history by reviewing photographs, trying to re-create the persona of his mother and the quality of his parents' early lives in those portraits.

Naming is another way of capturing, of possessing what is outside ourselves; the act of naming, both bestowing a name and recalling it, is significant in western literature. Many of the passages in Stegner's *Sound of Mountain Water*, Kesey's *Sometimes a Great Notion*, and Ehrlich's *Solace of Open Spaces* begin with lists of names. Names indicate not merely travel through a place but *into* a place: its physical qualities, its history.

Doig emphasizes the importance of places' having the right names. In his article "Lewis and Clark Were Name-Droppers," Doig chronicles the names with which the two explorers christened the streams, rivers, bluffs, mountains, and plains of a country new to them. He notes their humorous misnomers (Nightingale Creek for a bird not native to the Americas, No Preserves Island, Bald-Pated Prairie) and praises them for apt and musical names: the Yellowstone, the Marias (muh-RYE-us) River.

Names, to Doig, suggest history, personality, part of the past that remains in the present; they are a kind of folk poetry. His books abound with names. In *English Creek*, as Jick and Varick begin their yearly counting trip, Jick describes what he sees by naming it:

> Better country to look ahead to could not be asked for. Kootenai, Lolo, Flathead, Absaroka, Bitterroot, Beaverhead, Deerlodge, Gallatin, Cabinet, Helena, Lewis and Clark, Custer, Two Medicine—those were the national forests of Montana, totaling dozens of ranger districts, but to our estimation the Two Medicine was head and shoulders above the other forests, and my father's English Creek district the topknot of the Two. Anybody with eyes could see this at once, for our ride this morning led up the North Fork of English Creek, which actually angles mostly west and northwest to thread between Roman Reef and Rooster Mountain to its source, and where the coulee of the North Fork opened ahead of us, there the first summits of the Rockies sat on the horizon like stupendous sharp boulders. Only when our first hour or so of riding carried us above that west edge of the coulee would we see the mountains in total, their broad bases of timber and rockfall

gripping into the foothills. And the reefs. Roman Reef ahead of us, a rimrock half a mile high and more than three long. Grizzly Reef even bigger to the south of it, smaller Jericho Reef to the north. I don't know, are mountain reefs general knowledge in the world? I suppose they get their name because they stand as outcroppings do at the edge of an ocean, steady level ridges of stone, as if to give a calm example to the waves beyond them. (*EC* 1984, 14).

Doig focuses on etymology as well as aptness: Jick notes the derivation of the name of the Two Medicine River from the medicine lodges of the Blackfeet, comments with amusement on street names in Gros Ventre that repeat themselves—St. Mary St., St. Peter St.—because of the influence of a Catholic priest on a local landowner.

Doig also rejoices in the sound of names. In *Winter Brothers*, he records the names of ships that appear in Swan's diaries, arranging them for the play of consonance, assonance, alliteration, and rhythm:

Willamantic and *Alert* and *Flying Mist* and *Naramissic*. The *Toando Keller*, the *Lizzie Roberts*, the *Jenny Ford*. *Orion, Iconium, Visurgis*. *Torrent. Saucy Lass. Wild Pigeon. Forest Queen. Maunaloa. Growler. Quickstep.* Up from San Francisco, *Nahumkeag. Aguilar de Los Andes*, eagle of the Andes and homebound to Santiago. *Lalla Rookh* and *Wavelet* and *Jeannie Berteux* (*WB* 1980, 101).

"Nothing in our world is so richly, gaily named any more, unless it would be racehorses," Doig notes with a touch of regret. The music of the past is found in the names it goes by.

In the fact that names are not random but bear a human history lies some comfort for the newcomer, knowledge that someone was there before, that the landscape is not impervious to human influence. A place that is named has been marked by human consciousness and can be contained by the mind, becoming part of an I-Thou relationship that familiarizes the foreign and provides a human context for the non-human environment. Conversely, there is terror in being in a place so new that there are no names, or where names reflect a Native American relationship to environment, inaccessible to whites. In "Continuity in Northwest Literature," George Venn quotes a passage from William Clark's journal written 12 November, 1805. In it, Clark describes a night-long storm that soaked the men and their gear and sent branches crashing down around them. Clark describes moving camp "around a point to a Small wet bottom, at the Mouth of a Brook" and comments several times on the "danger" and "distress" of their "situation."

In this case, "situation" refers both to location and condition, and Clark felt keenly that both were dreadful. Venn notes:

> To dismiss Clark's writing as simple historical artifact or to say that all this was simply written for Jefferson is to miss what it expresses about the human condition in new space: the environment was upon Clark and his men, even intimidating them. Clark writes without specific names because he is new and not at home. He did not know what was out there, how it could be used, or how he and his men would have to change in order to survive. For settlers, diaries and journals show that in some cases men and women went mad under these conditions in which language, culture, and history had not yet established relationships between people and the environment that would allow them a greater chance for survival. Although the literal facts of such experiences seem to be their only significant dimension, what those facts *express* about the human condition in new space also needs to be understood (Venn 1979, 101).

In *The Sea Runners*, the Swedes find themselves in the same position as the men of the Lewis and Clark expedition: although narrator and reader know what the place-names signify, what the territory is like, the characters do not. They are lost in more ways than one as they paddle south through the treacherous waters of the Inland Passage. *The Sea Runners* opens with a map of the region, and from a godlike distance the reader can see the tangle of islands, bays, shoalwaters, inlets, and crossings that the men have to face from sea level, one at a time. Their maps are incomplete, and the names on them are Russian.

The significance of names is particularly clear in regard to the Indians whose territory the sea runners are crossing. The men have one name for the Indians—"Koloshes"—one name for Tlingits, Haidas, Makahs, Bellabellas, Bella Coolas, Tsimshians, Nootkas. All that Melander, Braaf, Wennberg, and Karlsson know about these people is that they take human heads and that they leave their villages for the fishing grounds every year. The men stumble on signs of these sophisticated cultures, witnessing the return of whale hunters to an island village, coming upon totem poles in the forest. But the ceremonies and the carvings are incomprehensible to them. Melander regards the carvings and says, "A kind of cathedral.... Whatever it is that these people believe is said in these carvings. Like rune stones, aye?" (*SR* 1982, 118). *The Sea Runners* is, in part, a book about facing the unknown, the unidentifed, the unnamed, and the price paid for ignorance. The fugitives pass through a space, a territory, without comprehending it and without leaving marks of their own. There is justice in their anonymity and the unintentional humility that accompanies it, for the land is not theirs to name. Naming is a privilege of relationship, if not ownership, and there is a great and dreadful irony in the arrogance with which whites imposed their own labels on a land named long before by the people who lived there. In the Americas, this chauvinism is most dramatically exemplified in tales of Spaniards who waded ashore from their ships, stuck flags into the earth of lands so vast the explorers could not even comprehend them, and declared that the land, the resources, and the people of that place were, from that moment on, property of the Spanish crown.

A similar, if subtler arrogance exists in the Anglo habit of renaming, a trait explored in *Winter Brothers*. Swan himself does the Makahs the courtesy of learning their language, studying their customs, reproducing their art. But the names of his Indian friends bespeak the dominance of an alien culture: Captain John, Jimmy, Peter, Boston Tom, the derisively titled Duke of York. And the places—Port Townsend, the Queen Charlotte Islands—are named for explorers who passed through, or for distant monarchs who regard the place only as an exploitable colony.

For Doig, "naming" something or someone is a moral prerogative, significant in characterization. In *English Creek,* for example, the origin of "Jick" as a nickname for "John Angus" is a mystery to the young narrator, and his parents are vague about who bestowed it on him. At the end of the summer he discovers that Stanley Meixell gave him his nickname, and that small detail affirms Stanley's role as a hero in the novel and clarifies his claim on the McCaskill family.

In *Ride with Me, Mariah Montana,* Mariah's name evokes both her unusual personality and her relationship to her home place. She was named for the Marias River, and Doig opens the novel with the citation from Meriwether Lewis's journal that explains the origin of the name:

> I determined to give it a name and in honour of Miss Maria W——d called it Marias River. it is true that the hue of the waters of this turbulent and troubled stream but illy comport with the pure celestial virtues and amiable qualifications of that lovely fair one; but on the other hand it is a noble river.

Clearly Mariah is much more like the turbulent river than she is like the lady for whom the river is named, and Jick muses about the connection:

> Not for the first time, more like the millionth, I wondered whether her behavior somehow went with her name. That *eye* sound there in

Mariah, while any other of the species that I'd ever encountered was always plain *ee* Maria. She was a singular one in every way I could see, for sure (*MM* 1990, 3).

The "Montana" appellation was tagged on when Mariah went back East to college and her classmates decided that her blue jeans and Blackfeet beaded belt made her a true daughter of the state. In Doig's work, names are invariably appropriate, evocative, sometimes ironic. Jick remembers that during haying season "you might put up hay with a guy called Moxie or Raw Bacon Slim or Candy Sam all season, then when he was paid off find out that the name on his paycheck was Milton Huttleby or some such" (*MM* 1990, 50). In *English Creek*, "Wisdom Johnson" is so tagged because he loved the town Wisdom, not because he demonstrated much perspicacity. "Good Help Hebner" was named for a silly comment on his part, ironic in the light of his selfishness, laziness, and dependency.

Sound and sense work together in the names Doig gives his characters. Jick comments that Riley "was truly well-named; he could rile me faster than anybody else ever could" (*MM* 1990, 28). Baxter Beebe, the *Montanian* editor, is nicknamed "BB," which immediately suggests "gun," and sure enough, he has a gallery of stuffed animal heads on his office walls. (Doig also had a more subtle pun in mind when he chose the name—"small bore".) Beebe's cerebral level is suggested by his never getting Jick's name right, coming out with "Jack," "Chick," or "Jiggs" instead. Leona lives up to the beauty and dignity of "lioness," and the sound of "Althea Frew" is as deliciously trivial as the lady herself. Some names are part of family tradition: Jick's full name is "John Angus," for his grandfather, "Lexa" is short for "Alexandra," for her uncle. All connote the characters' places in the world, the temporal, physical, and psychological spaces they occupy.

Chapter 15
Profane and Sacred Space

Western writers often talk about landscape in terms of profane and sacred space, and although Doig does not use those terms, the concept pervades his delineation of character through the ways his characters relate to the land.

The phrase "profane and sacred space" became known through the work of mythographer and theologian Mircea Eliade. Eliade defines personal experience of the sacred as "other": outside of daily life, often occurring in a space set apart. He defines sacred space as

> The holy places. . . . [I]n such spots [one receives] the revelation of a reality other than that in which he participates through his ordinary daily life. . . . Within the sacred precincts the profane world is transcended. . . . [I]n the sacred enclosure, communication with the gods is possible (Eliade 1959, 24–26).

Western American writers, however, have reshaped Eliade's formulation. "Transcendence," in their terms, is the realization of the sacred *in* ordinary daily life, and "communication with the gods" is a matter of awareness rather than a special set of circumstances. This concept is derived from the Native Americans' relationship to their world. For them the sacred is not idea but the energy and life that surround them in whose space they live.

Native people participate in the sacred through community rituals, storytelling, and ceremonies marking activities such as planting, harvesting, hunting, preserving food.

Max Westbrook asserts that the Native American worldview is accessible to all westerners if they are willing to let go of the perceived dichotomy between spiritual and physical realms and understand God as energy, the creative force that founded the world:

> The sacred man can find his rough and realistic God of energy in the beauty of a lake, the harsh heat of a desert, the blank and haunting eyes of a fresh-killed deer. This discovery, furthermore, is a literal one: the sacred man does not find a *symbol* of God; he finds God. He touches the thing itself (Westbrook 1968, 198).

Under Westbrook's analysis lies the assumption that the sacred is connected with wilderness; this is a common idea in western writing.

But wilderness is not a necessary precondition for the experience of sacred space; in the following definition by George Venn sacred space is determined not by environmental conditions but by inner receptiveness:

> *Sacred space* impl[ies] home, a heterogeneous landscape in which man has both privileges and responsibilities. . . . In sacred space, there is continuity between internal and external space; man seeks that continuity and binds himself to it. He claims space as part of himself, he identifies with it. Hence man is part of the landscape and knows his place in it. . . .
>
> *Profane space* impl[ies] a territory in which man believes he has all privileges and no responsibilities. . . . In profane space, man feels a profound discontinuity between internal and external reality, and confronted with that discontinuity over a period of time, man is emptied of himself and confronts absolute "other." (Venn 1979, 117).

The key to Venn's definition is the phrase, "in profane space, man feels a profound discontinuity between internal and external reality." To the twentieth-century mind, accustomed to organizing life according to Cartesian dualism, the distinction between internal and external reality seems inevitable. But western writers, familiar with the Native American worldview and sensitive themselves to the living world, have upon occasion articulated another state of being that John Milton calls "Emergence," which is actually a realization of the sacred:

The experience or ritual known as the Emergence is essentially an awareness that all of creation exists in the man, that all those forces which may be seen or sensed in this outer world are also present in an individual human being. This is a kind of knowledge, and it is arrived at through "realization and orientation," often a slow process although sometimes it occurs rather quickly in a moment of insight (Milton 1967, 278).

Sacred space, therefore, is a felt and lived relationship between a person and the world. Certainly the wilderness may be more conducive to "Emergence" than less prepossessing environments, but any place in which the individual is aware of continuity, renewal, personal responsibility, is sacred space.

But how does one translate a spiritual awakening into practical terms? How do people actually live in profane or sacred space? The answer is suggested in Bill Kittredge's memoir *Owning It All*, in which he grieves for the loss of the sacred in the pursuit of the pastoral yeoman dream. He describes his family's struggle to buy land and more land, then work it according to the received notions of order and control. He records their outrage and despair when they discovered that they had, in the process, destroyed the very thing they had sought to possess:

> As the fieldwork became more and more mechanical, we couldn't hire anyone who cared enough to do it right. The peat ground we had drained began to go saline. The waterbirds stopped coming in the great rafts we had so loved to hunt. Instead of creating a great good place, we were destroying our natural oasis. We had lived the right lives, according to mythology, and the mythology had lied (in Runciman 1987, 83).

In other words, living in sacred space means living *with* the land, in accordance with its laws and in harmony with its ecology; not trying to reshape it but allowing it to shape you. But how does one reconcile the demands of twentieth-century Anglo consciousness and a technological world with participation in the sacred? Doig explores that possibility in *English Creek*, where the psychological "inner scapes" of the characters reflect and merge with the "outer scapes" of the land. In this novel, and in *Dancing at the Rascal Fair*, which follows it, his heroes are characters who live in sacred space. They acknowledge their responsibilities to that space and have internalized the patterns of nature into their own physical and psychological rhythms.

The most obvious example of the blending of inner and outer landscapes is in the character of Varick McCaskill, father of the narrator and ranger for the Two Medicine National Forest. The patterns of his working life are determined by the rhythms of the wilderness. When spring begins, he watches the snow melt and the creeks fill: he keeps mental tally of the wildlife as bears come out of hibernation and deer start into the mountains, and he follows them on his summer counting trips to allot grazing land for sheep and cattle ranchers. He is a husbandman of the wilderness, his calendar established by its seasons. Varick is most comfortable by a camp fire or with a fishing rod in his hand. His appetite is stimulated by outdoor work, and his favorite foods are those provided by the land. Varick is so sensitive to the world he lives in that even his body functions according to seasonal changes:

> He never wintered well. Came down with colds, sieges of hacking and sniffing, like someone you would think was a permanent pneumonia candidate. Strange, for a man of his lengthy strength. . . .
>
> More than likely, all of my father's winter ailments really were symptoms of just one, indoorness. For stepping out a door somehow seemed to extend him, actually tip his head higher and brace his shoulders straighter, and the farther he went from a house the more he looked like he knew what he was doing. . . .
>
> When spring let him out and around, my father seemed to green up with the country. . . . The first roar of a chinook beginning to sweep down off the top of the Rockies signaled newness, promise, to my father (EC 1984, 34, 35).

Varick's complementary counterpart is Ed Heaney, father of Jick's best friend. Ed is a citizen of the town, a businessman. His calendar is determined by the economic year, his hunger dictated by the clock, his favorite place in front of the radio. Appropriately enough, it is Ed Heaney who brings the news of the war in Europe, the devastating intrusion of the outside world into the lives of the people in the valley.

If Ed Heaney is Varick's complement, Wendell Williamson is his opposite. Williamson lives in profane space. His relationship to the land is solely economic. He overgrazes the range, starves his own cattle in order to have larger numbers of them, exploits the men who work for him. Alec's choosing to work for Williamson is more than a career decision: it is a move from sacred to profane space, the most telling sign of which is Alec's refusal to help fight the fire at Flume Gulch.

Varick's wife, Beth McCaskill, is her husband's partner in sacred space. As he is attuned to the wilderness, she is attuned to the cultured land-scape: the fields that are farmed and ranched, irrigated and plowed. In her speech at the community Fourth of July picnic, she delineates her heroes and villains: those who cherish the land and make it fertile, as opposed to those who ravage it for profit. Her foods are from the garden, her calendar based on the canning and processing of the produce she raises.

Beth's opposite is Meredice Williamson, who is even more out of touch with the land than her rapacious husband. She spends only the sum-mers in Montana, and therefore "she never got clued in to the Two country; never quite caught up with its rhythms of season and livelihood and lore" (*EC* 1984, 261). She is unable to live responsibly or even responsively in the West; she seeks out quiet corners rather than enter into ranch life, tries to bring Culture to the cowboys by reciting poetry at the supper table. Mere-dice Williamson is finally pathetic because she is ultimately homeless, unlike Varick and Beth. Their association with sacred space is reflected in their centeredness, their sureness, their competence and generosity.

A more unusual hero is Stanley Meixell, whose reliability is constantly undermined by womanizing and alcohol. His love for, and knowledge of the land have drowned in the bottle. The scenes of the camptending trip that fo-cus on Stanley's recourse to the "doctor" (Dr. Al K. Hall) never achieve comic status as they might, for Stanley is a tragic figure; somewhere along the way he has lost his ability to be the caretaker of the wilderness, but his feelings for it have not diminished. Stanley's key role at the Flume Gulch fire is foreshadowed in his reminiscence about a boyhood impression:

"Take those fires—December of my first year in Kalispell. They burned along the whole damn mountains from Big Fork to Bad Rock Canyon and even farther north than that. Everybody went out on the hills east of town at night to see the fire. Running wild on the moun-tains, that way. Green kid I was, I asked why somebody didn't do something about it. 'That's public domain,' I got told. 'Belongs to the government, not nobody around here.' Damn it to hell, though, when I saw that forest being burned up it just never seemed right to me" (*EC* 1984, 96).

Stanley redeems himself at the end of the book when he gives up drink-ing to assist at the Flume Gulch fire, which climaxes the action of *English Creek*. It is he who tells Varick how to control it, saving both the forest and the fire crew from immolation.

Stanley's status as a hero in the Montana trilogy is confirmed in *Danc-ing at the Rascal Fair*, when as newly appointed ranger for the Two Medicine National Forest, he has to establish grazing allotments for the sheep and cattle ranchers who have previously made free with the mountain grass. The significance of Stanley's responsibility can best be understood in the context of the battle for free grazing land in the nineteenth century.

In the dry and mountain regions of the West, hundreds of acres were needed to support sheep and cattle; but even without privately owned land, ranchers could operate profitably by grazing their herds on range owned by the federal government but available for anyone to use. Congress had never regulated the use of these lands, so cattle and sheep ranchers competed for them, and sometimes their competition resulted in violence against animals, people, and the land. Ranchers set their herds to graze as early as possible, frequently before the grass could reseed, and often grazed more animals than the grass could support and still replenish itself. In the long run, the range was devastated, annuals and weeds replacing the once lush grasses, By the time Congress finally took steps to protect federally owned range areas, homesteaders and large ranchers alike were dependent on them.

When Stanley Meixell comes to the valley, he seems to the stockmen a harbinger of their economic demise. Homesteads were only 160 acres, too small to support stock without the summer range. Stanley has assured Angus McCaskill, the novel's protagonist, that grazing allotments would be fairly allocated, and Angus, trusting this straightforward, soft-spoken man, becomes his ally:

> There's one thing you've utterly got to do. . . . Somehow prove you're going to put a rein on Williamson as well as on the rest of us. If you're going to have the people of Scotch Heaven accept the notion of this national forest, prove to them it's not just going to be another honeypot for the Williamsons of the world (*RF* 1987, 242).

Stanley does just that. Guided by Angus, he scouts the ranges Williamson has been using and sees the damage overgrazing has done there. He promptly awards Williamson a grazing allotment for two hundred cows, the equivalent of what each sheepman will receive and far less than Williamson wants.

Stanley Meixell's standing up to Williamson is clearly an act of courage according to the history of frontier land use. Grazing allotments often did go to the large corporate ranches, squeezing out the homesteaders, as Doig makes clear in *This House of Sky*. Obviously Doig intends Stanley to be perceived as an unusual man, measured by his love for the land and his courage in preserving it from the greed of the stockmen.

The concept of profane and sacred space is also central to *Winter*

Brothers, in which Doig notes that the settlement of the West was too often more like a raid; motivated by greed, westerners have destroyed the very environment they came to live in. By doing so, they condemn themselves to the homelessness Venn describes as a characteristic of profane space. Doig writes:

> The occasional melancholy that whispers like wind in westerners' ears I think is the baffled apprehension of this; the sense that even as we try to stand firm we are being carried to elsewhere, some lesser and de-natured place, without it ever being made clear why we have to go. And the proper word for any such unchosen destination is exile (*WB* 1980, 137).

In *Mariah Montana,* Doig raises the question about whether return is possible, whether profaned space may be made sacred. Jick's inner confusion, anger, and unhappiness in *Mariah,* in contrast to the centeredness of his mother and father in *English Creek,* indicate that he has lost his sense of place and continuity. He cannot forgive Riley for refusing to take over the ranch and is sickened by indications that the days of the small rancher are coming to an end, partly because of the greed of ranchers who have despoiled the land. From the crossbar of the main gate to the WW hangs a cow skull, a pitiful reminder that the WW always took winter kills and yearly losses as part of the business: animals are "units" to them, and their deaths are business losses, doubtless recoupable through tax write-offs. Jick never passes the gate without longing, in an elaborate inner fantasy, to take a shotgun and blow the cowskull to smithereens. Although his own ranch is tidy and well run, he feels twinges of conscience over the domestic herds that graze land once black with buffalo. On the knee-deep grass of the buffalo range where ecology is so perfectly balanced the air is thick with birdsong and the scent of blooming plants, Jick experiences real anger when Riley asks, "Could you get grass to grow like this on that place of yours?"

Jick's anger comes from his feeling of helplessness against the ravages of the Montana landscape. "Yeah," he answers, "All it'd take is fantastic dollars." The government, they both know, could do it, but Riley brushes off that solution by noting that the government would rather spend money on "the death sciences." His rather cynical outlook serves him well as a newspaperman, a bee in the public bonnet. But Jick in his decision to sell his land to the Nature Conservancy is able to make a real change in things, to "give back to the earth some of the footing" it has given him and his family and to define that family in generous terms: "If we McCaskills no longer will be on that particular ground, at least the family of existence will possess it. That kind of lineage needs fostering too, I've come to think—our kinship with the land" (*MM* 1990, 314). Jick's decision not only impacts the land but returns him to sacred space. When he passes the dangling skull on his way to the centennial celebration, he has the perfect opportunity to demolish it as he has always wanted to, but he no longer feels the need. He is at peace with himself again, a dweller in sacred space.

Chapter 16
Meeting Adversity

The concept of profane and sacred space is useful but by no means the only way western writers perceive the relationship between character and landscape. Life lived in sacred space, after all, is not a pastoral idyll—the spiritual strength of characters like Beth McCaskill and Bessie Ringer is achieved at a price. Life in the West can be harsh and demanding. Doig himself left Montana to get away from conditions that had beleaguered his family for two generations. These conditions, particularly the violent extremes of weather, force onto westerners a relationship to the land that is frequently adversarial—they have to fight to save their crops, their stock, sometimes their lives. Gretel Ehrlich writes about cattle and sheep who freeze to death in their places and people who freeze to death outside their homes. Marilynne Robinson describes an outdoors that will not stay out but literally penetrates people's homes in the waters of a spring flood. Joe Ben in *Sometimes a Great Notion* is drowned by a rising tide, Charley Elwah of *Trask* plummets from a shoreline cliff; Doig himself was nearly drowned on the Northwest coast.

Life in the West is always a truce, and sometimes an uneasy one. Doig expresses the tension between landscape and character on the first page of *This House of Sky:*

It starts, early in the mountain summer, far back among the high spilling slopes of the Bridger Range of southwestern Montana. The single sound is hidden water—the south fork of Sixteenmile Creek diving down its willow-masked gulch. The stream flees north through this secret and peopleless land until, under the fir-dark flanks of Hatfield Mountain, a bow of meadow makes the riffled water curl wide to the west. At this interruption, a low rumple of the mountain knolls itself up watchfully, and atop it, like a sentry box over the frontier between the sly creek and the prodding meadow, perches our single-room cabin (*Sky* 1978, 3).

In this passage, the distance between the human and the nonhuman is tentatively bridged by language: the mountain is "watchful," the herding cabin a "sentry box." But in comparison to the eternal mountains, the cabin is "perched"—fragile, tenuous, temporary. The adversarial relationship between place and character hinted at in the opening passage develops in Charlie Doig's and Bessie Ringer's struggle to wrest a good living from the land and in their eventual defeat by the severe topography and climate. Charlie meets adversity with skill, knowing almost instinctively when to shear sheep, when to drive stock onto tender new grass, how to tactfully foreman crews made eccentric and touchy by isolation and endless work. Bessie meets adversity with endurance, throwing her body and her will against snow, against floods, against loneliness. Their economic success is never more than marginal. A severe winter forces Charlie to buy hay, eating up next year's profits. Ticks and coyotes take their toll on the ewes. A summer storm stampedes a band of sheep off the cliffs. Charlie and Bessie never achieve financial security, but their courage and determination against the forces of the landscape make them heroic figures.

In *Winter Brothers,* James Swan pioneers in the most rugged section of the Pacific Northwest and earns the admiration of author and reader as he assimilates himself to a new climate, new topography, and the Native American cultures there. In Neah Bay, he plants a garden and exchanges potatoes for Indian labor. He teaches school, trading his language and stories of Uncle Remus for the languages and legends of the people he lives among. But Doig most admires his calm intrepidness in the face of the climate and landscape of the Northwest. When Doig reads the portion of Swan's diaries that outlines his proposed journey by canoe along the treacherous western shore of the Queen Charlotte Islands, he comments: "Running a little late in life as usual, Swan at six and a half decades intends an expedition which I, twenty-five years younger and with the advantages of modern equipment, can never hope to duplicate" (*WB* 1980, 182).

The heroes in Doig's world are those who live with the rhythms of the land; the villains are those who abuse it. But there is a third character type—the victim. These are people who close themselves away from the landscape. They are citizens of neither profane nor sacred space but rather of some twilight world. They do not exploit, but neither do they rejoice in their world, and they are ultimately homeless. Foremost among these is Adair, Angus McCaskill's wife in *Dancing at the Rascal Fair*. Brought from Scotland by her brother, Rob, to marry Angus, she finds Montana an alien landscape:

> There already was a problem far at the head of the line of all others. Adair's lack of liking of the homestead and, when you came all the way down to it, for Montana.
>
> Again, her words were not what said so. I simply could see it, feel it in her when she went across the yard to fling out a dishpan of water and strode back, all without ever elevating her eyes from her footsteps. The mountains and their weather she seemed to notice only when they were at their most threatening. I counted ahead the not many weeks to winter and the white cage it would bring for someone such as Adair, and tried to swallow that chilly future away (*RF* 1987, 203).

Adair does survive the winter, largely by resorting to solitaire, a game symbolic of her isolation. Her disconnectedness is reflected in the fact that she often refers to herself in third person: "Adair would like a deck of cards" (*RF*, p. 208) and is at her happiest at community dances, when she disappears entirely:

> Dancing with Adair you were partnered with some gliding being she had become, music in a frock, silken motion wearing a ringleted Adair mask. It was what I had seen when she danced with Allan Frew after the shearing, a tranced person who seemed to take the tunes into herself (*RF* 1987, 209–10).

Homestead life in Montana is hard on Adair: winters cut her off from neighbors, a rough buggy ride brings on a miscarriage, wood chopping nearly costs her beloved son his eye, forest fires turn the air into choking heat. The fearsome outer scape chills her inner scape and she withdraws into herself, emerging at first only to care for her son and, later, to mediate between her husband and her brother. But Adair does not remain a passive victim of the landscape. She learns to ride a horse and handle a team and accompanies Angus on a long journey into the mountains to find a lost band of sheep. She emerges as a competent woman, finally able to come out of her self and survive in the environment.

Adair's sense of place, however, is dependent upon human relationships. In *Mariah*, Jick learns through the archived letters of his grandfather that, after Angus had died and Varick was settled with his family, Adair returned to Scotland, which her heart had never left and Montana could never replace. She was one of the immigrants American history books tend to ignore—the immigrant for whom the promises of the New World proved empty.

A different and more tragic journey is taken by her brother, Rob Barclay. Although he is enchanted with Montana at the beginning of the homestead years, his interest soon becomes economic rather than spiritual. He fights the land instead of living with it. He defies the stiff Montana winds by building his home at the top of a butte, digs a reservoir rather than using the creek water. Always eager to push his economic luck, Rob invariably wants to shear early, throw the sheep onto mountain pasture before the grass is ready, add new bands of sheep when he and Lucas and Angus can hardly support the ones they have. Rob's lack of sympathy for the land, his determination to live *from* it rather than *with* it, is epitomized by his becoming a "locator," a kind of real estate agent. Rob inveigles Angus into the same occupation for a time, defining it as a service for the new wave of dryland homesteaders who come west in 1910 to claim land that had remained unsettled because it was undesirable. Rob argues:

> "By our lights, maybe it isn't the best land there ever was. . . . But to these 'steaders it's better than whatever to hell they've had in life so far, now isn't it? Man, people are going to come, that's the plain fact of the matter. Whether or not we lead them by the hand, they're going to file homestead claims all through this country. They might as well be steered as right as possible, by knowledgeable local folk. Which is the same as saying us. In that way of looking at it, McAngus, we'll be doing them a major favor, am I right?" (*RF* 1987, 262).

But according to historians, the "service" Rob performs is largely parasitic:

> Most (homesteaders) came by rail, but others arrived in Studebaker wagons and lurching Model T Fords. At the depot, they often ran into the infamous "locators." These were classic frontier salesmen who, for a fee of usually twenty-five to fifty dollars, would find them a choice

homestead plot, or perhaps a lucrative piece of railroad land. Some of the locators were honest, of course, but others were not. As a result, many pioneer families ended up located on desolate lands (Malone and Roeder 1976, 187).

When his friendship with Angus is shattered, Rob becomes bitter and turns not only against Angus but against the land itself and the life it supports. He risks his stock, shoots coyotes, brutalizes an old horse. And finally, in the reservoir he built to defy the limits of natural forms, he drowns.

The definition of profane and sacred space is determined by how individuals regard the land they live on, but what that land consists of is not always a matter of individual choice. The federal government took a firm hand in the settlement and economic development of the West, and Doig records how people in Montana were affected by laws such as the Taylor Grazing Act, the establishment of the national forests, and the Homestead Act. Regarded one way, the Homestead Act opened up to settlement tracts of free land in the West, an irresistible lure to immigrants, landless in the old country for generations, and to Americans who had not been able to succeed in the East. On the other hand, the parceling of the land required that first the Native Americans who already lived there had to be removed. Following the signing of reservation treaties that remained in effect only as long as whites found no use for the land assigned to Indians, Indians were "removed" to less desirable land, died of smallpox and measles and starvation, or were massacred outright.

As the whites moved in, the face of the land that Blackfeet, Assiniboines, Sioux, Cheyennes, Crow, Nez Percé, Flatheads, and other tribes had lived on, hunted on, and regarded as sacred began to change. The buffalo were slaughtered, and sheep and cattle herds replaced them. Dry prairies became irrigated farms. The land was no longer divided according to natural forms—mountain, river, bluff, grassland—but according to the squares-within-squares established by the survey system. The pattern reflects the Anglo worldview, which perceives space in terms of straight lines and flat planes. From an airplane, the United States resembles nothing so much as a patchwork quilt, and for those who are used to this pattern, it seems natural:

> Most Americans and Canadians accept the survey system that so strongly affects their lives and perceptions of the landscape in the same way that they accept a week of seven days, a decimal numerical system, or an alphabet of twenty-six letters—as natural, inevitable, or perhaps in some inscrutable way, divinely ordained (Johnson 1976, i).

But the topography of the West does not yield so readily to a mathematical division of space. When the Homestead Act of 1862 adopted the grid system, Congress did not take into consideration that the western landscape, unlike the river valleys of the Midwest, was rugged and varied and that homesteaders might wind up on a patch of land without water or one that ran up the side of a mountain. When Rob and Angus are improving their homestead lots, they discover that "There were occasional consequences from nature for decreeing lines on the earth as if by giant's yardstick, and one of them was that the west boundary of my homestead claim went straight through a patch of rock that was next to impossible to dig in" (*RF* 1987, 96). The first Homestead Act ignored the physical features of the land and also the fact that in the arid West, 160 acres was far too small a piece of land to make a living on, a circumstance that was the ruin of Doig's own family's attempt at homesteading. In an interview, I asked Doig how he regarded the effect of the survey system. He replied:

> It's a dilemma in my own mind, and it's been a historical dilemma and turning out to be an environmental dilemma. I picked this up from Vernon Carstenson, . . . who used to talk about the American land system.[1] The survey system brought this great comparative ease of settlement, of definiteness, of measure and so forth, so we didn't have to try to settle the whole goddam continent so that it looked like Louisiana— where the line goes to this creek and then to that rock, and so forth. We simply put this big mesh of net across the country. And I don't know if there could have been a homestead system anything like ours based on anything else.
>
> In a way, my family's history is very closely tied back to that careful Jeffersonian geometric mesh of net. It is also tied into the fact that the mesh is much too small. That it ignored where the water flowed, where the grass should be used, where it shouldn't . . . my family just couldn't make it on those squares.
>
> [John Wesley] Powell argued that there should have been larger units in the West, much larger. Like four square miles instead of a quarter mile, for homesteads. And I can see [the sense of] that in Montana, which has fifty-six counties, some of them, including the county I grew up in, a county the size of Connecticut, with two thousand people. It's wonderful in a way; in a way it's absolutely absurd. . . . As the drought cycle comes to Montana, the environmental consequences have begun to play out pretty sharply. It's one of the contradictions that power us through life; one of the reasons I'm here is because

things were done a certain way. One of the reasons I have not gone on in my life in *that* life is because things were done a certain way.[2]

The irony of a well-intentioned system gone awry is manifested in human loss and tragedy in Doig's Montana books: the families of Scotch Heaven who prosper one season and are gone the next, the "dryland 'steaders" who haul water for miles and then must strain it through gunny sacks to remove only the grossest impurities, the little homesteads that become mere pieces of huge corporate ranches, turning out to be "not the seed acres for yeoman farms amid the sage, nor the first pastures of tidy family ranches," but "landing sites, quarters to hold people until they were able to scramble away to somewhere else" (*Sky* 1978, 29). People who did endure to success on their patches of land never did so in isolation. One of the terms of life in the West is the unwritten, often unspoken contract of mutual aid among neighbors, families, and communities. In order to survive, people must rely on one another.

Chapter 17
Landscape and Community

The Western myth, as promulgated by hundreds of formula novels and stories, depicts the westerner as a solitary hero, a single self against the wilderness. He may use wilderness skills to rescue schoolmarms or towns under siege but usually rides away again, scorning both woman and community. This myth depicts not social reality but a sort of collective fantasy that represents neither life in the West nor the present trend of writing in the work of authors like Doig and Maclean and Robinson and Ehrlich. One needs only to recall the fact that in *Sometimes a Great Notion* the Stamper family requires a collective effort to make a go of their logging business and that Hank, who appears to be a self-reliant hero, can actually only define himself as such in terms of his relationship to the town. *A River Runs Through It* is a story of the tragic loss of a brother, and so, in a different way, is *English Creek. This House of Sky* captures the struggle of three people to bond as a family.

The landscape of the West works both for and against the formation of communities, and the term must be redefined to encompass conditions in the West. Because of its aridity, much of the West is sparsely populated. The bulk of its population is urban, clustered in oases like Salt Lake City and Denver. But most contemporary Western writing re-creates life in rural areas in which the population density may be as low as three or four people to the square mile. In rural areas the word *community* takes on special meanings because living on the land isolates people. Ranches in Montana and Wyoming are widely separated: some are huge, encompassing entire counties. Weather, particularly winter weather, makes travel difficult, sometimes impossible. Because ranch and farm work are seasonal, many jobs, such as ranchhanding, sheepherding, and haying, are itinerant. People move from place to place, carrying most of their possessions with them.

But those same conditions also make community absolutely necessary. One of the prevelant themes of contemporary western writing is the physical and psychological danger of isolation. Even a light-hearted book like *The Egg and I*, set in rural Washington, takes the problem of loneliness seriously. As if in refutation of all of the novels that romanticize solitude, MacDonald writes:

> I used to harbor the idea, as who has not, that I was one of the few very fortunate people who was absolutely self-sufficient and that if I could just find myself a little haunt far from the clawing hands of civilization with its telephones, electric appliances, artificial amusements and people—people more than anything—I could be contented for the rest of my life. Well, someone called my bluff and I found that after nine months spent mostly in the stimulating company of the mountains, trees, the rain, Stove and the chickens, I would have swooned with anticipation at the prospect of a visit from a Mongolian idiot. (MacDonald 1945, 92).

Along the same lines, Doig and Ehrlich write about individuals who have become eccentric and unbalanced because of loneliness. Doig mentions stories told in the valley of "a herding dog bashed to death with rocks in some silent coulee, a haystack ablaze in the night when there had been no lightning, a man battered in an alley after an argument with a broody crewman" (*Sky* 1978, 45). Ehrlich recalls sheepherders who hoard piles of junk, who drink vanilla extract for its alcohol content or go on long binges, who are so strangled by customary aloneness they cannot talk when visitors do come. She remembers finding a ranch hand sitting in front of the badly decayed carcass of a cow, shaking his finger and saying, "Now, I don't want you to do this ever again!"

These stories, some horrifying, some comic, bespeak the need for communication, for society, for interaction with others that helps define the self. Understanding this need leads to a reevaluation of some of our cherished ideas in the James Fenimore Cooper tradition that society retards or subverts individuation. Richard Astro, in "*The Big Sky* and the Limits of

Wilderness Fiction," challenges the notion that individuals can mature by living alone in the wilderness. Astro argues that *The Big Sky* should be read not as a tragedy of Eden lost but as an exploration of the fact that humans are social beings and that resolution of conflicts, which results in self-realization, cannot take place in isolation:

> Huck Finn on and near the Mississippi, Ishmael on the *Pequod,* and Hester Prynne in Salem grow to a consciousness *in society.* . . . But in Western wilderness novels, particularly in those set in the times just before the closing of the frontier, a final resolution of the conflict is impossible, because the physical conditions necessary for that resolution do not exist. The best wilderness novelists—A. B. Guthrie, Vardis Fisher and Frederick Manfred—can create exciting plots which are true to history, and interesting, one-dimensional characters who live in unbounded space. And by so doing, they present a valuable record of what once was. But because their characters are cut-off and alone, by choice deprived of the kind of meaningful social contact which leads one from innocence to experience, they are limited by their medium. In short, the wilderness novel simply cannot transcend its occasion (Astro 1974, 113).

Given the need for community, westerners are faced with the problems presented by distance, climate, and itinerancy. They overcome these problems by sheer effort, sometimes walking, riding, or driving great distances to visit friends and neighbors, and by offering companionship to those who are alone. Gretel Ehrlich describes the response to Wyoming winters in terms of battling the frigid outdoors with inner warmth:

> Our connections with neighbors—whether strong or tenuous, as lovers or friends—become too urgent to disregard. We rub the frozen toes of a stranger whose pickup has veered off the road; we open water gaps with a tamping bar and an ax; we splice a friend's frozen water pipe; we take mittens and blankets to the men who herd sheep. Twenty or thirty below makes the breath we exchange visible: all of mine for all of yours. It is the tacit way we express the intimacy no one talks about (Ehrlich 1985, 72–73).

In the West, *community* takes on broader meanings and forms than it does elsewhere. We normally think of community in terms of a stable population—people living in the same small town for long periods of time, for example. A sense of community in that case grows from shared experience, a common body of knowledge. But those last two criteria can, and do, apply to the itinerant populations of the West—the ranch hands, farm hands and sheepherders who move from place to place. For one thing, they often move in the same patterns, coming back to work on the same places season after season, and often work with the same group at the same job. The men who form the haying crew in *English Creek,* for example, have been coming to Pete Reese's ranch for years. They know each other's strengths and weaknesses and therefore can work as an effective team.

Shared knowledge and traditions are the basis of occupation communities. Sheep ranchers, for example, all know the same things: the difficulties of finding good herders; how to dock lambs and castrate them; how to jacket a motherless lamb so that a new ewe will adopt it; when to shear and when to sell, when to throw a flock onto new grass, how to train a good sheepdog. These informally acquired traditions ranchers carry with them like a snail carries its house on its back. They will, therefore, have more in common with other sheep ranchers in other parts of the country than with the banker in their home town.

Community can exist diachronically, as well, and here the tie is the land itself. In Doig's work, this exists mostly in the resonance of the word *place,* used to designate a homestead, usually abandoned. In *This House of Sky,* Doig describes the stories of defeat and vanished hopes, of death or bankruptcy, represented by homesteads:

> By the time I was a boy and Dad was trying in his own right to put together a life again, the doubt and defeat in the valley's history had tamped down into a single word. Anyone of Dad's generation always talked of a piece of land where some worn-out family eventually had lost to weather or market prices not as a farm or a ranch or even a homestead, but as a *place.* All those empty little clearings which ghosted that sage countryside—just the McLoughlin place there by that butte, the Vinton place over this ridge, the Kuhnes place, the Catlin place, the Winters place, the McReynolds place, all the tens of dozens of sites where families lit in the valley or its rimming foothills, couldn't hold on, and drifted off. All of them epitaphed with that barest of words, *place* (*Sky* 1978, 22–23).

The fact that these old homesteads are named for the first families to try to live on them evidences the fact that their history lingers and becomes part of the lives of those next to try their luck there. In *English Creek* in the scene of the Fourth of July picnic, Beth McCaskill gives a speech that is in part a litany of names of places that have been sold at auction, abandoned, foreclosed on. In doing so, she honors those members of the community who are gone and condemns the Williamson family, who snatched up each piece of land after the banks had foreclosed on it and added it to their own property, whereupon it would slowly lose its name, its history, its uniqueness, its power to pass on memories of the families who had lived there.

The resonance of place and its power to create community are most pronounced in *Winter Brothers*, wherein Doig breaks the boundaries of the century that separate him from James Swan and rediscovers Swan by reviving the space he lived in:

> It is a venture that I have mulled these past years of my becoming less headlong and more aware that I dwell in a community of time as well as of people. That I should know more than I do about this other mysterious citizenship, how far it goes, where it touches.
>
> And the twin whys: why it has me invest my life in one place instead of another, and why for me that place happens to be western. More and more it seems to me that the westernness of my existence in this land is some consequence having to do with that community of time, one of the terms of my particular citizenship in it (*WB* 1980, 4).

Doig's "community of time" is created by space. He is able to enter imaginatively into Swan's life because they share a common landscape: Doig can walk the same beaches, look out over the same bluffs. He is a citizen of sacred space because he understands that the place itself "endures beyond any particular individual as a source of objective reality" (Venn 1979, 117). Doig transcends the barriers of time by using his imagination in the tradition of Coleridge, fusing materials in ways that have not been tried before. Doig binds the present and the past with language so that they exist simultaneously, all of the events that have ever happened in a place still lingering there:

> Nine twenty-one. Last night at this time, winter began. I noticed the numbered throb of the moment—the arrival of season at precisely 21:21 hours of December 21—which took us through solstice as if we, too, the wind and I and the fencetop cat and yes, Swan and the restless memories of departed Makahs, were being delivered by a special surf. The lot of us, now auspiciously into the coastal time of beginnings (*WB* 1980, 11).

Doig uses the places he shares in common with Swan to transcend the time that separates them, but he does not merely establish a community of two, isolated from their worlds, but also creates a language by which he and Swan come to share the same space across the separation of time.[1] From Swan's journals he re-creates the native and white communities Swan made himself part of and links them, thematically and historically, with the author's own community. He defines *community* elastically, sometimes narrowing it to his own Seattle neighborhood, sometimes expanding it to the West as a region. For Doig, nature itself creates and shapes communities, just as it shapes individuals. The interpenetration of character and landscape is manifested in the language Doig uses to describe both.

Part Four
Style

"An artist is committed to not abstracting the thing he loves."

—George Venn

Overleaf: *Ivan Doig and Norman Maclean at the Maclean family cabin on Seely Lake, Montana (1985).*

Chapter 18
Text and Context

Doig's books differ from one another in theme, genre, pace, tone, focus, narrative strategy, character, and setting. Nevertheless they form a distinct corpus because of the author's use of context to inform text, his choice of contextual materials, and his particular use of language to bring those contexts to life and show how they interact.

Doig's apprenticeship as a writer began with his boyhood in Montana. He grew up within the physical and cultural environs of northern Montana and learned in his boyhood the occupational and social skills of a rancher: how to herd sheep, cut hay, and mend fence, how to listen to and swap stories with the working people in the various communities he lived in. But by his junior year in high school Doig knew that his own future lay outside Montana, away from the winters and the grinding physical labor and the years of just getting by, and hence his moves to the Midwest and then the Far West. But Montana and the skills he absorbed there continue to inform his writing.

In 1985 Doig wrote an essay for *Montana: The Magazine of Western History* entitled, "You Can't *Not* Go Home Again," in which he sketched out events and discoveries in his life that took him away from Montana, then led him back in person time after time, and finally, artistically, brought him back to stay. In his article, Doig describes the specific contextual elements of life in Montana that have shaped his work: his grandmother's collection of family photographs that revivified his memories; people like Gertie Chadwick (who appears in *This House of Sky*) whose personal qualities are manifested in the strong, competent, caring women in Doig's fiction, such as Beth McCaskill in *English Creek*; the collective memories of Montanans preserved in historical museums and libraries and old WPA files; the turns and inflections of Montana speech. Doig ends his essay with an expression of indebtedness and gratitude to the enduring reminders of his home place:

> You can't go home again? You can't *not* go home again. Recollections constantly decree it. Language says it every time you open your mouth and utter, as at least one of your Montana parents did, "How you doin'?" What you like to eat or don't. Whiteness of the jackknife scar on your finger. The color of your eyes. Your name. Where does any of it come from but back there? And so, as a writer here I am, back where I have ever been. For I'm fully convinced that in my case—and I think even in Thomas Wolfe's, whose novels got gassier the farther he got from remembrance of his hometown in North Carolina and forthright experiences such as riding on trains—what I write best arises back there in time and memory (Doig 1985, "You Can't *Not* Go Home Again," 15).

What Doig absorbed from his life in Montana, however, goes beyond the specific memories and experiences and people that appear in his books about Montana. During his boyhood, Doig learned to listen to speech and to understand that character and place of origin are embedded in what people say and the way they say it. Above his desk is a quotation from John Rolfe Gardiner that attests to Doig's skill at recreating place, time, and character through language:

> Someone has said that history that tries to be fiction is boring, and that fiction that pretends to be history is specious. Ivan Doig seems to prevail over this dilemma of the historical novelist with the sure grace of his language. His work reminds us that style, after all, *is* substance, that *how* we say something is what we're saying (unpublished).

Doig's ability to fuse style and substance and his training in journalism taught him to write, as he says, "with his ear." All of Doig's works are filled with examples of the aural logic of spoken language. In *Mariah,* for example, when Jick thinks about the Pentagon's intentions to turn the dry country of Montana into an artillery range, he says to himself, "Why couldn't it be left alone? Left be empty?" "Left be empty" falls apart gramatically, but makes sense to the ear. Phrases like this force the reader to read Doig's books slowly, as one would poetry, to hear the language on the page.

In Montana, Doig learned that landscape can make or break people, that there is an interrelationship between the outer world and the inner self. Isolation can drive people to seek community with others or send them into near madness; fighting a harsh climate can foster self-reliance or despair. That, and his training as an historian, taught him that people's lives are irrevocably bound up with the place they live. As a writer, he has translated this lesson into complex artistic forms in which "text" and "context" interpenetrate.

Within Doig's work, "context" may best be understood as a kind of ecology, a set of interdependent forces that modify and define each other. Any given place can be perceived as a conglomerate of historical, ecological, geographic, demographic, economic, folkloristic, ethnographic, and topographic contexts. The discerning cartographer can map out these features separately or analyze them in various combinations in order to examine how they work together—to see, for example, how cycles of drought affect demographics. Doig uses the same kinds of contexts in much the same way, and to say that he writes *from context* is to realize his roles as craftsman and artist. As a craftsman, he selects his materials, relying most heavily on cultural history, cultural geography, folklife, and landscape. As an artist, he brings these factors to bear on his characters. The complexity of Doig's sense of context is suggested in the opening passage of his address to the Pacific Northwest American Studies Association in 1988:

> "I come from a *place*. I originate, as an American, from a place in a specific Montana sense of the word—place, meaning an abandoned homestead. Small ranch or farm, either one, but *abandoned*, given up on, because of the winter of 1919 or the bank failures that rippled through Montana in the early 1920s or the Depression, or death or disgust or any other of a hundred reasons."[1]

His first sentence, "I come from a *place*," is a declaration of the importance of origins, particularly to Doig the writer whose first book was a study of his own personal and professional evolution. "Place" in this case is not merely location, the cabin on the land, but the history of that cabin and land—specifically its abandonment. Doig recalls the local and national history behind abandonment, implying that abandoned homesteads were so common in Montana that they were designated by a special name. "Context," in this excerpt, is location, history, and emotion: abandoned homesteads resonate with accumulated human failure and loss.

In Doig's work, text and context are interdependent: specific contextual elements such as history, landscape, and folkways serve not only as subject matter but also as determinants of literary convention, shaping plot, structure, characterization, and theme. History is the most visible of these elements, and Doig's use of history has caused some critical grumbling because it makes his work difficult to place in traditional genre categories:

> Every once in a while I've been gently chided by academic reviewers about the amount of history that keeps creeping into my novels. Interestingly, those reviewers I think invariably have been English professors—the history profs don't seem to mind it that much. Well my history habit is even more serious than those reviewers thought, because it's *deliberate*. Although I've been writing fiction, in *The Sea Runners* and now in this Montana trilogy, I do want my characters' lives to respond to what might be called the historical laws of gravity.[2]

The plots in Doig's books are historically derived: in *Dancing at the Rascal Fair*, for example, the patterns of the characters' lives are determined by historical events. The Homestead Act gives Angus McCaskill and Rob Barklay the land they live on but demands that every moment of their time be spent in improving their claims, and a great deal of the action in the novel centers on the work they do. The establishment of the national forests and the enforcement of grazing acts restrict the ranchers' access to mountain pastures and their ability to make a profit, which leads to Rob's frustrated financial schemes and Angus's teaching school year after year. The First World War disrupts life in the valley and sends shock waves through the McCaskill family: Angus and Adair have maintained their marriage on the strength of their love for their son, and when he is drafted and sent to Fort Lewis, the loss both strains and strengthens their relationship. The influenza epidemic that ravaged Montana in 1918 and 1919 decimates the community and takes the life of Anna, Angus's lifelong love, but also restores Varick to his father.

Doig's use of history challenges the traditional concept of plot if we think of plot as an artificial construct of a series of actions. Doig has no need to create extraordinary events in his fiction: instead, he allows history to take its course, and his characters respond in ways that illustrate the impact of the times they live in. It should not be assumed, however, that Doig's books are "historical novels," using fictional techniques to enliven past events: his focus is on the characters who come to life in his pages. In the following passage, for example, the motivating force is the influenza epidemic of 1918, but the focus is on the human response to that epidemic:

> People were resorting to whatever they could think of against the epidemic. Out on the bare windy benchlands, 'steader families were sleeping in their dirt cellars, if they were lucky enough to have one, in hope of keeping warmer than they could in their drafty shacks. Mavis and George Frew became Bernarr McFadden believers, drinking hot water and forcing themselves into activity whenever they felt the least chill coming on. Others said onion syrup was the only influenza remedy. Mustard plasters, said others. Whiskey, said others. Asafetida sacks appeared at the necks of my schoolchildren that fall. When a newspaper story said masks must be worn to keep from breathing flu germs, the Gros Ventre mercantile sold out of gauze by noon of that day. The next newspaper story said masks were useless because a microbe could pass through gauze as easily as a mouse going through a barn door (*RF* 1987, 338).

The passage is not merely a list of the odd and desperate measures people took against infection; it captures the feeling of helplessness that overwhelmed them. Passages describing the death toll do not include the statistics Doig worked from but rather convey the emotions and experiences of people who saw their friends and families die:

> From all we heard and read, the influenza was the strangest of epidemics, with different fathoms of death—sudden and selective in one instance, slow and widespread in another. Donald Erskine's fatality was in the shallows, making it all the more casual and awful. One morning while he and Jen were tending Davie, he came down with what he thought was the start of a cold, and by noon he was feeling a raging fever. For the first time since childhood, he went to bed during the day. Two days after that, the uneasy crowd of us at the Gros Ventre cemetery were burying that vague and generous man (*RF* 1987, 337).

Influenza makes strangers of the people in the valley—neighbors have become potential carriers of death, and the social gatherings that enlivened their seasons and created their sense of community are abandoned. Their isolation is poignantly expressed in a scene where Angus and Adair, missing their friends and aware of their new dependence on each other, dance alone in their cabin to a tune they hum from memory.

These passages are historically accurate, but what the reader carries away from them is not factual information about the flu epidemic but the human story of fear and grief and loss.

Doig's awareness of the complexity of social contexts—the bonds created and broken by love and hatred, distance and proximity—is reflected in the unusual human communities that arise in his books. *This House of Sky* is among other things about very different people learning how to live together, finally forming a family that enriches and sustains all three of its unlikely members. *Winter Brothers* examines the life of a man who leaves his own wife and children in the civilized East but finds family among the Indians of the Northwest coast and among other pioneers like himself. Swan remains, nonetheless, an outsider to the societies he has chosen, maintaining his sense of self by compulsively recording the minutia of his daily life, resorting often to the bottle and, once, to a fantastic courtship of a sixteen-year-old girl. In *The Sea Runners,* four men of different backgrounds and personalities make themselves into a community out of mutual desire to escape indentureship, and the constant stresses of their relationships threaten to destroy them even as they work together for a common goal.

English Creek examines the shattering of a family. *Dancing at the Rascal Fair* traces the ebb and flow of lives as friendship is forged and then betrayed, as love is sought and denied. In *Mariah*, Doig comments on the composition of modern families, which are often not bonded by bloodline. A service station attendant comments cheerfully that it's nice to see a family traveling together these days, and Jick is suddenly struck by the oddness of their situation:

> It surprised the daylights out of me, the notion of the four of us as a brood. I was briefly tempted to tell the stationman that yeah, we were just your normal vanilla American household these days; the silver-haired lady and I weren't married, at least to each other, but she'd once almost married my brother before thinking better of it, whereas the younger two, she mine (by my second wife) and him hers, *had* been married to one another but weren't any more, although they intended to be again. Family tree, hell. We were our own jungle (*MM* 1990, 244–45).

But such jungles may be entirely satisfactory, if occasionally awkward. The Bago bunch work together effectively, and Jick feels enriched by the results of living in the hour-by-hour centennial trip: "Across county after county I put on the miles, Leona put on the meals, and Mariah and Riley kept on scouring that upper righthand corner of the state" (*MM* 1990, 256). As in *This House of Sky,* Doig makes us reexamine traditional definitions of family. In both books, human ties are determined not by blood and law, but by people's ability to work together, talk together, support each other.

Behind the personalities that clash and bond in Doig's books is always historical context: life on the frontier, he asserts, was no paradise: people could not survive in isolation and the communities they created out of economic and personal necessity were seldom free from conflict. But on the other hand, those communities usually lasted. This quality is particularly clear in *Dancing at the Rascal Fair*: individuals come and go, but the thing that brought them, the place itself, endures. Personal relationships, such as Angus and Rob's friendship, Angus and Adair's marriage, undergo tremendous pressures, but the need for economic cooperation, for family and companionship, keep those relationships alive.

Doig is aware of the potential for individuals to grow because of (or in spite of) their social contexts, and his own empathy for people is reflected in the way he portrays his characters: sometimes humorously, sometimes wryly, but always with respect for their dignity and complexity. "I do not use irony in my writing," he says, "because I write about people. People do not live in irony; they live in earnest."[3] The reader senses that even Doig's minor characters have full lives, histories, stories to tell, and that those stories come to life in the process of their interaction with each other and with the world they live in.

Doig's interest in the play of historical forces on the lives of individuals result in his books' emphasis on characterization and human conflict rather than on action, and Doig has strong feelings about the overuse of action in the construction of plot. "Literature," he says, "ought to try to be a medium of emotions and sensibilities, rather than a display of horrific effects:"[4]

> I don't believe you have to be goosing the reader with outlandish surprises all the time, the notion that fiction has to be hyped up—Ho! Here comes an axe murderer! Huh! Here's a Russian submarine! Jesus! Here's the killer comet from outer space! Life is vivid enough in itself. Look what happens to people as they go through their years. Everybody's got a story, everybody's got drama, good times and bad. There's a lot of intrinsic drama, and I think it cheapens fiction by having artificial sweetener in the plot all the time (O'Connell 1987, 303).

As Doig's plots and characters respond to historical and social contexts, his narrative structures respond to what may be called environmental contexts—the subjects he is writing about and the specific milieus that give rise to them. The second half of the title of *This House of Sky* is *Landscapes of a Western Mind*, a reminder that *Sky*'s formal principles are patterned on personal narrative and the mechanics of memory. The personal narrative structure has been discussed in chapter 11: embedded within that are passages of recall where sensory stimuli such as the creak of a desk chair, the image in a photograph, a remembered voice inspire the author's recollection of specific scenes and conversations.

The narrative structures of *Winter Brothers* are also derived from contexts related to the subject. The form of the book is that of a journal: Doig keeps his own diary in response to Swan's, and passages quoted from Swan are followed by recordings of Doig's experiences, observations, comments, until the book resembles a conversation written across time. The temporal structure, in which Doig moves forward through the winter season but also back and forth between centuries—often in the space of a single sentence— was inspired by Native American art in which disparate life forms occupy the same space at the same time; the art itself replicates the lush, tangled growth of the Indians' rainforest home. The spacial structure of the book, in which similar units (week-long passages from Swan's diaries, for example) are repeated at different intervals, recalls the templates Indian carvers used for their totem poles, which enabled them to use the same motif for different purposes, to establish a pattern of repetition and variation of a single theme.

The language that Doig uses in each book is also contextually derived. In *This House of Sky*, language alternates between the author's "literary" voice, filled with allusion, metaphor, and imagery, and the more colloquial language of his father, grandmother, and neighbors. This alternation reinforces the structures of storytelling and memory: personal narrative, as David Stanley points out, is always a movement from redaction of experience to evaluation of experience. Doig uses colloquial speech to reconstruct the experiences of his life and those of his father and grandmother and his own mature literary voice to comment on those experiences from the perspective of adulthood. In the following passage, for example, Doig reconstructs his father's inner conflicts about bringing Bessie into their lives, then reinforces the memory with his father's own words:

> Dad began to try to talk me—and himself—into forgetting Bessie Ringer. And at the same time, I suppose, to chant himself into a rightness about what he was doing, for along with all else borne in him since my mother's death, he had been living with twin fears. The first, that he would lose me, somehow be unable to keep me with him and

raise me amid his zigzagging ranch life. Second and worse, that if he was forced to give me up, it would have to be to the mother-in-law he had been at spear-point with so much of the past.

It must have represented the last loss possible to his life: that his one son would be made a stranger to him. Dad tried to twine his other bereavement onto that one, as if he could knot together from the two a talisman of some sort: *Your mother would of wanted me to raise you instead of your grandma doing it, I can tell ye that. She said . . . she said just as much. She talked about it sometimes, after she'd had one of her bad spells. . . . She went through hell on this earth, your mother. And she never would want me to give you up, I'm-here-to-tell-you* (*Sky* 1978, 121).

Doig's use of the vernacular varies from book to book, appearing most strongly in *English Creek* and *Mariah Montana* where his characters speak the "Montanese" Doig grew up hearing. His use of the vernacular is significant for the authenticity it provides, but western language is also a code that conveys the quality of western life and implies the influence of western space. Rural westerners are often laconic, as if they have absorbed the silences of the outer world. In *The Solace of Open Spaces,* Gretel Ehrlich describes this characteristic:

The solitude in which westerners live makes them quiet. They telegraph thoughts and feelings by the way they tilt their heads and listen; pulling their Stetsons into a steep dive over their eyes, or pigeon-toeing one boot over the other, they lean against a fence with a fat wedge of Copenhagen beneath their lower lips and take in the whole scene. These detached looks of quiet amusement are sometimes cynical, but they can also come from a dry-eyed humility as lucid as the air is clear.

Conversation goes on in what sounds like a private code; a few phrases imply a complex of meanings. . . . Sentence structure is shortened to the skin and bones of a thought. Descriptive words are dropped, even verbs; a cowboy looking over a corral full of horses will say to a wrangler, "Which one needs rode?" People hold back their thoughts in what seems to be a dumbfounded silence, then erupt with an excoriating perceptive remark. Language, so compressed, becomes metaphorical. . . .

What's behind this laconic style is shyness. There is no vocabulary for the subject of feelings. It's not a hangdog shyness, or anything coy—always there's a robust spirit in evidence behind the restraint, as if the earth-dredging wind that pulls across Wyoming had carried its people's voices away but everything else in them had shouldered confidently into the breeze (Ehrlich 1985, 6–7).

For all his own command of language, Doig appreciates the silent communion of westerners, describing, for example, the comfortable silences he shared with Tommy Chadwick, the son of the family with whom he boarded in Dupuyer. He also records westerners' tendency toward understatement, their ability to convey a great deal in a few words. In *This House of Sky* Pete McCabe, bartender at the Stockman saloon, has a habit of sizing people up and evaluating them in a few well-chosen words.

He had a tribute for the few best men he knew. Glancing off into the glass hodgepodge behind the bar, Pete would say slowly: *He's a nice fellow.* Slow nod, and slower again: *A real nice fellow.* When that was said, you knew the fellow must be a prince of the world (*Sky* 1978, 58–59).

The fact that such statements are a kind of code, decipherable only to other insiders, reinforces the sense of community in Doig's West. People can be spare with their words when they know each other well. Doig indicates the close relationship between two of the minor characters in *English Creek* by indicating their use of such a code. Dode Withrow, a sheep rancher, knows that his herder, Pat Hoy, needs to go on a bender when Pat declares he's going to quit. He knows just where and how Pat will spend his time and at what point Dode can go collect him to start the new herding season.

The contrast between silence and eloquence is most fully developed in *Ride with Me, Mariah Montana* in the split between Jick as a character and Jick as a narrator. The difference is not, as it is in *This House of Sky,* one of literary as opposed to colloquial speech—Jick speaks colloquially in his interior monologues as well as in his conversations—that is, not between *how* things are said but *what* things are said, between the inner and outer skins of a person. In this contrast, Doig accurately replicates one aspect of regional speech patterns: the western tendency to be laconic rather than verbose, to express emotion in understatement rather than overstatement. Hereby he also reinforces his theme of how our silences can keep us from knowing each other.

Doig also knows how to read western character from language. In *Winter Brothers,* for example, he comments on a phrase overheard in a Seattle cafe:

There you go: that western byphrase from waitresses and bartenders, sometimes from friends or just people in conversation. I hear it in Montana as I do here and like it immensely, the friendly release in the saying, the unfussy deliverance it carries. A very independent little trio of words, encouraging yet declaring okay-I've-done-my-part-it's-up-to-you-now. The best of benedictions (*WB* 1980, 122).

In western dialect, understatement is sometimes punctuated by over-statement, bits of tall tale creeping into stories and speech. About mosquitos—"Bastards are so big this year they can stand flatfooted and drink out of a rainbarrel... saw one of 'em carry off a baby chick the other day"... "yah, I saw two of 'em pick up a lamb, one at each end." About fishing—"Hide behind a tree to bait your hook, or they'll swarm right out of the water after you"... "I'm just corraling them first. What I intend is to get fish so thick in here they'll run into each other and knock theirselves out." Hyperbole, like understatement, is a response to environment. Barre Toelken discusses its function in the form of "local lies," which are hyperbolic statements or tall tales told by local characters:

Local lies allow local people to focus on the emotional and personal factors of their environment in ways not normally countenanced or encouraged in everyday discourse. One is not supposed to complain loud and long about weather and circumstance; one is not supposed to crow unduly about his successes in farming. In the local lie, however, both the negative and the positive aspects of the region are expressed in humorous hyperbole. In eastern Oregon the wind blows so hard that cattle have to stand on their hay to keep it from blowing away... in central Oregon it gets so dry... that their rain water assays out at 31% moisture (Toelken 1979, 30).

Doig's westerners express their feelings about the environment in hyperbolic terms that allow them to comment on its rewards and difficulties without forcing them to either brag or complain.

As well as dialect, Doig also uses idiolects, individualizing his characters by assigning them particular habits of speech. Beth McCaskill's background as a schoolteacher is reflected in her use of standard English: her rather prickly personality and habit of command are conveyed by the use of capital letters in her speeches. After Jick and Ray get into a scrap and spoil their clothes, for example, Beth separates them with, "Jick, I believe you would like To Read in the Other Room. Ray, I think you would like To Put

Together the Jigsaw Puzzle I Am Going to Put Here on the Table for You" (*EC* 1984, 174). Stanley Meixell is characterized by his use of understatement, facing tasks with, "Well, we got it to do," summing up the disaster at Flume Gulch with, "Kind of looks like a forest fire, don't it?"

Idiolects convey not only personality but place of origin. In the haying scene in *English Creek*, for example, the crew members announce their arrivals and their origins simultaneously: "How do, Jick," from an old Texas cowpuncher; "How's she going, Jick?" from an Anaconda smelter hand; "Hey, Jick!" from a Great Falls hay stacker; "Hello there, Jick!" from a Gros Ventre resident. Doig's delight in accuracy extends to exact reproductions of the way different characters say "sonofabitch":

> Some say it with an "f" in the middle, some with a "v," some say the plural as "sonsabitches," some say it as "sonofabitches"—my idea here being to differentiate the speakers somewhat according to their nationality, Scottish, French-Canadian, or Missourian. All in all, I think there are five deliberately different spellings of it, single or plural, in *English Creek*.[5]

Doig's talent for finding the right phrase that will accurately reflect a personality and his insistence that that phrase be contextually precise, recreating the way people talk (and therefore interact with each other and the natural world) are part of the ethos of context. Through the use of contextual materials in his art, Doig brings the imagination back to its sources in the physical world. Avoiding abstraction, embedding themes and ideas always in the physical image, the concrete metaphor, he uses language as a link between internal and external worlds, between self and other.

Chapter 19
Language

In any discussion of his work, Ivan Doig foregrounds language. Interviewers find that he readily answers questions about landscape or pace or character or theme, inquiries about his research and writing processes or publishing experiences, but left to his own devices, he will turn the conversation to his passion for words: "Above all, I'm interested in the language," he says. "Language is the alpha and omega" (O'Connell 1987, 299). Doig's crafting of language speaks to the diversity of his personal background: rancher, scholar, journalist, historian, poet. Passionate about sound, rhythm, etymology, and connotation, Doig delights in word play.

The term *play* may be deceptive. The poetic power of Doig's language intimates a faith in the ability of words to convey life, reality, the "thingness" of things. Implicit in his attitude toward language is a sense that the writer is ethically responsible not only for deft craftsmanship but also to the world he reflects in his writing. Doig perceives that language is alive and that its vitality is bound up in the lives of people who create words and endow them with meaning:

> Language is the river of experience we live in . . . it's changing and alive
> and a kind of folk poetry. . . . It's the terrific *life* of language that inter-
> ests me. . . . Kids on every street corner invent new uses of the lan-

guage. Sheepherders who are barely sober enough to put their shoes on invent new ways words can go together or have some kind of a flip or a nudge to them.[1]

Doig dips into that river of language, and, as he puts it, "sluices out" the nuggets that bring to life the characters who use that language and the world their words articulate. But Doig is not merely a recorder of speech: he achieves his own poetry in the sound and rhythm of his prose, in the way his phrases are packed like suitcases to carry more than one thing at a time. He uses language to control pace and tension in his books: he reflects the shape of an event with syntax. He plays with parts of speech, using nouns as verbs, verbs as adjectives, conveying action with a prepositional phrase. These manipulations slow the reader down, force the mind's attention from story to experience. Doig's use of language resonates with the contexts he writes from, not only in his interest in vernacular speech but also in his own figures of speech: most of his images and metaphors are drawn from the landscape. Carl Bredahl writes:

> One of the great pleasures in reading Ivan Doig is the discovery of a language that touches the world's surfaces. The more one reads of Doig, the stronger the sense that Doig uses language as a vital point of contact between the individual and the natural or social world (Bredahl 1989, 140).

Doig creates those points of contact partly through sound. His style appeals to the ear in the interaction of vowels and consonants, the way words echo or ricochet off each other. He uses alliteration, assonance, consonance: "sea of sage," "gold out of every gravel gulch," "the loss of whatever thin livelihoods there had been in laboring on a laird's estate," "shadowless smothering snow," "the astral glance of a cat," and the sounds reinforce semantics. The alliterative g in "gold out of every gravel gulch" is harsh, evoking both the hard labor of gold panning and the disappointment of most of the gold-seekers; the sibilant s in "shadowless smothering snow" reproduces the soft hiss of a Montana blizzard, the hypnotic feel of watching it fall. In *Mariah*, Riley writes,

> They named the place Butte, in the way that the night sky's button of light acquired the round sound of moon or the wind took to itself its inner sigh of vowel. Butte was echoingly what it was: an abrupt up-shoot of earth, with the namesake city climbing out of its slopes (*MM* 1990, 57–58).

Here Doig interweaves two contexts—the city named after a landform, the sound of both suggesting extrusion and abruptness, reflecting the rough and aggressive life of the miners there.

It is important to note, however, that sound by itself does not convey meaning. According to Leech and Short, it is a mistake to assume that there is a meaningful connection between a particular sound and a particular reference, such as *s* and the sighing of wind in the trees. Onomatopoeia is better understood as a combination of evocative sound and denotation or connotation. Doig does make sound work in combination with other linguistic features, and certain passages suggest that meaning and sound are interdependent. In *English Creek,* for example, he writes:

> I recall Pete, just right out of the blue, telling me about the Noon Creek Kee-Kee bird. "You never heard of the Kee-Kee bird we got around here? Jick, I am surprised at you. The Kee-Kee bird shows up the first real day of winter every year. Lands on top of the lambing shed over there and takes a look all around. Then he says, 'Kee-Kee Keerist All Mighty, this is c-c-cold c-c-country!' and heads for California." (*EC* 1984, 220).

The syntax of many of Doig's phrases and sentences is structured to suggest the physical rhythm of the experience he is describing. At the Fourth of July dance in *English Creek,* for example, Jick and his mother are square dancing to "The Dude and Belle," called by Jick's father. Doig sets up the rhythm of the dance by quoting a verse of it:

> First gent, swing the lady so fair.
> Now the one right over there.
> Now the one with the sorrel hair.
> Now the belle of the ballroom.
> Swirl and twirl. And promenade all.

Doig maintains that rhythm in Jick's description of the dance:

> You begin with everybody joining hands—my mother's firm feel at the end of one of my arms, Arleta's small cool hand at my other extreme—and circling left, a wheel of eight of us spinning to the music. Now to my father's call of "You've done the track, now circle back" the round chain of us goes into reverse, prancing back to where we started (*EC* 1984, 211).

Although Jick's sentences are longer than the phrases of the caller, they could be chanted to the rhythm of the dance:

> First gent swing the lady so fair;
> You begin with everybody joining hands. . . .

In *This House of Sky* the scene of the sheep stampede is re-created kinesthetically as well as visually:

> Before we could reach the corral, a sharp rain began to sting down. The mountains had vanished, and the gray which blotted them already was taking the ridgeline. Chill sifted into the air as the rain drilled through. Now a wind steadily sharpening the storm's attack. The sheep milled in the corral as if being stirred by a giant paddle, quickening and quickening. A stalled wave of them had begun to pack so tightly against the wooden gate that Dad and I together couldn't undo the wire that held it closed; the gate bowed, snapped apart against the tonnage of the hundreds of struggling bodies (*Sky* 1978, 218–19).

Of this passage, Bredahl notes: "Varying sentence structures and lengths—one sentence incomplete; one sentence nicely balanced against the semicolon like the sheep against the gate so that the sentence itself seems to bow as the gate does—reinforce the portrayal of two men struggling" (Bredahl 1988, 142).

Stylistic features of Doig's work may be examined separately but do their work in combination. In this scene from *English Creek,* for example, Doig uses sound, syntax, and narrative viewpoint to re-create Wisdom Johnson's tumble from a haystack and Jick's sensations in watching him fall:

> The hay. The hay was airborne. And Wisdom was so busy glowering he didn't realize this load was arriving to him as if lobbed by Paul Bunyan. I yelled, but anything took time to sink in to Wisdom. His first hint of doom was as the hay, instead of cascading down over the pitchfork Good Help was supposed to be sighting on, kept coming and coming and coming. A quarter of a ton of timothy on a trajectory to the top of Wisdom's head.
>
> Hindsight is always twenty-twenty. Wisdom ought to have humped up and accepted the avalanche. He'd have had to splutter hay the next several minutes, but a guy as sturdy as he was wouldn't have been hurt by the big loose wad.

But I suppose to look up and see a meteorite of hay dropping on you is enough to startle a person. Wisdom in his surprise took a couple of wading steps backward from the falling mass. And had forgotten how far back he already was on the stack. That second step carried Wisdom to the edge, at the same moment that the hayload spilled itself onto the stack. Just enough of that hay flowed against Wisdom to teeter him. The teetering slipped him over the brink. "Oh, *hell*," I heard him say as he started to slide (*EC* 1984, 249).

Doig creates Jick's "freeze-frame" sensation as he sees what is about to happen in the brevity and repetition of the first two sentences: "The hay. The hay was airborne." Jick's attention then shifts to Wisdom, and he sees that Wisdom is oblivious to his situation, the comic nature of which is captured in the allusion to Paul Bunyan, the giant hero of American tall tales. Observation yields to action—"I yelled," and then Jick shifts perspective from his own position on the ground to Wisdom's on the haystack and slows the pace of the action by subordination and repetition: "The hay, instead of cascading down over the pitchfork Good Help was supposed to be sighting on, kept coming and coming and coming." The next sentence also slows the pace by restating what is about to happen, and the alliterative "t" reinforces the comic tone of the passage: "A quarter of a ton of timothy on a trajectory to the top of Wisdom's head." The next paragraph, because it pauses in retrospect instead of moving the scene forward, stops action entirely. In the final paragraph, the action moves in tiny increments, marked by the repetition of key words: "Steps...step; hayload...hay; teeter...teetering."

A similar passage in *The Sea Runners* describes Braaf's tumble from a rock into the ocean. But this scene is tragic, not comic, and the narrative pace is swift. The narrator is outside of the action, so there is no shifting of perspective—the motion of the passage is forward, unlike the passage in *English Creek*, where the action stops while Jick comments on it.

Of what happened next, only this much is sure. That amid a climbing stride by Braaf as he began to cross the wrist of rock, surf burst its power in front of him. That a startling white weight of water leapt, seemed to stand in the air. That it then fell onto Braaf.

Comical, this ought to have been. A drenching, an ass-over-earhole tumble as Wennberg might have said, and there the sum of it, Braaf bouncing up now with a grin of rue. But the topple of water slung Braaf backward more than that and the hand he put down to halt himself met the wet slickness of brown rockweed.

Braaf slid on into the tidal trough.

Above, Karlsson and Wennberg, half-turned in stare to the crevasse water, were twins of disbelief.

Braaf was vanished (*SR* 1982, 230–31).

In this passage, Doig moves the action forward relentlessly, quickening the pace near the end by creating separate paragraphs for each sentence and abbreviating phrases: "Above, Karlsson and Wennberg, half-turned in stare to the crevasse water, were twins of disbelief." Their momentary motionlessness is captured in the prepositional phrase "in stare." The phrase that follows is truncated and tortured—two prepositional phrases (to the crevasse in the water) are supported by only one preposition, and a noun serves as an adjective: "the crevasse water." This deliberate paring of words creates the bareness and brevity of the passage. The momentary halting of action as Karlsson and Wennberg stare at the water is reinforced by the word "crevasse," a term usually used to describe an immobile fissure in ice. In the last sentence of the scene, Doig's use of the word "was" rather than the more conventional "had" emphasizes situation rather than action. "Had vanished" would imply the possibility of return; "was vanished" connotes the permanence of the loss. As brief and unadorned as the passage is, it reads very slowly. The reader literally has to "make sense" of the sentences, supply the missing prepositions, figure out the grammar. The effect of the language is to replicate the swiftness of the event, the frozen helplessness of the witnesses. Overall, Doig's economical style makes *The Sea Runners* a swift book but one that cannot be read swiftly.

The pace of *English Creek*, by contrast, is leisurely. The emphasis is on scene rather than action, on *examined* experience rather than experience by itself. Jick narrates action in context and gives context its full measure. He seldom foregrounds action but rather what that action signifies: its relevant history, how it may be interpreted, what it may lead to. The considered pace recapitulates the seasons within a season that compose its time-frame. The novel takes place in a single summer, but each of the seasons within that—early June and the counting trip into the mountains, the Fourth of July, August's haying season, forest-fire season—is carefully explored. The significance of the events of this summer is clarified in the final section where Jick as a grown man talks about what happened to his family afterwards, particularly the disaffection and death of his brother.

Doig reinforces the reflective tone of *English Creek* by "layering" passages. That is, a single event will be considered a number of times, observations elaborated:

My personal theory is that a lot of misunderstanding followed my mother around just because of her way of saying. Lisabeth Reese McCaskill could give you the time of day and make you wonder why you had dared to ask. I recall once when I was about eleven that we were visited for the morning by Louise Bowen, wife of the young ranger at the Indian Head district to the south of us. Cliff Bowen was newly assigned onto the Two, having held down an office job at Region headquarters in Missoula all the time before, and Louise was telling my mother how worried she was that her year-old, Donny, accustomed to town and a fenced yard, would wander off from the station, maybe fall into the Teton River. I was in the other room, more or less reading a *Collier's* and minding my own business, but I can still hear how my mother's response suddenly seemed to fill the whole house:

"Bell him."

There was a stretch of silence then, until Louise finally kind of peeped: "Beg pardon? I don't quite—"

"Put a bell on him. The only way to keep track of a wandering child is to hear him."

Louise left not all too long after that, and that was the extent of our visits from her. But I did notice, when my father drove down to borrow a saw set from Cliff a month or so later and I rode along, that Donny Bowen was toddling around with a lamb bell on him (*EC* 1984, 112–13).

The core information in the passage is delivered in the first sentence. It is elaborated in the second sentence with a general example, then illustrated in a detailed, specific example, complete with background on the visitor, her husband and child, the overheard conversation, and its eventual outcome. In this novel, unlike *The Sea Runners*, event and action assume their significance and take on life within multilayered contexts.

Doig's books are all quite different from one another, but each is demanding. Doig's experiments with language force the reader to examine the prose carefully, to visualize scenes, to see the unfamiliar clearly, to understand the familiar in new ways. Doig often plays with parts of speech, particularly verbs: "The one thing that would *pulse* her alive for me ... a difference *sloped* between us ... [he] *fathered* hard until the family finally numbered nine children ... Dad *seared* himself loose that way a number of times ... a country which had *tumbleweeded* so many families out of desperate foothills ranches ... we *deigned* into the Grand Central ... you needed risk, needed somehow to *sizzle* ordinariness by dropping danger into it now and then . . . what that *tokened* to me." This evocative use of verbs is representative of how Doig thinks about words: "A word is like a section of telephone cable, a sheath with several conduits inside it. Each of the conduits can carry different meaning, but all within the same unit" (Doig and Doig, *News*, 1972, 144). Doig exploits many conduits in a single word: its denotations, connotations, etymology, and sound. With some verbs, Doig conveys tone as well as action: "We *deigned* into the Grand Central" has a humorous ring of superciliousness, particularly in context: the Grand Central was a saloon Ivan and his father rarely went into, because the place was frequented by sour, hopeless men, and those two "had standards about saloons." The verb in the phrase "a country which had *tumbleweeded* so many families" invokes the helplessness of those families by comparing their movement to the small, uprooted bushes that roll across the West at the mercy of the wind. The use of *sear* to indicate Charlie's routine of leaving ranches that were badly run conveys the anger and abruptness of his departures.

Doig also manipulates parts of speech, using nouns as verbs, verbs as nouns, prepositional phrases as gerunds: "the earliest of them *wagoned* in," "in their daily *sift* through the forest," "as for this crew *in evening dawdle* all around him." His language calls attention to itself and thereby calls attention to the scene, the mood, the context of the event.

Doig's style reflects his belief that language is a conduit into which multiple meanings, conveyed by sound and sense, rhythm and meter, are packed. In *Mariah*, this conviction is most clearly reflected in his playful use of puns. For example, Jick fixes himself a Bago breakfast of scrambled eggs with some slices of baloney slivered into them. He turns on the radio for company and catches the latest pop tune by the "Roadkill Angels," which describes the sublime destiny of birds and animals slaughtered by cars: "Up along the High Line, on Route 2 east of Shelby! / The guardian in action is Angel Number Three! / Now chrome collides with pheasant, sending feathers in the air! / But heaven's breeze collects them with a whisper of a prayer!" As Jick listens, he asks himself what he is doing sitting in the Bago eating "eggs a la baloney," a perfect description of the lyrics if not the sentiment of the song. In a later scene, Riley, trying to settle on a topic for the centennial series, spots a comely bartender and announces, "I see the piece!" and Jick, trying to extract his ex-son-in-law from his entanglement with "the piece," which is clearly painful to Mariah, comments glumly to himself that it is not his style to "sit around in a tourist bar into the whee hours." When Jick picks up a volume of Churchill's speeches to inspire him for the composition of his centennial speech, Riley groans, "*Winnie*, in the *Bago*?"

At the wedding in the Billings Holiday Inn, Jick stares in fascination at a re-volving statue of Elvis Presley at three different stages of his career—as a young artist, at the height of his fame, then in his years of decline—and de-cides that the statue must represent Elvis as "Hound dog, top dog and pound dog." Fun puns, these, but Doig also uses the form for irony, as in his measuring the Berkeley Pit by the height of the Empire State Building and in his wry naming of the hunting-fiend editor Baxter Beebe, "BB."

Like a poet, Doig avoids abstractions. His is not a literature of ideas but of experiences, events, human lives. His work is certainly not devoid of ideas, but he nails them down with concrete images and metaphors. In his description of his father's family's immigration from Scotland, he writes, "The one clear fact about the route from Dundee is that a number of Scots came in succession, like a chain of people steadying one another across a rope bridge." In *The Sea Runners,* an angry Wennberg stops talking: "His mouth now clamped until his lips all but vanished. Words were having their spines snapped here, the other three could see." In *Winter Brothers,* Doig contemplates his passages through time, saying, "Our perimeters are strange, unexpectedly full of flex when we touch against them just right." Doig's insistence on the physical image—people on a rope bridge, words as living things, containers of time that move at a touch—remind the reader of the sensuality of knowledge. That is, we take in the world through our senses and lose a certain relationship to it when we abstract it or describe it with words that refer not to the world we live in but to other words.

In this respect, Doig's work is intensely moral. His books remind us that Americans have justified to themselves the rape and slaughter and ex-ploitation of the western landscape by abstracting that landscape, by making it both more and less than it is. Thinking about environment in terms of profit enables people to strip it for profit. The buffalo were wiped off the Great Plains because they were perceived not as buffalo but as a larder for Indians who could be eliminated more easily if their food supply was de-stroyed. Whites assumed (falsely, as it turns out) that buffalo did not pro-vide as much meat as cattle, and that raising cattle would bring more profit to the ranchers.[2] It is symptomatic of the "unreality" of the buffalo that thousands of them were shot from moving trains. It can be said that whites abstracted the buffalo and destroyed them without ever having perceived them in the first place.

By insisting on the "thingness" of things, Doig fulfills Carl Bredahl's assertion that contemporary western writing can contribute a healthy moral palliative to the American canon. Bredahl argues that contemporary western writers, Doig among them, "value surface . . . the physical skin of the world of which we are all a part," and that they use concrete, sensual language to put readers in touch with that surface. This results in a privileging of human experience over abstract idea, which Bredahl feels is a major contribution to American writing:

> Response to surface has long troubled the human imagination; it is so much easier to deny and look beyond (or beneath) surface in an intellectual search for absolutes and ultimates—this is the argument set forth by Alfred North Whitehead in his discussion of "misplaced concreteness." Rejection of surface, Whitehead argues, leads inevitably to rejection of individuals and the environment—the most obvious instances of which would be the destruction of lives and land in the name of such absolutes as religion or patriotism. Consequently, that western experience necessitates a valuing of surface and discovery of what Harold P. Simonson calls "place" indicates the importance of a western story as part of the larger cultural framework of America (Bredahl 1989, 31).

In Bredahl's terms, Doig uses language to keep the reader in touch with surfaces, to re-present the physical world and our experiences in it. One of his means to this end is the use of the human body as image and metaphor. Feminist critics speak of "writing the body," and Doig often seems to do precisely that. In this passage from *This House of Sky,* for example, Doig has the reader re-create the macrocosm of a landscape by using the microcosm of human hands:

> A moment, cup your hands together and look down into them, and there is a ready map of what these homesteading families had in mind. The contours and life lines in your palms make the small gulches and creeks angling into the center of the Basin. The main flow of water, Spring Creek, drops down to squirt out there where the bases of your palms meet, the pass called Spring Gulch. Toward these middle crinkles, the settlers clustered in for sites close to water, and they hoped, under the wind. The braid of lines, now, which runs square across between palms and wrists can be Sixteenmile Creek, the canyoned flow which gives the entire rumpled region its name—*the Sixteen country.* Thumbs and the upward curl of your fingers represent the mountains and steep ridges all around. Cock the right thumb a bit outward and it reigns as Wall Mountain does, prowing its rimrock out and over the hollowed land below (*Sky* 1978, 23–24).

In such passages, Doig keeps the reader close to the landscape, making the unfamiliar accessible by using a metaphor the reader can literally create with his or her own body.

In passages that deal with moral or ethical problems, Doig is equally concrete. In *English Creek*, for example, Jick describes the fracture of his family in terms of a broken bone:

> It is like one of those worst bone breaks, a shatter. You can mend the place, peg it and splint it and work to strengthen it, and while the surface maybe can be brought to look much as it did before, the deeper vicinity of shatter always remains a spot that has to be favored (*EC* 1984, 19).

The use of the body as a metaphor for family indicates that Doig regards the family as a living, integrated whole. The individual's relationship to his or her family, particularly the tension between the need for self-realization and independence and the need for bonding and loyalty is one of his major themes. And the use of such a forceful image is particularly important in this section of *English Creek*. For all his apparent stylistic pyrotechnics, Doig tends to use understatement rather than overstatement in conveying human conflicts and relationships. In this instance, it would be easy for the reader to dismiss the family quarrel as minor, but the image of the shattered bone indicates the seriousness of Alec's conflict with his parents.

Doig also uses active verbs and human references in many of his descriptions of landscape: "autumn *tanned* the valley," "clear air *lensed* close the details" "the mountain *knolls itself up watchfully,*" "as the creek *makes* its *shying mutter,*" "the foothill country *hunkered* all around it," "wind and storm *liked to work* in that country, gladly *nubbing* down a boulder." Associated with action and vitality, the landscape becomes a living force, personified but not romanticized, intimately related to human beings.

Doig strengthens the bond between humans and landscape by describing humans with images drawn from the environment: "Webster was granitic" . . . "With his feathered name and that migratory nature he was something of a Boston bird himself" . . . "a sudden alert center of face amid the jaw-and-forehead expanse as if peering in wily surprise out of the hole of a tree trunk" . . . "Rob could hold that smile effortlessly the way a horse holds the bit between his teeth" . . . "his skin color with a dangerous hint of bluing in it, like some dark seepage beneath ice" . . . "this grandmother was an oak stump." Crowds of people in motion are described as "rivering"; Charlie's brothers scatter from the failed homestead "like seeds flying on the Basin's chilly wind." Physical descriptions, motions, emotions—Doig ties human appearance, action, and motivation, to the landscape by metaphor, a tool of language that crafts reality:

> Metaphor is not fanciful embroidery of the facts. It is a way of experiencing the facts. Metaphor denies us a literal sense, and so induces us to *make* sense, i.e. to find interpretations beyond the truth—functional meaning captured by paraphrase (Leech and Short 1981, 24).

What Doig shows in his use of metaphor is the shaping power of the landscape; human life is tied to environment in the West, and he makes us *experience* that fact through metaphors that force the reader to see human beings in terms of the land. Doig also uses images of landscape to describe other kinds of landscape: "a high-nosed cedar canoe, nimble as a seabird, atop a tumbling white ridge of ocean"... "hill of water"... "dark-treed islands schooled like furry whales"... "spruce slopes like green avalanches into the seawater"... "Dabs, driblets, peninsulas, spits and spatters, this portion of coastline when rendered into linework looks startlingly like a breathing moil of sea things, jellyfish and oysters and barnacles and limpets and anemones"... "two dozen Olympic peaks alive in jagged white rhythm like lightning laid sideways"... "Sound's prairie of water."

Interestingly, landscape metaphors for people occur most often in *This House of Sky;* landscape metaphors for landscape occur most often in *The Sea Runners.* Doig mentions one reason for their numerical weight in the latter: "I fairly consciously regarded the NW coast as the fifth character in that book."[3]

Although he attempts to capture experience in language, one might say *replicate* experience in language, Doig is aware that language is a closed and self-reflexive system—it can only approximate life as we live it and take it in through our senses. This awareness is articulated in a narrative portion of *Sky* where Doig describes his frustration that the uniqueness of the Charlie-Bessie-Ivan family can only be hinted at in the words at our disposal. General as they must be, they have all their corners rubbed off:

> *What I miss in our special blood-words is a sense of recasting themselves for each generation, each fresh situation of kindredness. It seems somehow too meager that they should merely exist, plain packets of sound like any other, and not hold power to texture each new conformation with the bright exact tones that are yearned for (Sky 1978, 238).*

In *Ride with Me, Mariah Montana,* Doig underscores the problem of language by focusing on the problem of communication: characters sometimes speak cryptically, signaled by phrases like "Riley's latest codegram," or "How do you say that in American?" or "I knew I should have brought a translator along when I hooked up with you two." Part of Doig's point is that all folk groups—families, ranchers, journalists—have their own abbreviated and special ways of talking that outsiders won't readily understand. But the other point of these phrases is that communication between people is ever only partial.

Imperfect as it is, however, language is finally all we have. It is our means of telling stories, our tool for shaping and expressing experience. Doig's love and respect for the power of language precludes his adopting certain contemporary theories of language and literature. In a speech called "Passion, Precision and Vice Versa," given before the Western History Association (Reno, October 1990), Doig said: "There was a phase of our leading lights in fiction trying out self-conscious mannerisms which tended to produce plots about a writer writing about what he was writing about." Doig classifies that phase as "hermetically experimental fiction without connection to the workaday world." He feels that self-conscious literature ignores the reader: "In terms of investigating, say, roots of social class, this fiction that yawned condescension toward people who have to shop at K-Mart instead of at Banana Republic was . . . unpassionate on the page." "Passion," in Doig's terms, lies in language that captures the way people express themselves, that tells us about how they live, and why. Doig sees cultural and moral vacuity in writing that acknowledges only self-referential language, and in a system of thinking that denies the physical world. He quotes Charles Newman: "One cannot help seeing much contemporary fiction as literary slideshow, holding in common a purposive lack of scale and depth and altogether predictable coloration, and a transparency of surface, encoded by narration that advertises in advance that it will not sustain itself."[4] Doig goes on to point out that aesthetic neutrality creates a cultural flat earth, a despairing milieu where, if all values are equal, then, truly, *nothing counts.*

Implicit in theories that regard language as an arbitrary, self-reflexive system are two assumptions: first, that personal and cultural values expressed in language are equally arbitrary, and second, that literature, like language, has no connection with life beyond what we may choose to assign it. While Doig is aware of contemporary language theory, he is wary of the ethical negation that such theory suggests. As Carl Bredahl demonstrates,

Doig's language, in sound and syntax as well as in denotation and connotation, touches the surfaces of the world. Any study of Doig's work must recognize the interrelationship between *text* and *context*.

Doig the craftsman who selects certain contexts to explore and Doig the artist who expresses those contexts in concrete, sensual, poetic language are supported by Doig the scholar and researcher. Although a historian himself, he does not pursue theories of history nor does he often rely on secondary texts:

> I tend to go back to the detailed sources and original sources rather than the theoretical or survey sources.... I tend not to spend much time or thought on historical schools, I don't think. You know, too much the journalist, the Scotch pedant, the detailist, to be much of a cosmic thinker. I'm simply trying to find some kind of record in front of me of what people actually ate and spent and did day by day.
>
> And out of that, at least in the periods I know anything about from first-hand experience, I try to gauge and judge, at least hint at in the books, what some of these things meant in historical terms. *English Creek*—I don't think there's any surprising view of the Depression in it, but I thought it was time to make the point how tough the Depression was on some of those High Line farmers and others. The homesteading stuff in *Rascal Fair* is not generally known; it's not much known that Montana was the leading homestead state, the numbers involved, how late it was into this century.
>
> I'm not groundbreaking here, I'm using the groundbreaking stuff of Malone and Roeder, some of it in their book and some in other sources, and a lot of homesteader memoirs and oral histories and so on.... I put in the details, and let the details make the arguments.[5]

Doig, then, works from large to small, small to large. Ideas for books strike him—writing a novel (*The Sea Runners*) after fifteen years of writing nonfiction, for example, or writing a trilogy about Montana—and then he does the research, gleaning library stacks, gaining information from correspondence and newspapers and oral histories and diaries and journals, cultural geographies and folklore files, until he has formed a sense of the period, the place, the people he wants to write about. Doig says that he is a "magpie," a "plunderer" of his sources, and his findings are recorded on file cards, scraps of paper that are like the scraps of cloth his grandmother pieced into quilts. Doig works these bits and pieces into patterns that are determined in part by his knowledge of human nature and cultural history and landscape, in part by his own ethical system: his dislike for "big money from afar" running huge ranches and running them badly, his admiration for courageous and competent people. After he has achieved a "critical mass" of the text he works both forward and backward, writing the next sections and revising earlier ones for language, for texture, for character development, guided by his vision of what this particular book should be and do.[6]

Doig's passion for detail and skill with concrete language, his refusal to include material that is inaccurate or that does not reflect in some way the quality of western life, also manifests his refusal to abstract the thing he loves. In this regard, Doig is, in the most inclusive sense of the term, a regional writer: one who weaves the history, the landscape, the folklore, the language of his home place into stories that articulate major themes in American life.

Works by Ivan Doig

Books

Dancing at the Rascal Fair. New York: Atheneum, 1987.

Early Forestry Research: A History of the Pacific Northwest Forest and Range Experiment Station, 1925–1975. Washington: Forest Service, U.S. Department of Agriculture, 1976.

English Creek. New York: Atheneum, 1984.

"John J. McGilvra: The Life and Times of an Urban Frontiersman, 1827–1903." Ph.D. diss. University of Washington, 1969.

(With Carol Doig.) *News: A Consumer's Guide.* Englewood Cliffs, N.J.: Prentice-Hall, 1972.

Ride with Me, Mariah Montana. New York: Atheneum, 1990.

The Sea Runners. New York: Atheneum, 1982.

The Streets We Have Come Down: Literature of the City. Compiled and edited by Ivan Doig. Rochelle Park, N.J.: Hayden Book Company, 1975.

This House of Sky: Landscapes of a Western Mind. New York: Harcourt Brace Jovanovich, 1978.

Utopian America: Dreams and Realities. Compiled and edited by Ivan Doig. Rochelle Park, N.J.: Hayden Book Company, 1976.

Winter Brothers: A Season at the Edge of America. New York: Harcourt Brace Jovanovich, 1980.

Articles

"About Some of Us Being Less Equal." *Seattle Times,* 8 February 1970.

"Are You a Poet?" *Modern Maturity,* June-July 1977, 15–16.

"Article Research Sources." *Writer's Digest,* January 1970. "Astor's Town at Land's End." *New York Times* (Travel), 25 June 1978.

"The Baedeker of Idaho." *Pacific Search,* June 1978, 21–23.

"Bag and Baggage." *Passages,* March/April 1970, 25–26.

"Barney McPhillips, Citizen of the Outdoors." *Pacific Search,* October 1976, 17.

"When the Douglas Firs Were Counted: The Beginning of the Forest Survey." *Journal of Forest History* 20, no. 1 (January 1976): 20–27.

"Be Kind to your Local Planet." *The Rotarian,* April 1971, 39–40.

"The Bob Marshall: A Memorial Wilderness." *Pacific Search,* July/August 1978, 63.

"Borrowing a Forum: A Public Critic's Letters to the Editor." *Journalism Quarterly* 48 (Winter 1971): 763–64.

"Building a Black History." *College Management,* April 1970, 36–37.

"The Care and Handling of the Forest Gene Pool." *Pacific Search,* June 1976, 7–9.

"A Cure for Blue Snow." *Everett Herald,* 23 December 1967, 2–3.

"Did T.V. Camera Help Shatter McCarthy Image?" *Add 1: Reports in Professional Journalism,* Spring 1961, 38–41.

"Diverse Readership." *Editor and Publisher,* 22 May 1971, 44–45.

"Eastern Washington's Hills of Wheat." *Pacific Search,* December 1974, 6–7.

"An Ecotopian Skeptic Views the Tricentennial." *Pacific Search,* July/August 1976, 18.

"Elizabeth Buehler, Envoy to the Past." *Pacific Search,* May 1977, 13.

"Expo '74: Seeking Harmony with Nature." *Chevron U.S.A.,* Spring 1974, 6–9.

"The Far Edge of Nowhere." *Cascades,* Fall 1971, 18–21.

"Fenciful Artwork at the UW." *Everett Herald,* 29 November 1969, 11.

"Firemen from the Sky." *Pacific Search,* November 1976, 15–16.

"Following Oliphant Tracks through Idaho." *Pacific Search,* February 1976, 45.

"Footnotes to History." *Idaho Yesterdays,* 14, no. 2 (Summer 1970): 29–30.

"Forest by the Sea." *Pacific Search,* February 1975, 41.

"Forest Grove: On the Way to Omnipolis?" *Pacific Search,* March 1977, 17–18.

"Fox among the Modocs." *Pacific Search,* May 1976, 12–13.

"Fred Martin, Neighbor to Eagles." *Pacific Search,* December/January, 1977–1978, 10.

"From Norway to the North Pacific." *Pacific Search,* November 1977, 8–9.

"Good-by to the Windmill." *NRTA Journal,* July/August 1971, 11–13.

"Green Lake's First Century." *Seattle Times,* 5 July 1970, 4–5.

"Happy Birthday, George!" *Everett Herald,* 21 February 1970, 3 ff.

"Heigh-Ho to Expo." *Pacific Search,* March 1974, 42.

"The Home Town Boy." *Seattle Times Magazine,* 18 April 1971, 4 ff.

"Hot Lines to Help." *Bell Telephone Magazine,* March/April 1971, 27–29.

"Houses, Water, and Ships Spell New England." *Portland Oregonian,* 7 December 1969.

"How to Resolve Your New Year." *Everett Herald,* 27 December 1969, 2 ff.

"If Only Once." *Powder Magazine,* Fall 1975, 15–17.

"Indian Giver." *Seattle Magazine,* April 1967, 15–17.

"Interracial Adoptions: How Are They Working?" *Parents' Magazine,* February 1971, 63–65.

"It's a Great Place to Live, But Would You Want to Visit?" *New York Times,* 17 October 1976, 5 ff.

"James M. Trappe and the Truth about Truffles." *Pacific Search,* June 1977, 8–9.

"The Jogger as Traveler: How, Why, Whether." *New York Times* (Travel) 29 May 1977.

"John Jay McGilvra." *Cascades,* December 1967, 22–25.

"John J. McGilvra and Timber Trespass: Seeking a Puget Sound Timber Policy, 1861–1865." *Forest History* 13, no.4 (January 1970): 7–17.

"Keepers of the Light." *Ladycom,* April 1971, 18–22.

"Kefauver versus Crime: Television Boosts a Senator." *Journalism Quarterly* 39 (Autumn 1962): 483–90.

"King Columbia's Troubador." *Pacific Search,* September 1978, 16.

"Lewis and Clark Were Name Droppers." *Chevron U.S.A.,* Spring 1976, 33–37.

"Liberation or Else!" *Yankee,* August 1970, 81 ff.

"Lieutenant Puget on the Sound." *Pacific Search,* April 1979, 10–12.

"Lincolniana Notes: The Genial White House Host and Raconteur." *Journal of the Illinois State Historical Society* 62, no. 3 (Autumn 1969): 307–11.

"Look in on the Fish at Seattle's Chittenden Locks." *Chevron U.S.A.,* Spring 1976, 6–7.

"Loony Squiggles from a Writer's Notebook." *Seattle Times Magazine,* 14 July 1974, 3 ff.

"'Madam, I'm Adam': Backward or Forward, Palindromes Read Same." *Seattle Times Magazine,* 14 July 1974, 10 ff.

"The Mapping of America." *American Legion Magazine,* December 1978, 10 ff.

"The Moving History of Metlakatla." *Seattle Times Magazine,* 15 September 1974, 26 ff.

"Mr. Doig Buys His Dream House." *Seattle Times Magazine,* 20 February 1977, 3–5.

"Mr. McGilvra from Flint Creek." *The Crackerbarrel,* October 1968.

"The Murky Annals of Clearcutting." *Pacific Search,* December/January 1975–1976, 12–14.

"Music—Hope for the Ghetto." *Music Journal,* November 1965, 43 ff.

"My Seattle." *Seattle Times,* 24 March 1968, 4–5.

"Naturalists along the Columbia—Lewis and Clark." *Pacific Search,* November 1974, 9–10.

"The Navy vs. Oil." *Ladycom,* April 1972, 60.

"Nights on the Fish Traps." *Pacific Search,* February 1977, 12–13.

"Ol' Dan'l Said it All T'day." *Yankee,* July 1971, 64 ff.

"Old Washington Forts Big Attractions." *Everett Herald,* 25 April 1970, 4 ff.

"Oregon's Neahkahnie Mountain Lures an Acrophobe." *Pacific Search,* March 1975, 42.

"Our Bicentenntial Symbols." *Seattle Times Magazine,* 7 December 1975, 7 ff.

"Passing the Test or Flunking Out?" *Together,* June 1970, 26–29.

"The Passport vs. Freedom to Travel." *New York Times,* 6 June 1976, Section 10, 22 ff.

"Prairie America." *Minutes,* Summer 1970, 4–6.

"A President Visits Alaska." *Seattle Times,* 15 February 1970, 21.

"Puget Sound's War within a War." *The American West,* May 1971, 22–27.

"Rainbow Families." *Ladycom,* September 1970, 9 ff.

"Records Never Die, Nor Do They Fade Away." *Seattle Times,* 31 August 1969, 7–9.

"The Rights of Nature." *Pacific Search,* March 1976, 13.

"Rodeo: Sport of Flings." *The Rotarian,* April 1966), 50 ff.

"A Romantic Interlude in Seattle for Robinson Jeffers." *Seattle Times Magazine,* 23 September 1973, 3 ff.

"The Rumor Fighters." *Kiwanis Magazine,* June 1972, 31–33.

"Running the Sand." *Pacific Search,* July/August 1977, 42–43.

"Rx for the Country Doctor." *The Lion,* February 1972, 17–18.

"Seattle's Monorail Plan—1918." *Seattle Times Magazine,* 21 December 1969.

"Seattle's Pacific Science Center—Or How to Square a Bubble." *Chevron U.S.A.,* Fall 1974, 8.

"Self-Portrait of a Landscape Artist." Review of *Ansel Adams: An Autobiography,* by Ansel Adams. *Washington Post,* 10 November 1985, 1 ff.

"The Sharpest Shopper." *Tacoma News Tribune,* 30 November 1969, 2 ff.

"Smokejumpers." *Pacific Search,* n.d., 14.

"Sound Reflections." *Seattle Times,* 1 June 1969, 12 ff.

"A Spooky House and a Strange Trial." *Seattle Times,* 9 February 1975.

"Stanley Park: Vancouver's Thousand Acre Arcadia." *Pacific Search,* June 1974, 38–40.

"'A Steam Vessel Would Afford Us Incalculable Savings.'" *Pacific Search*, May 1979, 18–20.

"Stone Spirits." *Washington: The Evergreen State Magazine* 3, no. 2 (September/October 1986): 45–51.

"Strokes of History from Lewis and Clark." *Pacific Search*, November 1978, 54–55.

"Sunday's Town." *Aloft*, Summer 1972, 27–29.

"Timber and the Law: A Civil War Chapter." *Pacific Search*, July 1974, 18–20.

"There's a Flag Flying Everywhere." *The Rotarian*, June 1971, 15–18.

"A Time to Ask the Question: Am I My Brother's Jailer?" *The Kiwanis Magazine*, April 1972, 19–21.

"Tracking the Sasquatch Trackers." *Pacific Search*, July/August 1978, 16–17.

"Trade Secrets of a Regular Editorial Page Letter Writer." *Editor and Publisher*, 22 July 1972, 18.

"Treat Your Family to a Funny Festival." *Chevron U.S.A.*, Spring 1972, 10–15.

"The Tribe That Learned the Gospel of Capitalism." *The American West*, March 1974, 42–47.

"Trying to Place It." Paper published by Montana State University Lectures, 8 June 1984.

"The Two Legends of Lew Wallace." *Empire Magazine*, 19 July 1970, 17–21.

"A Utopian Tale of Hood Canal." *Seattle Times Magazine*, 29 June 1975, 4 ff.

"Visits to the Past with Human Landmarks." *Seattle Times Magazine*, 11 January 1976.

"A Voice for Birds." *Pacific Search*, October 1977, 14–15.

"Voices of Yesterday." *Pacific Search*, March 1978, 10–11.

"Washington's First Smoke Jumper." *Seattle Times*, 5 July 1970, 11 ff.

"Welcome (cough) to the Pacific (wheeze) Northwest, Mark Twain." *Pacific Search*, September 1977, 22–23.

"Wellington, 1910: Avalanche!" *Everett Herald*, 11 April 1970.

"What's Doing in Seattle." *New York Times*, 8 May 1977.

"When Death Wore White at Wellington." *Pacific Search*, April 1975, 9–10.

"When Forests Went to Sea." *Oceans*, July 1974, 24–29. Reprinted in *Castoff*, 4, no. 1 (1976), 12 ff.

"When the Bitterroots Burned." *Pacific Search*, September 1975, 9–11.

"When the Law Came West." *Everett Herald*, 25 May 1968, 4 ff.

"Where a Southpaw is Really a Southpaw." *Midwest*, 27 April 1972.

"Wine-Growing Comes to the Willamette." *Pacific Search*, October 1976, 54–55.

"Yesterday's Town." *Everett Herald*, 4 October 1969, 3 ff.

"You Can't *Not* Go Home Again." *Montana: The Magazine of Western History*, 35, no. 1 (Winter 1985): 2–15.

Notes

Chapter 1: Early Writing

1. See, for example, the file on "The Rainbow Families," *Ladycom*, September 1970, in the Doig Files, Special Collections, University of Washington Libraries, Seattle. Despite the difficulties of free-lancing, Doig enjoyed it and has commented that it is the quickest way into print. The main problem with free-lancing, he says, is that it pays so little. Ivan Doig, interview with author, Seattle, Wash., 9 February 1989.

2. See Works by Ivan Doig for specific citations.

3. Letter to Bill Bevis, 1 November 1984, the Doig Files

4. Doig, interview with author, Seattle, Wash., 2 March 1988.

Chapter 2: *This House of Sky*

1. In a letter to Mike Olsen, January 1979, Doig wrote, "I consider *Sky* a memoir—'a narrative of experiences that the writer has lived through'—rather than an autobiography. That is, it is the experiences rather than the life that I wanted to write about. I found it hard to put much of myself into the book, and would quite possibly not have done it in first-person except for the technical advantages of that." The Doig Files, University of Washington.

2. Ibid.

3. For the significance of photographs in the research for *This House of Sky*, see Doig's introductory comments in Duncan Kelso, *Inside This House of Sky: Photographs of a Western Landscape.* Kelso, a professional photographer, was so taken with Doig's memoir that he traveled to western Montana to photograph the region, and his work was published with Doig's collaboration.

4. Doig to Olsen, 28 January 1979, the Doig Files.

5. Doig, interview with author, 2 March 1988.

6. For a theoretical discussion of this process, see Hayden White, *Metahistory: The Historical Imagination in Nineteenth Century Europe,* (Baltimore: The Johns Hopkins University Press, 1973), especially chapter 3.

7. Doig's reluctance to assign a particular cause to the failure of homesteaders reflects the fact that homesteaders were of diverse origins and backgrounds. About 17 percent immigrated from Europe (especially Germany and Scandinavia), the rest from other parts of the United States. Many homesteaders lacked farming experience, and for that reason many of them failed. Malone and Roeder cite the agricultural expert M. L. Wilson, who found that of fifty-eight farmers in one section of Montana, only twenty-three listed their occupation as "farmer." Among the others, Wilson found two physicians, two school teachers, three "Maiden Ladies," six musicians, two wrestlers, and one "World Rover." But Malone and Roeder also note that Wilson's sample may be misleading because it fails to take into account how many of

the homesteaders in his group came originally from farm families and thus had farming experience (Malone and Roeder 1976, 187).

8. Doig, interview with author, 9 February 1989.

9. See, for example, reviews by Thomas Lyon in *Western Historical Quarterly* 11, no. 2 (April 1980): 229–30, and David Remley in *Western American Literature* 14. no. 4 (Winter 1980): 324–25.

Chapter 3: *Winter Brothers*

1. *The Northwest Coast; or, Three Years' Residence in Washington Territory* (New York: Harper & Brothers, 1857; Seattle: University of Washington Press, 1972) and *The Indians at Cape Flattery,* The Smithsonian, 1868.

2. For interesting discussion of Doig's relationship to Swan, see Kerry David Ahearn, "Ivan Doig's Self Narratives: The West, Wilderness, and the Prophetic Impulse," *South Dakota Review* 20, no. 4 (Winter 1983): 7–22.

3. In a taped interview with Professor Eugene Smith of the University of Washington, (Seattle, Autumn 1984), Doig expounded on the inspiration for this structural device, the templates used for carving totem poles:

> Smith: You mentioned that one of the reasons for adopting that format was to make it manageable . . . so you wouldn't have to feel . . . obligated to include all or most of Swan's stuff, which you couldn't have done anyway, because a lot of it is trivial. . . . Were there other reasons as well, aesthetic reasons, for adopting that format?
>
> Doig: Well, I guess it turned out to be some, what I would call technical reasons. In finding Swan among the coastal Indians and his interest in their art and the interplay between what he would show them—books with dragons in them—which then would show up in the Indians' art eventually (much to the dismay, I hasten to say, of a lot of anthropologists and Northwest art historians) . . . I didn't know much about Northwest art. . . . I tried to figure out what Swan saw by looking at it more closely and reading, and talking to Bill Holm. Bill's book [*Indian Art of the Northwest Coast: A Dialogue on Craftsmanship and Aesthetics,* Holm and Bill Reid] was a revelation to me, where he pointed out that these wonderful designs, the ovoids and the other patterns that run through this art are not absolutely free play; they're done with templates made of cedar. These guys would have a set of templates; if they wanted an ovoid or some other design of a certain size, by God they'd reach in the rack and pull out a template . . . when you look at it completed, it's wonderfully imaginative, it has all this force and creativity to it. So I was interested in that, that you could use set elements and yet come out with a remarkable explosion of creativity. So . . . I tried to use some patterns, I would call them, in writing *Winter Brothers*. Early in the book there's a week of Swan's life, during the Neah Bay years, later in the book there's another week of Swan's life . . . it's a deliberate attempt to bring seven days here, seven days here, these are templates, to my mind. I used individual words every so often in the same way. I tried to go back with phrases, once in a while.
>
> Smith: To keep it from rambling?
>
> Doig: To bring this stuff back. In the Indian art the eye catches this wonderful design up here which might be the eye of an eagle on the top of the totem pole and then you get to looking at the bottom of this seventy-foot carved column,

here's the same eye which might be the tooth of a beaver, it's the same template down here. Part of the wondrousness of the Northwest artists... is the way they subtly, but powerfully, use these similar elements. They do different things, maybe, in the specific piece they appear in, but they give you continuity. I tried not to get drunk on that idea.

Smith: I don't think you did, because until you mentioned it I wasn't aware that you were doing that.

Doig: Nobody mentions it, which makes me hope it worked, although maybe it didn't work at all, and that's why.

I wish to thank Professor Smith for generously making the tapes from his interview available to me.

4. The theme of exploitation runs throughout contemporary western writing. In his introduction to *The Sound of Mountain Water,* Wallace Stegner notes: "the entire history of the West, when we hold at arm's length the excitement, adventure, romance and legendry, is a history of resources often mismanaged and of constraining conditions often misunderstood or disregarded. Here, as elsewhere, settlement went by trial and error; only here the trials were sometimes terrible for those who suffered them, and the errors did permanent injury to the land" (Stegner 1980, 19).

5. See Geoffrey Cowley's interview, "A Talk with Ivan Doig," in *The Weekly's Reader,* (Seattle), December 1980, 1 ff.

6. See Harold Simonson's review of *Winter Brothers* in *Western American Literature* 14, no. 2 (August 1981): 169–70.

Chapter 4: *The Sea Runners*

1. Ivan Doig, from a presentation to graduate students in library science, University of Washington, 2 March 1988.

2. Doig found the diary in the Bancroft Library at the University of California, Berkeley.

3. Doig has pointed out that of all the questions routinely posed to him the first is, "Why don't you use a word processor?" and the second is, "Why did you kill off Melander?" so he feels that there is great reader identification with that particular character.

4. Ivan Doig kindly made his journal available me, and I would like to express my gratitude for his generosity.

Chapter 6: *Dancing at the Rascal Fair*

1. Malone and Roeder point out:

Two smaller Indian groups lived beyond the Blackfeet in northeastern Montana: the Atsina and the Assiniboine. The Atsinas spoke an Algonquin language. They were very close relatives of the Arapaho, who had earlier moved southward into Wyoming and Colorado. Misunderstanding sign language, as they so often did, the French traders named them the "Gros Ventre," meaning "big bellies." This was doubly unfortunate, both because the Atsinas had ordinary stomachs and because the Hidatsas of Dakota also became known as "Gros Ventre," leading to much confusion (Malone and Roeder 1976, 13–14).

Doig notes that Montanans routinely flatten town names of French origin in their own idiosyncratic way: i.e., GROVE-on for Gros Ventre, SHOW-toe for Choteau. Doig, interview with author, 9 February 1989.

2. Because the major immigrant group in Doig's works consists of Scots, who did not have to learn a new language in order to live in a new country, Doig deals very little with the problems of immigrants who had to choose between complete assimilation in the new country and the maintenance of linguistic and cultural ties with the old. The problems experienced by other groups are glimpsed in minor characters such as Isaac Reese in *Dancing at the Rascal Fair,* whose Danish accent is cause for much joking among the other characters. Little pressure to assimilate was exerted on immigrant groups until World War I, when fear for national security raised concern about immigrants who might feel more loyalty for their homeland than for their adopted country. In an address in 1915, Teddy Roosevelt said:

> The one absolutely certain way of bringing this nation to ruin...would be to permit it to become a tangle of squabbling nationalities, an intricate knot of German-Americans, Irish-Americans, English-Americans, French-Americans, Scandinavian-Americans or Italian-Americans, each preserving its separate nationality, each at heart feeling more sympathy with Europeans of that nationality than with other citizens of the American Republic. The men who do not become Americans and nothing else are hyphenated Americans; and there ought to be no room for them in this country.

Quoted in Carl H. Crislock, "Introduction: The Historical Context," in *Cultural Pluralism vs. Assimilation: The Views of Waldemar Ager,* ed. Odd S. Lovoll, (Northfield, Minn.: Norwegian-American Historical Association, 1977), 25.

Chapter 8: Recent Developments in Folklore Theory

1. No detailed studies have yet been done on folklore in Puritan or colonial literature, although discussions of individual historians and theologians (William Bradford and Cotton Mather particularly) reveal a wealth of folk beliefs, local legends, folk remedies, and other folklore. John Flanagan notes:

> Folklore in American literature is almost as old as folklore in American life and certainly as constant. When Cotton Mather recorded how divine providence violently interfered with ordinary New England life, he thought he was writing ecclesiastical history but he was actually reporting folklore. Mather easily accepted spectre ships, heavenly signs, the tormenting of innocent people by witches and devils; and he constantly gave allegorical interpretations to unusual phenomena. When Benjamin Franklin ironically remarked that the grand leap of the whale up the falls of Niagara was, to all those who had seen it, one of the most amazing events in nature, he was simply telling one of the best American tall tales (Flanagan et al. 1959, 50–1).

A systematic examination of folklore would be very useful to understanding the development of the Puritan world view from the perspective of its adaptation to the American environment. Studies of early writers such as Washington Irving and

Benjamin Franklin show two trends: the adaptation of European folklore to the American scene, and samples of native forms, such as the tall tale. (Dorson 1957, 5).

2. For a more detailed discussion of the evolution of the discipline, see Dan Ben-Amos, "The Seven Strands of Tradition: Varieties in Its Meaning in American Folklore Studies," *Journal of Folklore Research* 21 (1984): 97–131.

3. Nineteenth-century assumptions about who the folk were and how their traditions should be considered lead to complex functions of folklore in certain texts. Although the "folk" were often regarded as simple, rural, and unsophisticated, their traditions were sometimes esteemed as the repository for human values that had escaped their more sophisticated urban counterparts, and sometimes in American writing the initiation of an outsider into a folk group was a positive moral experience. This is the case with Sarah Orne Jewett's stories in *Country of the Pointed Firs,* for example. With Southern writers like Mark Twain and Charles Chessnut, the distinction between "folk" and genteel reader becomes even more complex, because folklore is used to establish ethnic and cultural differences. In *Huckleberry Finn,* for example, Jim is characterized by his dialect and by aphorisms and beliefs that white readers regard as "ignorant": in fact, much of the humor of the book rests on that response. Yet Jim emerges as a sympathetic character, morally superior to many of the whites in the book. Even more arresting is the figure of Uncle Julius in Chessnut's *The Conjure Woman.* A superficial reading of the book allows the reader to adopt the narrator's "enlightened" scientific worldview, according to which Uncle Julius is a superstitious old huckster who tells his stories for material advantage. A closer look, however, reveals that the tradition Uncle Julius represents is vital and passionate, while the culture of the whites in the book (and perhaps in the audience) is marked by appalling dullness and insensitivity. (Hemenway 1976, 283–309).

4. In his collection of essays about farming in Southeastern Oregon, William Kittredge notes this change:

> We wanted to build a reservoir, and litigation started. Our laws were being used against us, by people who wanted a share of what we thought of as our water. We could not endure the boredom of our mechanical work, and couldn't hire anyone who cared enough to do it right. We baited the coyotes with 1080, and rodents destroyed our alfalfa; we sprayed weeds and insects with 2–4–D Ethyl and Malathion, and Parathion for clover mite, and we shortened our own lives.
>
> In quite an actual way we had come to victory in the artistry of our playground warfare against all that was naturally alive in our native home. We had reinvented the valley according to the most persuasive ideal given us by our culture, and we ended with a landscape organized like a machine for growing crops and fattening cattle, a machine that creaked a little louder each year, a dreamland gone wrong (Kittredge 1987, 61).

5. An example of this kind of scholarship at its finest can be found in Alan Dundes's study of a traditional riddle in James Joyce's *Ulysses* (Dundes 1965b, 136–41).

6. For a discussion of this problem in Ken Kesey's *Sometimes a Great Notion,* see Simpson 1988, 30–35.

Chapter 9: Making It Work

1. Although folklorists argue that by studying literary texts we can get a reliable picture of folklore of the past that has been otherwise unrecorded, the fact remains that folklore serves the writer, not the other way around.

2. Ken Kesey uses another much more charming variant of this story in *Sometimes a Great Notion* to illustrate the naivete and optimism of one of his characters. Of this story Doig says it was "simply a joke I've heard in Montana many times, from probably the time I was a kid out there." Doig, interview with author, Seattle, Wash., 19 April 1989. Note: all of the following information about Doig's sources for the folklore that appears in his books was gathered at this interview.

3. The "Moose-Turd Pie" variants of this story can be found in Barre Toelken's *Dynamics of Folklore*, 66–67, 179–80. Doig gleaned the story from the oral histories of forest rangers recorded by the Forest History Society (now based in Durham, North Carolina, formerly at Santa Cruz), which he had perused in order to catch the rhythms and phrases of the speech of forest rangers. In the version he came across, a logging crew strikes the bargain to change cooks at the first complaint.

> Putting Methuseleh in is my own doing, and the amount of years and so forth.... I find "Methuselah" kind of a wonderful prance of a word on paper, and the notion of someone living that long, and I think both my folks and my grandmother would talk about somebody being "as old as Methuselah"... I think Methuselah shows up in each of these books.... It *was* salted coffee in the version that I read, by the way; you academics tell it with moose turds, eh? Big hearty loggers just use salted coffee!

4. The recreational preferences of what folklorists call "high context" occupation groups, such as loggers, cowboys, and fishermen, often derive from the skills they use in their work. For an excellent example, see Ellison 1988, 36–43. In *The Solace of Open Spaces*, Gretel Ehrlich explains the finer points of various rodeo events and discusses them in terms of community between people, and between people and animals. (Ehrlich 1985, 91–101).

Chapter 10: Realizing the Country

1. In one of the most widely used textbooks on the study of folklore Alan Dundes defines the field as follows:

> It is possible... to define both folk and lore in such a way that even the beginner can understand what folklore is. The term "folk" can refer to *any group of people whatsoever* who share at least one common factor. It does not matter what the linking factor is—it could be a common occupation, language or religion—but what is important is that a group formed for whatever reason will have some traditions which it calls its own. In theory a group must consist of at least two persons, but generally most groups consist of many individuals. A member of the group may not know all other members, but he will probably know the common core of traditions belonging to the group, traditions which help the group have a sense of group identity. Thus if the group were composed of lumberjacks or railroadmen, then the folklore would be lumberjack or railroadman folklore. If the group were composed of Jews or Negroes, then

the folklorist would seek Jewish or Negro folklore. Even a military unit or a college community is a folk group (Dundes 1965a, 2).

2. For a complete discussion of patterns of initiation, see Campbell 1944, 245–51.

3. Bessie's speech is often unique to her: "*I'll have a sipe more coffee, but if I eat another bite, I'll busticate.... Get the swatter and dead that fly for me, pretty please?... Hmpf, I been settin' so long my old behinder is stiff....*" Such turns of phrase are not folkloric, and certainly not clichéd. Doig speculates that this "private language" originated during Bessie's "islanded times of childhood, her own growing up on the Wisconsin farm and her children's years at Moss Agate" (*Sky* 1978, 130).

4. See Arewa and Dundes for a discussion of the use of proverbs as a teaching device.

Chapter 11: Personal Narrative

1. See Stahl, 1977, p. 19.

2. The link between author and audience in the performance of a personal narrative, as the reader stands ready to contribute his or her own thematically similar story, has been strong in Doig's case. He has received hundreds of letters from readers describing their families' homesteading experiences in response to *This House of Sky* and *Dancing at the Rascal Fair,* or recalling their own canoe trips in response to *The Sea Runners.* The fact that readers write their own stories, or tell them to Doig at book signings or public readings, creates what amounts to a long-distance storytelling session. The grizzly story in *Mariah,* which Doig read at a Western Literature Association meeting in Coeur d'Alene in 1989, set up an impromptu storytelling session then and there. Doig noted that after the reading, "As somebody would be telling me their bear story, I would overhear other people telling their bear story to somebody else while they waited to tell it to me!" Doig, interview with author, Seattle, Wash., 25 March 1991.

3. That legends are often recorded as formal history is demonstrated in Jay Gurian's "Literary Tradition and the Mining Romance," 1975.

Chapter 12: Solving Problems

1. Doig found the story of the Bell Rock Lighthouse in the collected work of Robert Louis Stevenson.

2. It is Doig's custom to adapt the words and rhythms of likely looking ballads to dance tunes. "Sir Patrick MacWhirr" was originally titled "Sir Patrick Spens." Doig changed the title because "Spens" looked strange to him on the page and chose "MacWhirr" in honor of Conrad's *Typhoon* captain.

3. Doig made up "Dancing at the Rascal Fair." He had found the phrase "Rascal Fair" (referring to "hiring fairs" in Scotland where workers and craftspeople made themselves available to prospective employers) in a book of Scottish sociology and took it from there.

4. "Zebra Dun" is a western folksong, altered slightly here because Doig "ran it through the typewriter" to improve its prosody. This particular song is a sad comment on the fate of Davie Erskine, who is dragged and crippled by a horse.

For the celebration in Scotch Heaven of "Hogmanay," Scottish New Year, Doig found the "good luck" tradition that the "first foot" through the door should be that of a tall, dark, unspeaking stranger, who tends the household fire. Doig said he allowed his characters to "rig" the tradition a little, asking Angus to perform the rite; considering where they were, they could wait forever for a stranger of the right description to come along.

Doig found the story of the "fillyloo bird" in the oral history archives of the Forest History Society.

Chapter 14: Re-Visioning the West

1. There is no agreement among scholars as to how many regions there are in the United States, what principles should define them, what political boundaries comprise them. For my own definition, I am indebted to Wallace Stegner's introduction to *The Sound of Mountain Water*.

2. Doig, interview with author, Seattle, Wash., 9 February 1989.

Chapter 16: Meeting Adversity

1. Vernon Carstenson teaches history at the University of Washington. The dedication of *Dancing at the Rascal Fair* reads, "For Vernon Carstenson, Who Saw the Patterns on the Land."

2. Doig, interview with author, Seattle, Wash., 9 February 1989.

Chapter 17: Landscape and Community

1. Richard White discusses this approach: "The past may be another country, but for some authors a transcendent nature can wash away the boundaries that time creates. Instead of a search for historical context, there is an attempt to find a universal language shared by author and subject." (White, 1985, 305).

Chapter 18: Text and Context

1. Doig addressed the Pacific Northwest American Studies Association on the topic of "Place" at their annual meeting in 1988, University of Washington. He kindly made his written speech available to the author.

2. Ibid.

3. Doig, interview with author, Seattle, Wash., 10 October 1989.

4. Address to Pacific Northwest American Studies Association annual meeting, 1988, University of Washington.

5. Ibid.

Chapter 19: Language

1. Doig, interview with author, Seattle, Wash., 10 October 1989.

2. I am indebted to Professor Louie Attebery for this information.

3. Doig, letter to the author, 2 May 1989.

4. The quote from Charles Newman is from "What's Left Out of Literature," *New York Times Book Review,* 12 July 1987.

5. Doig, interview with author, Seattle, Wash., 10 October 1989.

6. Doig, letter to author 16 February 1989, taken from a file card he kept while working on *English Creek*:

10 June '82: Each book has some great technical challenge which the solving of enriches the work. In Sky, it was to maintain a poetic flavor thruout the book; W Bros, to work with patterns and make the work mimic its source, to be a diary-of-a-diary; Runners, to do a big story scene by scene. In Eng Crk, it's going to be forming a completeness, a textured whole, of the details. To make a forest of the trees.

Selected Bibliography

Primary Sources

Doig Collection, Shoreline Community College, Seattle, Wash.
Doig File, Special Collections, University of Washington Libraries, Seattle, Wash.
Doig, Ivan. Interviews with author. Seattle, Wash. 2 March 1988, 9 February 1989, 19 April 1989, 10 October 1989, 25 March 1991.
Doig, Ivan. Interviews by Professor Eugene Smith, Seattle, Wash. Autumn 1984. Tape recordings provided by Professor Smith.

Secondary Sources

Abbott, Lee K. "Love in the Back 40" Review of *Dancing at the Rascal Fair,* by Ivan Doig. *New York Times Book Review,* 1 November 1987, 20.
Abrahams, Roger D. "Folklore and Literature as Performance." *Journal of the Folklore Institute* 9 (1972): 75-94.
——. "A Rhetoric of Everyday Life: Traditional Conversational Genres" in *Southern Folklore Quarterly* 22 (1968): 44-59.
Ahearn, Kerry David. "Dancing at the Rascal Fair" *Magill's Literary Journal* (1988): 228-32.
——. "Ivan Doig's Self-Narratives: The West, Wilderness, and the Prophetic Impulse." *South Dakota Review* 20, no. 4 (Winter 1983): 7-22.
——. Review of *The Sea Runners,* by Ivan Doig. *Western American Literature* 18/4 (Fall, 1984), 347-8.
Arewa, E. Ojo and Alan Dundes. "Proverbs and the Ethnography of Speaking Folklore." *American Anthropologist* 66, no. 6 (1964): 70-85.
Astro, Richard. "*The Big Sky* and the Limits of Wilderness Fiction." *Western American Literature* 9, no. 2 (Summer 1974): 105-14.
Barnes, Daniel R. "Toward the Establishment of Principles for Study of Folklore and Literature." *Southern Folklore Quarterly* 43 (1979): 5-16.
Bauman, Richard. "Differential Identity and the Social Base of Folklore." *Toward New Perspectives in Folklore,* edited by Americo Paredes and Richard Bauman. Austin: University of Texas Press, 1972.
Ben-Amos, Dan. "The Seven Strands of Tradition: Varieties in Its Meaning in American Folklore Studies." *Journal of Folklore Research* 21 (1984): 97-131.
Bevis, William. "*English Creek* and Western Historical Fiction," In *Montana: The Magazine of Western History* 35/2 (Spring 1985): 76-77.
——. *Ten Tough Trips: Montana Writers and the West.* Seattle: University of Washington Press, 1990.
Bingham, Edwin R. "Pacific Northwest Writing: Reaching for Regional Identity," in *Regionalism and the Pacific Northwest* edited by William G. Robbins,

Robert J. Frank and Richard E. Ross. Corvallis, Oregon: Oregon State University Press, 1983.

Blevins, Winifred. Review of *Dancing at the Rascal Fair*, by Ivan Doig. *Los Angeles Times* (Books), 18 October 1987, 15.

Bredahl, A. Carl. *New Ground: Western American Narrative and the Literary Canon*. Chapel Hill: University of North Carolina Press, 1989.

——. *"This House of Sky*: A Consumer's Guide." Paper presented at the annual meeting of the Western Literature Association, Eugene, Oregon, October 1988.

——. "Valuing Surface" *Western American Literature* 24, no. 2 (August 1989): 113-20.

Brenner, Jack. "Ivan Doig: Looking for a Kindred Soul." Review of *Winter Brothers*, by Ivan Doig. *Pacific Northwest* 14, no. 8 (November 1980): 41.

Brown, Richard Maxwell. Review of *Winter Brothers*, by Ivan Doig. *Montana: The Magazine of Western History* 32, no. 2 (Spring 1982): 71.

Brunvand, Jan Harold. "Regional Folk Speech and Sayings" in *Handbook of American Folklore*, edited by Richard Dorson, 201-7. Bloomington: Indiana University Press, 1983.

——. *The Study of American Folklore: An Introduction*, 2d ed. New York: Norton, 1978.

Campbell, Joseph. *The Hero With a Thousand Faces*. Cleveland and New York: The World Publishing Co., 1949.

Clark, Malcolm. Book Review of *Winter Brothers*, by Ivan Doig. *Oregon Historical Quarterly* 86, no. 1 (Spring, 1985): 102-3.

Clark, Norman. Introduction to *The Northwest Coast; or, Three Years' Residence in Washington Territory*, by James G. Swan. New York: Harper & Row, 1969. Reprint. Seattle: University of Washington Press 1972.

Cole, Douglas. *Captured Heritage: A Scramble for Northwest Coast Artifacts*. Seattle and London: University of Washington Press, 1985.

Cole, Douglas, and Maria Tippett. "Pleasing Diversity and Sublime Desolation: The Eighteenth-Century British Perception of the Northwest Coast." *Pacific Northwest Quarterly* 65, no. 1 (January 1974): 1-7.

Cowley, Geoffry. "A Talk With Ivan Doig." Interview in *The Weekly's Reader* (Seattle), December 1980, 1 ff.

Critchfield, Richard. "Ivan Doig: The Old West and the New." Review of *Dancing at the Rascal Fair*, by Ivan Doig. *Washington Post* (Book World), 18 October 1987, 1 ff.

Dally, John, "Interpreting the West: An Interview with Ivan Doig." *Elliot Bay Booknotes* (Seattle: The Elliot Bay Book Co.), Fall, 1983, 1 ff.

Dorson, Richard. *American Folklore and the Historian*. Chicago: University of Chicago Press, 1972.

——. "The Identification of Folklore in American Literature." *Journal of American Folklore* 70 (1957): 1-8.

Dundes, Alan. *The Study of Folklore*. Englewood Cliffs, N.J.: Prentice-Hall, 1965a.

——. "The Study of Folklore in Literature and Culture: Identification and Interpretation." *Journal of American Folklore* 78 (1965b): 136-41.

Ehrlich, Gretel. *The Solace of Open Spaces*. New York: Penguin Books, 1985.

Eliade, Mircea. *The Sacred and the Profane*. New York: Harcourt, Brace, 1959.

Ellison, Diane. "Log Rolling" in *Northwest Folklore* 7, no. 1 (Fall 1988): 36-43.

Etulain, Richard W. Review of *This House of Sky,* by Ivan Doig. *Montana: The Magazine of Western History* 29, no. 3 (July 1979): 79.

Flanagan, John T., Mody Boatwright, and Robert B. Davis. *The American Family Saga and Other Phases of American Folklore.* Urbana: University of Illinois Press, 1959.

Gish, Robert. Review of *This House of Sky,* by Ivan Doig. *Chicago Tribune* (section 7), 17 September 1978, 3.

Gullard, Pamela. Book Review of *Dancing at the Rascal Fair,* by Ivan Doig. *San Francisco Chronicle,* 30 August 1987, 3-4.

Gurian, Jay. *Western American Writing: Tradition and Promise.* Florida: Everett Edwards, 1975.

Gorner, Peter. "Big Sky Guy," in *Chicago Tribune* (Tempo), 10 December 1987), 1 ff.

Grobman, Neil R. "A Schema for the Study of the Sources and Literary Simulations of Folkloric Phenomena." *Southern Folklore Quarterly* 43 (1979): 17-37.

Hays, Samuel P. *Conservation and the Gospel of Effeciency: The Progressive Conservation Movement, 1890-1920.* Cambridge: Harvard University Press, 1959.

Hemenway, Robert. "The Functions of Folklore in Charles Chessnut's *The Conjure Woman" Journal of the Folklore Institute* 13 (1976): 283-309.

Hoffman, Daniel G. "Folklore in Literature: Notes Toward a Theory of Interpretation." *Journal of American Folklore* 70 (1957): 15-24.

Horgan, Paul. "The Pleasures and Perils of Regionalism." *Western American Literature* 8, no. 4 (Winter 1974): 167-71.

Johnson, Hildegard Binder. *Order Upon the Land: The U.S. Rectangular Land Survey and the Upper Mississippi Country.* New York: Oxford University Press, 1976.

Jones, Suzi. "Regionalization: A Rhetorical Strategy." *Journal of the Folklore Institute* 13 (1976): 105-20.

Kaufmann, James. Review of *English Creek,* by Ivan Doig. *Los Angeles Times* (Book Review), 9 December 1984, 11.

Kelso, Duncan. *Inside This House of Sky: Photographs of a Western Landscape.* New York: Atheneum, 1983.

Kernan, Michael. "How Montana Was Won." Review of *Dancing at the Rascal Fair,* by Ivan Doig. *Washington Post* (Book World), 28 November 1987, 1 ff.

Kesey, Ken. *Sometimes a Great Notion.* New York: Viking, 1964.

Kirsch, Robert. "Ivan Doig: Hewn from Montana." Review of *This House of Sky,* by Ivan Doig. *Los Angeles Times* 13 September 1978, (Part 4), p. 4.

Kittredge, William. *Owning it All.* Saint Paul, Minn.: Graywolf Press, 1987.

Kittredge, William, and Steven M. Krauzer. "Writers of the New West." *Tri-Quarterly* 48 (Spring 1980), 5-14.

Kline, Marcia B. *Beyond the Land Itself: Views of Nature in Canada and the United States.* Cambridge: Harvard University Press, 1970.

Lee, Hector H. "Tales and Legends in Western American Literature." *Western American Literature* 9, no. 4 (Winter 1975): 239-54.

Leech, Geoffrey N., and Michael H. Short. *Style in Fiction: A Linguistic Introduction to English Fictional Prose.* London: Longman, 1981.

Lewis, Mary Ellen B. "The Study of Folklore in Literature: an Expanded View." *Southern Folklore Quarterly* 40 (1976): 343-51.

Lewis, Merrill and L. L. Lee, eds. *The Westering Experience in American Literature.* Bellingham, Wash.: Bureau for Faculty Research, 1988.

Libecap, Gary. *Locking Up the Range: Federal Controls and Grazing Land*. Cambridge, Mass.: Ballinger Publishing Co., 1981.

Lightfoot, William E. "Regional Folkloristics." In *Handbook of American Folklore*, edited by Richard M. Dorson, 183-93. Bloomington: Indiana University Press, 1983.

Lyon, Thomas. Book Review of *This House of Sky*, by Ivan Doig. *Western Historical Quarterly* 11, no. 2 (April 1980): 229- 30.

MacDonald, Betty. *The Egg and I*. Philadelphia and New York: Lippincott, 1945.

Maclean, Norman. *A River Runs Through It*. Chicago: University of Chicago Press, 1976.

Malone, Michael P. and Richard B. Roeder. *Montana: A History of Two Centuries*. Seattle: University of Washington Press, 1976.

Marovitz, S. E. *"This House of Sky:* Western Portraits of a Literary Mind." Paper presented at the annual meeting of the Western Literature Association, Eugene, Oregon, October 1988.

McDonald, Lucile. *Swan among the Indians: Life of James G. Swan*. Portland, Oreg.: Binfords and Mort, 1972.

Meldrum, Barbara, ed. *Myth Under the Sun: Myth and Realism in Western American Literature*. Troy, N.Y.: Whitston Publishing Co., 1985.

Milton, John R. "The American West: A Challenge to the Literary Imagination." *Western American Literature* 1, no. 4 (Winter 1967): 267-84.

Morris, Wright. "Times of the Males." Review of *This House of Sky*, by Ivan Doig. *New York Review of Books*, 7 January 1979, 14.

O'Connell, Nicholas. *At the Field's End: Interviews With 20 Pacific Northwest Writers*. Seattle: Madrona Publishers, 1987. The interview with Ivan Doig was published earlier in *Seattle Review* 8 (Spring 1985): 33.

Putnam, Jackson K. "Historical Fact and Literary Truth: The Problem of Authenticity in Western American Literature." *Western American Literature* 15, no. 1 (Spring 1980): 17-23.

Remley, David. Book Review of *This House of Sky*, by Ivan Doig. *Western American Literature* 14, no. 4 (Winter 1980): 324-25.

Robbins, William G. "The Historian as Literary Craftsman: The West of Ivan Doig." *Pacific Northwest Quarterly* 78, no. 4 (October 1987): 134-40.

Robinson, Marilynne. *Housekeeping*. New York: Farrar Straus Giroux, 1980.

Roripaugh, Robert. Review of *English Creek*, by Ivan Doig. *Western American Literature* 20, no. 4 (February 1986): 353-54.

Runciman, Lex and Steven Sher, eds. *Northwest Variety: Personal Essays by 14 Regional Authors*. Seattle: Arrowood Books, 1987.

Satterfield, Archie. "Memoirs from beneath the Big Sky." Review of *This House of Sky*, by Ivan Doig. *Seattle Post Intelligencer*, 1 October 1978, G-7.

Settle, Mary Lee. "Novels of History and Imagination." Review of *The Sea Runners*, by Ivan Doig. *New York Times Book Review*, 3 October 1982, 9.

Simonson, Harold P. *Beyond the Frontier: Writers, Western Regionalism, and a Sense of Place*. Fort Worth: Texas Christian University Press, 1989.

———. Review of *Winter Brothers*, by Ivan Doig. *Western American Literature* 14, no. 2 (August, 1981): 169-71.

Simpson. Elizabeth. "Voices of the Folk: Northwest Traditions in *Sometimes a Great Notion*." in *Northwest Folklore* 7, no. 1 (Fall 1988): 30-35.

Smith, Wendy, "Ivan Doig," Interview. *Publishers Weekly*, 18 September 1987, 156-57.

Sokolov, R. A. Review of *Winter Brothers,* by Ivan Doig. *New York Times Book Review,* 11 January 1981, 12.

Stahl, Sandra K. D. "Personal Experience Stories." In *Handbook of American Folklore,* edited by Richard M. Dorson, 268-76. Bloomington: Indiana University Press, 1983.

——. "Personal Narrative as Folklore." *Journal of the Folklore Institute* 14 (1977): 9-30.

——. "Studying Folklore and American Literature" In *Handbook of American Folklore,* edited by Richard M. Dorson, 422-33. Bloomington: Indiana University Press, 1983.

Stanley, David H. "The Personal Narrative and the Personal Novel: Folklore as Frame and Structure for Literature." *Southern Folklore Quarterly* 43 (1979): 107-20.

Stegner, Wallace. "History, Myth and the Western Writer." *The American West* 4, no. 2 (May 1967): 61-62 ff. Reprinted in *The Sound of Mountain Water.* Lincoln: University of Nebraska Press, 1980.

——. "On the Writing of History." *The American West* 2, no. 4 (Fall, 1965): 6-14. Reprinted in *The Sound of Mountain Water* Lincoln: University of Nebraska Press, 1980, 181-90.

——. *The Sound of Mountain Water.* Lincoln: University of Nebraska Press, 1946. Reprint, 1980.

Suplee, Curt. "The Hardpan World of Stoic Westerners." Review of *This House of Sky,* by Ivan Doig. *Washington Post* (Book World), 11 December 1978, 11.

Swan, James G. *The Northwest Coast; or, Three Years' Residence in Washington Territory.* Harper & Brothers, 1857. Reprint. Seattle: University of Washington Press, 1972.

Toelken, Barre. *The Dynamics of Folklore.* Boston: Houghton Mifflin, 1979.

——. "Folklore in the American West" In *A Literary History of the American West.* 29-63. Fort Worth: Texas Christian University Press, 1987.

——. "Northwest Regional Folklore." In *Northwest Perspectives: Essays on the Culture of the Pacific Northwest* Compiled and edited by Edwin R. Bingham and Glen A. Love. Seattle: University of Washington Press, 1979.

Trippett, Frank. Review of *This House of Sky,* by Ivan Doig. *Time,* 11 September 1987, 90 ff.

Tyburski, Susan J. "Wallace Stegner's Vision of Wilderness." *Western American Literature* 18, no. 2 (August 1983): 133- 42.

Van Strum, Carol. "Chronicles of a Changing Country." Review of *Winter Brothers,* by Ivan Doig. *Washington Post* (Book World), 6 January 1981, 2.

Venn, George, "Continuity in Northwest Literature." In *Northwest Perspectives: Essays on the Culture of the Pacific Northwest,* compiled and edited by Edwin R. Bingham and Glen A. Love. 98-118. Seattle: University of Washington Press, 1979.

Westbrook, Max. "The Authentic Western." *Western American Literature* 13, no. 3 (Fall 1978): 213-25.

——. "Myth, Reality, and the American Frontier." In *Myth under the Sun: Myth and Realism in Western American Literature,* edited by Barbara Meldrum, 11-19. Troy, N.Y.: Whitstun Publishing Co., 1985.

——. "The Practical Spirit: Sacrality and the American West." *Western American Literature* 3, no. 3 (Fall, 1968): 193-205.

White, Richard. "Historiographal Essay: American Environmental History: the Development of a New Historical Field." *Pacific Historical Review* 54, no 4. (November 1985): 297-335.

Yurkovich, Sally. "Conversational Genres" in *Handbook of American Folklore*, edited by Richard M. Dorson, 277-81. Bloomington: Indiana University Press, 1983.

Index

and tradition, 76, 77, 79, 82, 84
and worldview, 78, 79
as performance, 82–83, 86, 100
changes in theory, 75–79
definition of, 75, 77–79, 88–89, 194–95,
  Ch. 10, n. 1
family saga, 82, 106–107
in literature, 76–79, 80–113, 105–109,
  192–93, n. 1
legend, 82, 97, 102–104
material culture, 81–82
proverbs, 93–95
tall tale, 82, 98, 109, 167, 173, 192–93, n. 1
toasting, 104, 108
traditional stories (jokes), 83–84, 96, 98
See also Doig's works, links between
Forest Rangering, 41, 42, 44, 56, 91, 113, 137
Forest Service, 5, 45, 48, 56, 60, 69
Frontier, xv, 9, 17

Garland, Hamlin, 23
Grazing acts, 108, 139, 146, 160
Great Depression, 41, 42, 57, 65, 66, 81, 105,
  159, 182
Guthrie, A. B. (*The Big Sky*), xiii, 23, 117,
  122, 151

History:
  and characterization, xv, 45–46, 68,
    161–63
  and folklore, 110–13
  and memory, 65, 68, 102
  and plot, 27, 160–63
  and the role of "remembrancer," 46, 65,
    111–12
  and verisimilitude, 5, 7, 75
  as theme, 13, 22, 30, 56, 57, 65–66, 72, 84,
    86, 101–102, 110–13
  as story, 47, 65–66, 84, 112
  as structural device, 24, 30
  continuity of, xiv, xv, 50, 59, 110–13
  definition of, 6, 19, 46, 65–66
  of Montana, 6, 53–54, 71, 72, 84, 86, 112
Homesteading, 23, 91, 110, 112, 139,
  147–48, 178, 182
  in *Rascal Fair*, 19, 54, 105, 139, 144,
    145–46, 147, 148, 159
  in *Sky*, 13, 22, 152
Homestead Act, 19, 146, 147, 160
Hutterites, 21, 90

Ideolects, 167–68
Immigration, xiv, xv, 9, 24–25, 54, 55,
  107–109, 145, 189–90, n. 7
  in *Rascal Fair*, 51–53, 56, 57, 86, 107, 109,
    192 n. 2
  in *Sky*, 11, 20–21, 91
Indian art (as structural device in *Winter*

Brothers), 28, 30, 32, 100, 164, 190–91,
  n. 3
Indians:
  and sacred space, 134–35
  Blackfeet, 46, 53, 130, 133
  Haida, 25, 30, 102
  in Montana, 53–54, 65–66, 112, 146
  Makah, 25, 28, 102, 132, 153
  Names for, 53, 191, Ch. 6, n. 1
  Nez Perce, 65–66
  Northwest Coast, 37, 125, 131, 132, 143,
    146
  Tlingit, 30, 34, 38
Influenza Epidemic of 1918–1919, 56, 160,
  161–62

Jefferson, Thomas, 24, 147
Jewett, Sarah Orne (*Country of the Pointed
  Firs*), 193, n. 3
Johnson, Hildegard, 146

Kesey, Ken, (*Sometimes a Great Notion*),
  117, 119–20, 122, 123, 124, 129, 142,
  149, 194, n. 2
Kittredge, William (*Owning it All*), 23, 123,
  126, 136, 193 n. 4
  and Steve Krauzer, 123
Klintberg, Bengt af, 82

Landscape, xiv–xv, 3, 5, 43, 45, 72, 112–13,
  115–54
  and character, xv, 119, 122–27, 142–46,
    159
  and community, 123, 127, 129, 148,
    149–54
  and identity, 19
  and naming, 129–33
  as adversary, 6, 19–20, 37, 38–40, 42, 53,
    54, 55, 125, 142–48, 159
  as metaphor, 40, 41, 170
  as structural device, 28–29, 32
  destruction/exploitation of, 24, 31–32,
    46–47, 57–58, 72, 120–21, 140, 177,
    191, ch. 3, n. 4, 193, n. 4
  in western writing, xv
  perception of, 39–40, 119–21, 123,
    125–29, 178
Lawrence, D. H. (*Portrait of the Artist as a
  Young Man*), 100
Leech, Geoffrey N., and Michael H. Short,
  171, 180
Lewis and Clark, 6, 11, 27, 129, 130–31, 132
Lytle, Andrew, 123

Maclean, Norman (*A River Runs Through
  It*), 23, 122, 123, 149
MacDonald, Betty (*The Egg and I*), 150
McDonald, Lucile (*Swan Among the